PERGAMON INTERNATIONAL LIBRARY
of Science, Technology, Engineering and Social Studies

*The 1000-volume original paperback library in aid of education,
industrial training and the enjoyment of leisure*

Publisher: Robert Maxwell, M.C.

Prescriptive Psychotherapies

Publisher's Notice to Educators

THE PERGAMON TEXTBOOK
INSPECTION COPY SERVICE

An inspection copy of any book published in the Pergamon International Library will gladly be sent without obligation for consideration for course adoption or recommendation. Copies may be
retained for a period of 60 days from receipt and returned if not
suitable. When a particular title is adopted or recommended for
adoption for class use and the recommendation results in a sale of
12 or more copies, the inspection copy may be retained with our
compliments. If after examination the lecturer decides that the
book is not suitable for adoption but would like to retain it for his
personal library, then our Educators' Discount of 10% is allowed on
the invoiced price. The Publishers will be pleased to receive suggestions for revised editions and new titles to be published in this
important International Library.

PERGAMON GENERAL PSYCHOLOGY SERIES

Editor: Arnold P. Goldstein, *Syracuse University*
Leonard Krasner, *SUNY, Stony Brook*

TITLES IN THE PERGAMON GENERAL PSYCHOLOGY SERIES
(Added Titles in Back of Volume)

The terms of our inspection copy service apply to all the above books. A complete catalogue of all books in the Pergamon International Library is available on request.

The Publisher will be pleased to receive suggestions for revised editions and new titles.

PRESCRIPTIVE PSYCHOTHERAPIES

Arnold P. Goldstein
Norman Stein
Syracuse University

PERGAMON PRESS INC.

New York · Toronto · Oxford · Sydney · Frankfurt · Paris

Pergamon Press Offices:

U. S. A.	Pergamon Press Inc., Maxwell House, Fairview Park, Elmsford, New York 10523, U.S.A.
U. K.	Pergamon Press Ltd., Headington Hill Hall, Oxford OX3 0BW, England
CANADA	Pergamon of Canada, Ltd., 207 Queen's Quay West, Toronto 1, Canada
AUSTRALIA	Pergamon Press (Aust.) Pty. Ltd., 19a Boundary Street, Rushcutters Bay, N.S.W. 20011, Australia
FRANCE	Pergamon Press SARL, 24 rue des Ecoles, 75240 Paris, Cedex 05, France
WEST GERMANY	Pergamon Press GMbH, 6242 Kronberg/TS, West Germany

Library of Congress Cataloging in Publication Data

Goldstein, Arnold P
    Prescriptive psychotherapies.

    (Pergamon general psychology series ; PGPS-55)
    1.   Psychotherapy--Addresses, essays, lectures.
2.   Psychiatric research--Addresses, essays, lectures.
I.   Stein, Norman, joint author. II. Title.
[DNLM: 1. Psychotherapy. WM420 G624pe]
RC480.5.G599 1975   616.8'914   75-5620
ISBN 0–08–019506–7
ISBN 0–08–019505–9 pbk.

Printed in the United States of America

To Cindy, a very special person, with loving and liking
and
To Judy, with love and devotion

Contents

THE AUTHORS

Arnold P. Goldstein (Ph.D., Pennsylvania State University) is professor of psychology at Syracuse University, Syracuse, New York. He has authored several books in behavior modification, including *Therapist–Patient Expectancies in Psychotherapy, Structured Learning Therapy, The Lonely Teacher*, and an earlier volume in the Pergamon General Psychology Series, *Psychotherapeutic Attraction*. Dr. Goldstein has written more than 40 articles on staff training, management training, and behavior change.

Norman Stein (Ph.D., Pennsylvania State University) is Associate Professor of Psychology at Syracuse University. He has published numerous articles in the area of learning and conditioning in professional journals.

Preface

This book is addressed to both clinicians and researchers concerned with the conduct and effectiveness of psychotherapy. Simply stated, it is our view that psychotherapeutic treatment may not succeed, in full or in part, much more often than is necessary. Viewing and applying treatment more prescriptively, we would hold, is a major corrective to this frequent failure.

In its earliest days, psychotherapy research sought answers to such global questions as: "Does it work?" or "Is treatment A superior to treatment B?" Even when answered in the affirmative, such comprehensive questions yielded little or no information regarding how to improve the success rate of the given treatments studied, or for whom the treatment was most appropriate. The second stage of psychotherapy research, the process stage, did examine the "innards" of psychotherapy, but not much else. The "success" of psychotherapy was generally assumed, and the process dimensions studied were generally not linked to outcome evidence. In its third and most progressive stage thus far, the stage of "outcome-related process studies," psychotherapy research began more fully to identify the patient, therapist, and treatment variables relevant to increasing the success of therapeutic outcomes. It is these active therapeutic ingredients – these characteristics of the participants, the treatment offered, and the outcomes obtained – which form the building blocks for the theme of the present book. We address ourselves here not to the outdated outcome questions noted above but, instead, to "Which type of patient, meeting with which type of therapist, for which type of treatment will yield which outcomes?" This patient X therapist X treatment interactionist view of the outcome question lies at the heart of a prescriptive viewpoint. This viewpoint is examined in depth in Parts I and II of this book; its diagnostic, research, and therapeutic implications are all explored. Attention is also devoted to the question of how prescriptive psychotherapy research might be most advantageously conducted to yield prescriptive information leading to increasingly successful treatment outcomes.

But today's patient can't wait for tomorrow's answer. We must offer him the best we have now. Current research does yield beginning psychotherapeutic prescriptions, and these are presented in Part III. We have examined relevant psychotherapy and psychopathology research and, in Part III, these findings are summarized and the currently most optimal psychotherapeutic prescriptions are derived. It is our hope that the therapeutic value of these current prescriptions and our schema for the development of even more adequate combining of patients, therapists, and techniques will stimulate others to function prescriptively and thereby contribute in some appreciable degree to the successful treatment of both today's and tomorrow's patients.

We would like to acknowledge the helpful assistance of John Healy for gathering some of the material in preparing this book and to extend our appreciation to Patricia Prindaville for her valuable critiques and comments.

PART I

Introduction

Introduction

Understanding of the nature of psychotherapy, in its several contemporary forms, has advanced significantly since its formal beginnings less than 100 years ago. We are increasingly able to differentiate active from inert psychotherapeutic ingredients. Therapist, patient, and treatment dimensions that are relevant to treatment outcome are increasingly differentiable from those that are not. Criteria of successful treatment outcome are being defined and measured with growing clinical sensitivity and methodological sophistication. Several diverse bodies of psychological knowledge are being drawn upon for their psychotherapeutic relevance. Research designs now in use for the study of psychotherapeutic phenomena are both more elegant and more utilitarian. Yet, the *clinical* utility of such investigative progress has been minimal. While several types of research strategies may eventually be successful in making research more useful for practice, one such strategy is already obvious, if markedly underutilized: research reflecting much greater concern with psychotherapeutic prescriptiveness. Researchers have been insufficiently oriented toward conceptualizing, building, and testing outcome-enhancing therapist-patient-treatment matches. Researchers have but barely begun to ask, much less answer, approximations to the proper therapy outcome question: Which treatment procedures, administered by which therapist to which patient, with which specific problems are predicted to yield which outcomes?

Many clinicians are equally culpable. They too have retarded the advance of therapeutic practice by gross inattention to prescriptive concerns. Instead, what we have described elsewhere as the "one-true-light assumption" has prevailed (Goldstein, 1969). This is essentially a nonprescriptive stance which holds, in the absence of supportive evidence, that one's preferred treatment approach is equally and widely applicable to most or all types of patient-candidates. It is an orientation in which diagnosis is largely a functionally autonomous activity – i.e., diagnostic procedures are implemented and summary formulations rendered, but treatments are instituted essentially independent of such diagnostic information. Psychotherapy, we would hold, is optimally conceptualized and conducted when it is viewed prescriptively. We are urging that treatments be designed to be responsive to "diagnosis" broadly defined, that the therapist-patient-treatment match be optimized, or, more generally, that both researchers and practitioners become increasingly oriented

3

toward an individualized, differential, tailored, focused, or prescriptive strategy in both the study and the use of psychotherapeutic methods.*

PSYCHOTHERAPIES VERSUS PSYCHOTHERAPY

As noted above, a one-true-light assumption has dominated much of our thinking about the conduct and conceptualization of psychotherapy. Stimulated by the unidimensionality or "unimethodology" of many clinical training centers, and abetted by the practitioner need to hang one's procedural hat on a consistent theoretical framework, most practitioners essentially know, practice, are committed to, and overtly champion a single therapeutic approach. While such singularity of orientation may be therapeutically beneficial for patients for whom the given treatment has been shown to be appropriate, concerns arise when it is utilized with patients for whom it is either inert or counterproductive. Skilled eclecticism is both difficult to develop and difficult to implement. This is an eclecticism of therapeutic techniques, procedures, and instrumentalities, rather than an eclecticism of theory construction and conceptual systemization. A "technical eclecticism" (e.g., Lazarus, 1967) does not preclude formal subscription to a single system at the assumptive and theoretical level. Failure to recognize this fact has done much to foster and promulgate the myth of the "one true light" and has led to extreme positions, polemics, and protestations that serve only to antagonize those of other persuasions. Specific psychotherapeutic techniques that serve to differentiate psychotherapeutic systems are not, regardless of their school of origin, inevitable or exclusive deductions from that theoretical system, ". . . since the same theory may suggest several techniques and a single technique [may] be deduced from many theories" (London, 1964, p. 32). This has been aptly illustrated by Weitzman (1967), in his analysis of Wolpean systematic desensitization in terms consistent with Freudian, Jungian, and Sullivanian theoretical systems. For example, he argues that, from a Freudian perspective, the therapeutic effects of systematic desensitization may be understood as deriving from the ego's confrontation with anxiety-evoking impulses during periods of

---

*Our focus throughout this book will be upon maximizing the prescriptive utilization of individual psychotherapy. This is a major, largely unmet clinical goal. A second and even more desirable ultimate target is the prescriptive blending of individual psychotherapy with other treatment modes. We will not, in the present book, address ourselves to such blending of approaches in the belief that a satisfactory prescriptive use of a single approach (individual psychotherapy) must precede its use in combination with other approaches. The reader wishing to pursue issues relevant to the prescriptive blending of approaches may wish to examine the following articles dealing with individual psychotherapy as it interacts with drug therapy (Uhlenhuth *et al.*, 1969), group therapy (Guttmacher & Birk, 1971), physical therapy (Alexander, 1966), nutritional therapy (Stuart, 1971), ward atmosphere (Kellam *et al.*, 1967), and nonspecific therapy effects (Ludwig, 1968).

attention to hierarchically arranged images as well as to the reality-oriented binding of cathexes resulting from the inhibition of anxiety while the patient is in a state of deep muscular relaxation. Similarly, for a Sullivanian, systematic desensitization acts to preclude the arousal of anxiety and the clouding of consciousness, which maintain defensive parataxic thought. In this fashion, systematic desensitization provides the conditions for rational, syntactic thought processes to emerge.

There are yet many other examples in the literature in which the technique of systematic desensitization — originally conceived, refined, and popularized within a Pavlovian learning theory framework — has been reconceptualized and integrated into the "cognitive" psychologies (e.g., Brown, 1967; Wilkins, 1971). Significantly, such reformulations of the effects of systematic desensitization may go beyond mere rhetoric and restatements, by suggesting revisions on both procedural and theoretical levels (e.g., D'Zurilla & Goldfried, 1971; Goldfried, 1971; Wilkins, 1971; Wilson & Davison, 1969). We concur with Weitzman's (1967) position that

> The consequences, for a psychotherapist, of acknowledging the possible utility of systematic desensitization, bear illustration. One may tentatively accept the data which report the effectiveness of this technique and which deny contraindicating consequences. One may use the technique to give relief to one's patients. When the use of this technique is allowed, and when its implications are permitted to interact with an existing analytic, or other, orientation, possibilities occur which, while quite foreign to the behavior therapists, may lead to technical and theoretical growth. . . . Dynamic points of view also suggest possible technical innovations in the desensitization procedure itself which are not likely to present themselves to a behavior therapist of a learning theory persuasion.* (pp. 310–311)

Important advances and innovations in psychotherapy theory and technique (e.g., problem solving, self-control and self-regulation, convert control, biofeedback) have in part occurred when a therapeutic procedure of demonstrable effectiveness has been examined, explained, and expanded upon from a theoretical orientation at variance with the rationale originally used to understand the technique. We urge and support efforts by clinicians to explain through their theoretical orientations the empirically demonstrated effects of therapeutic procedures derived from different and often antithetical positions, to remain receptive to ensuing accommodations that may be indicated at both the procedural and theoretical level, and to maintain a continuous feedback between the technology of therapeutic change and the scientific theories accounting for the change process.

Perhaps almost as difficult as the implementation of skilled eclecticism among persons choosing to function as professional helpers is the ability to

---

*From B. Weitzman, Behavior therapy and psychotherapy, *Psychological Review*, 1967, *74*, 300-317. Copyright 1967 by the American Psychological Association.

know when one's approach is not appropriate for a given patient. Yet it is patently true that the most effective therapeutic approach for a given patient differs both from patient to patient and within a given patient at different points in his treatment career. Stated this way, the foregoing seems to be a truism, a viewpoint with which few would disagree. Yet training philosophies and practitioner needs typically mitigate against a more appropriate prescriptive stance. Instead, what Kiesler (1966) has cogently described as the "patient uniformity myth" largely prevails — and treatments continue to be dispensed on bases insufficiently relevant to prognostic considerations. Heller (1965) has commented that our field is in need of precision rifles, not therapeutic shotguns. We would similarly urge that our need is for psychotherapies and not psychotherapy; that our need, furthermore, is for psychotherapies that fit the patient — that is, prescriptive psychotherapies.

SPECIFIC THERAPEUTIC INGREDIENTS

While we do not wish to carry an analogy between our present focus and pharmacological terminology too far, it will be useful to examine the subject of active versus inert and specific versus nonspecific psychotherapeutic ingredients. This examination of the "components" of successful psychotherapies will later permit us to reflect more adequately upon (a) the bases for prescriptiveness, (b) prescription building and utilization, and (c) prescription testing and revision.

Psychotherapy outcome research has passed through three stages. The first was the global outcome stage, during which treatments were compared for their overall efficacy, but little or no information was obtained which identified and distinguished the therapeutic wheat from the inert chaff of whichever approaches seemed globally effective. The minimal usefulness of such research for clinical practice, for improving the clinical value of psychotherapy, led to a flight from global outcome studies to studies of the psychotherapy process. While this strategic reorientation did represent a step in the direction of prescriptiveness (since patient, therapist, and treatment variables more fully became the targets of study), the flight from global outcome concerns had gone too far. Means and ends became confused. Patient, therapist, and treatment dimensions were investigated primarily in a manner *independent* of their consequences for patient change. Astin (1961) has correctly described this as a time during which a functional autonomy of psychotherapy research prevailed. This was a period in which psychotherapy research became the study of "a rich interpersonal laboratory," but one in which the patient and his concerns somehow became essentially lost. A third outcome research strategy eventually developed, and prevails today. It may be described as the study of outcome-related process variables. Therapist, patient, and treatment dimensions remain the targets of study, but now are increasingly related in a systematic manner to a wide array of outcome criteria. A research strategy oriented toward the identification, development, and utilization of prescriptive psychotherapies is wholly consistent with this contemporary view of outcome research. Such outcome-related process research may, in fact, be appropriately viewed as a necessary precondition to prescriptive research attempts. It seeks to identify the therapeutic components (patient, therapist, therapy) which subsequent prescriptive studies attempt to combine optimally.

Investigations of outcome-related process variables, combined with parallel advances in psychotherapeutic theory, have led to the identification of a number of potential active therapeutic ingredients. We have termed these processes *potential* active ingredients because, while each has frequently been identified as associated with favorable outcomes on one or more criteria, each has rarely been so identified in a prescriptive manner. Most of the research supporting the therapeutic impact of the following ingredients (Bergin & Strupp, 1972) is pre-prescriptive in that it points to the potency of the given processes with little regard to its selective action — i.e., to identifying with which types of patients it does and does not have its typical impact: (a) counterconditioning, (b) extinction, (c) cognitive learning, (d) reward and punishment, (e) transfer and generalization, (f) imitation and identification, (g) persuasion, (h) empathy, (i) warmth, and (j) interpretation. Further work obviously is necessary toward the goal of a continuing development of our understanding of potential active therapeutic ingredients. Additional ingredients must be identified, their individual and combined actions delineated, the types of patients for whom each process is most appropriate specified, and the types of therapists most effective with each process determined. That is, in this pre-prescription phase of psychotherapy research (on patient, therapist, and treatment dimensions) the active and inert must be identified, examined, and maximally understood.

Even if most of the methodological difficulties characteristic of psychotherapy research could be wished away, other difficulties would remain to hinder the task of identifying the components of effective therapeutic prescriptions — i.e., potential active ingredients. To identify and utilize a therapeutic prescription for a given patient, one needs information not only regarding which processes or ingredients are or can be "active," but which are or can be *specific* active ingredients. Potential active therapeutic ingredients, once differentiated from the typically inert, can be further differentiated into specific and nonspecific in order that the therapeutic development of each class of ingredient be maximized. Specific active ingredients refer to those aspects of a therapeutic approach which differentiate it from other approaches and which are purported to be responsible in part for the approach's effectiveness. Included here are the pairing of relaxation and imagined approach to feared objects in desensitization therapy, nonrelaxed and intense imaginal involvement with feared objects characteristic of implosive therapy, psycho-analysis' free association, role reversal in psychodrama, etc. Each such technique has been explicitly declared "central, therapeutic, and idiosyncratic" for the given therapeutic approach by its proponents. Yet, for reasons including, but certainly not limited to, the one-true-light assumption, the validity of such specific active ingredient claims remains only partially substantiated.

NONSPECIFIC THERAPEUTIC INGREDIENTS

Psychotherapy researchers and theoreticians have also made beginning progress in identifying nonspecific active ingredients. In contrast to specific active ingredients, held to be idiosyncratic to particular approaches, nonspecific ingredients refer to those active therapeutic ingredients purportedly held in common by most or all psychotherapies. The therapist's communication skills may be viewed as one such ingredient. He may be ". . . an expert conversationalist whose specialized equipment include: sensitivity to the emotional nuances of the patient's communication, an ability to listen selectively, facility in encouraging the patient to start and continue conversation, deftness in leading the patient to particular topics, capacity both to tolerate the patient's silences and to use his own silence in communicating"* (Schofield, 1964, p. 106).

A second nonspecific active therapist ingredient may be the ascendant or power position of the therapist relative to that of the patient, particularly during the earlier phases of therapy (Schofield, 1964). The status and stature of the therapist are enhanced through a variety of conditions that are operative within all psychotherapies (Haley, 1963). Patients seek help from a socially sanctioned healer, and their very distress leads to viewing him as a person of considerable potency and status. During the initial interviews, the patient may be further inculcated with his diminutive role when instructed to talk about his inadequacies, his hurts, his failures, and his symptoms to an individual whose overt behavior appears adequate, competent, and confident. Moreover, during these early sessions, the therapist largely specifies the rules for treatment, the nature of the contract, the manner in which the patient will conduct himself (e.g., free association, dream reports, muscular relaxation, etc.), and the amount of money to be paid to meet with him. In the background are the professional trophies and paraphernalia (e.g., titles, diplomas, certificates, furniture arrangements, etc.) which augment the therapist's superior position.

---

*From William Schofield, *Psychotherapy: The purchase of friendship,* © 1964, Prentice-Hall, Inc., Englewood Cliffs, N.J.

We may also view the "asocial and unengaged" quality of the therapist's behavior as an important nonspecific active ingredient underlying positive gains in most psychotherapies. Beier (1966) has proposed that

> The uniqueness of the psychotherapy hour lies in the fact that the therapist is a social human being who will respond to the conventions of our language and will therefore necessarily become engaged by the patient. But he is also trained to look at himself, to use himself as an instrument, and to learn from his own engagements what ails the patient. Rather than respond within the emotional climate expected of him and reinforce the present adjustment of the patient (as most of the patient's respondents will usually do), he can disengage from the patient's expectations. ... It is this unexpected response of the therapist, which represents concern for the patient rather than self concern, that forces a change in the patient's experience.* (p. 247)

Such beneficial disengagements and asocial responses by the therapist may be expressed as reflections of feeling (client-centered specific active ingredient), interpretations of unconscious meanings (psychoanalytic specific active ingredient), identification of previously unarticulated assumptions (rational-emotive specific active ingredient), or instructions to relax one's muscles and imagine feared situations (systematic desensitization specific active ingredient). From this perspective, specific active ingredients originating from different schools of therapy may be conceptualized as instances of a common nonspecific active therapeutic ingredient. Thus, while the means of communicating beneficial disengagements and asocial responses differ systematically between psychotherapies, the essential nonspecific active ingredient may be embraced by all psychotherapies.

Another nonspecific active patient ingredient is the arousal of favorable expectations for change through dependence upon the psychotherapist (Frank, 1961; Goldstein, 1962). Even in systematic desensitization therapy, in which an array of specific active ingredients has been tentatively identified, the effect of positive expectancies is an additional determinant of therapeutic outcome (Marcia *et al.,* 1969). "Increasingly in our society because of the improved education of the public the patient brings to his therapist a readiness to be helped and some faith in the process" (Schofield, 1964, p. 108). Recent evidence suggests that patients' faith is more informed than blind, that they may have accurate expectations about which treatment they view will have greater therapeutic benefits for them (Devine & Fernald, 1973). Not only patient expectancies but also those held by the psychotherapist may be viewed as an active, nonspecific ingredient.

The most celebrated nonspecific active ingredient discussed in the psychotherapy literature involves the interpersonal relationship between therapist and patient. Unlike other social relationships, the therapeutic relationship is lim-

---

*From E. G. Beier, *The silent language of psychotherapy*. Chicago: Aldine, 1966.

ited and controlled. When it occurs, where it occurs, how frequently it occurs, its potential duration, and, to some extent, what will transpire may all be specified beforehand. According to Schofield (1964), ". . . . this fact of definite controls on what the patient may do or fail to do, and what he can require of the therapist, constitutes what may be the most distinctive feature of the therapeutic relationship. This feature of controlled relationship is espoused in nearly all methods of psychotherapy" (p. 109). In each method of therapy, the sincerity, honesty, concern, utilitarian purposefulness, and confidentiality of the therapist-patient relationship provide the catalyst for new social and personal learning to occur.

Therapeutic nonspecific ingredients are relevant to the general aims and outcomes that are common to diverse forms of psychotherapeutic intervention. Parloff's (1967) differentiation between mediating and ultimate goals of psychotherapy may be useful for understanding the nonspecific effects of psychotherapy. Mediating goals are learned changes in patients that are deemed necessary by a particular school of psychotherapy for the course of that treatment to be considered progressive. As such, they represent the effects produced by the specific active ingredients of that therapy (e.g., resolution of the transference neurosis, changing convictions about one's self, extinction of maladaptive anxiety and emotional habits, etc.). Ultimate goals, on the other hand, are value judgments about what is deemed to be ultimately desirable for the final outcomes of therapy to be considered effective.

> There is ample evidence that the statements of mediating goals are quite different, depending on the therapist, school, evaluation of the patient's needs, concepts of mental health, and moral values; however, there is a reasonable basis for the speculation that there may be relatively little difference in the goals regarding ultimate change. Such differences as exist regarding the ultimate goals appear to concern not the nature of the changes but rather their durability and their extent. (Parloff, 1967, p. 16)

Most schools of psychotherapy view as a desired outcome the reduction of psychopathology (symptomatology). This has been expressed in terms of providing the patient with opportunities ". . . to learn new and more appropriate responses to the symbols that are evoking in him what we call neurotic behavior" (Hobbs, 1962, p. 744). In a similar fashion, as Harper (1959) observes, the sources of overconcern, guilt, and worry that originally were seen by the patient as centrally important become viewed as less important and unnecessary. At the least, the patient gains a perspective on his fears and anxieties and comes to find future anxieties less threatening and attention-compelling.

In addition to reducing sources of discomfort, most psychotherapies work toward improving the patient's personal and interpersonal functioning. Primarily through the nonspecific relationship factors, the patient learns to become involved in an intimate relationship without getting hurt; he learns that it is possible to have an open, honest, and disclosing interpersonal encounter; he learns more realistic ways of coping with life's problems from a more rational and adaptive person (therapist); and he typically acquires a new set of assumptions, constructs, values, beliefs, or myths from the therapist that are more functionally congruent with social reality. In this fashion patients become more sensitized to perceive and experience new sources of pleasure in the form of enhanced external (interpersonal) and internal (self) relationships.

Since one of our purposes in underscoring the importance of identifying active therapeutic ingredients, specific and nonspecific, is to urge their more adequate prescriptive use, we strongly support and encourage the several lines of research by many investigators which have led to the identification of these ingredients. Yet it must be noted that such pre-prescription progress continues to be attenuated by the fact that one man's specific ingredients are another man's nonspecific ingredients. For example, a psychoanalytic patient reclines on a couch, shares with his analyst (week after week) thoughts and feelings never previously verbalized to another (or himself), and receives calm and accepting responses from the analyst rather than the feared criticism. What shall this series of events be called? Or, stated more prescriptively, what shall this series of events be called in order to improve its therapeutic impact with given patients? Shall we describe it in largely nonspecific terms, as the analyst might, and thus invoke primarily relationship constructs? Or is it more psychotherapeutically heuristic to view such events as a sort of "unsystematic desensitization," an approximation to another man's specific ingredient?

When the desensitizer, while spending several early sessions in gathering information for hierarchy construction purposes, communicates to his patient in a variety of ways that he (the therapist) has high expectations of a favorable outcome, mastery of a set of procedures of apparent value with past patients, and so forth, how shall we explain later positive outcomes? Shall we do so strictly in terms of specific ingredients or, perhaps more appropriately, by also invoking relationship, expectancy, and other placebo-like constructs? We do not know the answer in these specific instances, and are simply urging that such questions be asked and empirically answered.

The realignment of specific and nonspecific active ingredients may occur in well-established forms of therapy depending upon changes in the theoretical understanding of the treatment. For example, Goldfried (1971) has recently advanced a mediational interpretation of the active ingredients in systematic desensitization. In contrast to Wolpe's (1958) formulation of reciprocal inhibition to account for the effects of the desensitization procedure, Goldfried proposes that successful desensitization be construed as a self-control procedure which teaches the patient a general coping skill for reducing anxiety. Derived from this framework are specific active ingredients which are different from those in Wolpean desensitization and which are suggestive of several changes in the treatment procedure. For example, in the traditional form of desensitization, items reflecting a particular theme are hierarchically arranged from situations that evoke minimal levels of anxiety to situations that evoke intense levels of anxiety. Thus, in the Wolpean framework, the presentation of an anxiety hierarchy around a selected topic is a specific active ingredient. In contrast, the mediational viewpoint proposes that the specific active ingredient is the evocation of progressively more intense feelings of anxiety, irrespective of the thematic consistency of the stimuli producing the tension. Similarly, Wolpe considers it necessary for successful desensitization that the imagery of tension-producing scenes be terminated immediately, and concentrated thoughts and attempts at muscular relaxation be substituted. The prepotency of relaxation in comparison to feelings of anxiety is considered by Wolpe as another specific active ingredient in desensitization therapy. Within the mediational framework, however, maintaining the anxiety-arousing image and learning to control and attenuate its intensity is considered more veridical with actual life situations and thereby provides the patient with practice in effective coping. Thus, extended exposure in imagery to feared situations followed by relaxation-coping is proposed as an alternative specific active ingredient in systematic desensitization.

We are proposing here that the task of developing and utilizing prescriptive psychotherapies must be preceded or accompanied by considerably more activity in a research direction in which we already seem to be headed. This research is characterized by the empirical differentiation of active and inert therapeutic ingredients, as well as the sub-task of differentiating active specific from active nonspecific ingredients for given treatment approaches. Only as we succeed in such ingredient identification can we effectively constitute our most useful prescriptive psychotherapies — that is, only then can we turn to identifying the *selective* action of given ingredients: with *which* patients is the set of ingredients active? The identification of active therapeutic ingredients is but part of the precondition to prescriptive psychotherapies. We must not only have an array of potentially active procedures in our "psychotherapeutic pharmacy," but we must also have appropriate bases for identifying and describing who our treatment receivers and treatment dispensers will be. That is, before seeking to match treatments, patients, and therapists (i.e., before prescribing), we must not only know the treatments of potential value, but must also develop languages or classification systems relevant to the prescription process, languages or systems that may be used to more relevantly describe patients and therapists. We must develop bases for prescription.

PRESCRIPTIVE BASES — THE PATIENT

A number of ways of describing patients in a manner relevant to treatment prescription can be conceptualized. A medical model immediately suggests psychodiagnosis as one such descriptive approach. Unfortunately, psychodiagnosis as traditionally implemented may often be described as a largely treatment-irrelevant activity. With obeisance to the medical model, diagnostic procedures and formulations continue to be actively pursued, with very few of its implementers asking "diagnosis for what?" Therapists refer for diagnostic work-ups, duly file the resultant reports, and largely offer whatever is most prepotent in their therapeutic repertoire — independent of the psychodiagnosis.

Diagnosticians, therapists, and researchers concerned with both processes — diagnosis and psychotherapy — have done exceedingly little to relate the two in a meaningful way. Yet a few important beginnings in this direction are apparent. Within the behavior therapies movement there has been an increasing concern with behavioral classification, analysis, or diagnosis as an appropriate precondition to treatment selection and implementation (Goldfried & Pomeranz, 1968; Kanfer & Saslow, 1969). Equally rigorous assessment relevant to the selection and implementation of the insight-oriented or the existential therapies has been much less in evidence.

But therapists *do* use prescriptive bases other than their own theories. If they are typically not using psychodiagnosis, what are they using? Sanua (1966) claims, and we have marshaled concurring evidence (Goldstein, 1973), that patient social class is indeed a frequently, if implicitly, used prescriptive basis. For example, the lower-class patient in the United States and elsewhere strongly tends to be offered a more directive, concrete, and brieter psychotherapy than his middle-class counterpart. A less experienced therapist is also often "prescribed" for the lower-class patient. We and others have dealt elsewhere with questions regarding the appropriateness of such prescriptions (Goldstein, 1973). We simply wish here to underscore the reality that social class is, in fact, a very frequently used basis for choice of treatment decisions. The patient-candidate's cultural background, race, age, and sex appear to be additional, often implicitly used, bases upon which treatment dispensers make their prescriptive decisions.

Beyond the diagnostic-psychopathology and sociocultural realms, there appear to be both enduring trait and more transient state determinants of the treatment a patient will be offered. By trait critieria we refer to those predispositions or attributes that are believed to be relatively stable and enduring aspects of an individual's behavior. The potential usefulness of patient trait variables as a predictor of differential success in psychotherapy has been demonstrated by DiLoreto (1971). This study compared the relative effectiveness of systematic desensitization, rational-emotive, and client-centered group psychotherapy in introverts and extroverts seeking treatment for interpersonal anxiety. In terms of the relationship between treatment type and the trait variables of introversion-extroversion, it was found that client-centered therapy was approximately two and one-half times more effective in reducing anxiety with extroverts as opposed to introverts. In contrast, rational emotive therapy was three times more effective in alleviating anxiety with introverts than with extroverts. Interestingly, there were no reliable differences between introverts and extroverts treated by systematic desensitization, which also proved to be the most efficacious form of therapy. These results suggest the possibility that with "prescriptively powerful" or optimal treatments the contributions of trait factors relevant for positive therapy outcome are minimized. In contrast, with "weaker" or nonoptimal forms of treatment, trait factors may play a more predominant and significant role in determining the outcome of therapy.

We believe that there are at least two other patient determinants of the prescription that is offered. Both are rarely discussed or written about. One is the physical attractiveness of the patient. The second is the specific type of setting in which patient and treatment-prescriber find themselves. We would propose that prescriptions vary, in ways yet to be sufficiently elucidated, for the young attractive female, the elderly unattractive male, the obese adolescent, etc. We would also propose that an (in)patient newly arrived at a state hospital will frequently receive a different prescription than would the *same* patient presenting himself at any one of a number of other types of treatment settings, perhaps even including the outpatient clinic at the same hospital! Furthermore, Braginsky, Braginsky and Ring (1969) and Kelly, Farina, and Mosher (1971) have demonstrated that patients are resourceful and effective impression managers, able to willfully convey and manipulate intended levels of pathology, likableness, and mental health to professional clinicians whose dispositional judgments may be affected by these variables.

Even the development of new theories and techniques of psychotherapy can be understood in terms of the type of patient they are specifically designed to treat. New approaches typically appeal to and are tailored to the needs, characteristics, and consumer demands of previously untreated groups of potential patients (Lyons, 1973). Classical psychoanalysis was responsive to the psychologically constricted, guilt-ridden, European middle-class professional; ego and character analysis was shaped to accommodate the concerns of independence, lifestyle, and identity formation of early 20th-century Americans; neo-analysts spoke to the alienated and depressed women of this country; client-centered therapy reflected the optimism, freedom-seeking, and achievement orientation of the college campus clientele; rational-emotive therapy taught passive and ineffectual urbanites how to assertively cope with their overbearing and pressured environment; and behavior modification responded to the needs of the chronic mental patient with a technology for teaching basic self-help and socializing skills.

We are not faulting any of these bases for treatment prescription decisions. Each may indeed be of incremental value when used for such purposes, but each must be used *explicitly*. It is reasonable to conceptualize different treatments for persons of different social class levels or for persons differing in certain trait or state characteristics. However, such differences and their relevance to treatment must be overtly hypothesized, systematically examined, and then either sustained and used or refuted as a sociological or psychological myth and discarded. As we will elaborate later, beyond the point of "validation" of single patient prescriptive bases is their utilization in combination, as Magaro (1969) has urged with regard to patient social class and level of premorbid functioning. In essence, we would agree with Blocher (1968) that diagnosis and psychotherapy are ideally reciprocally contingent processes and that, as far as prescriptive psychotherapies are concerned, one can advance only as fast as the other.

PRESCRIPTIVE BASES – THE THERAPIST

We observed earlier that the most useful manner, clinically and investigatively, to frame the question of therapeutic outcome is: which treatment procedures, administered by which therapist to which patient, with which specific problems are predicted to yield which outcomes? Issues relevant to the pre-prescription treatment and patient components of this question have, in part, been addressed above. The therapist, too, is a matter of equal consequence for the optimal therapeutic prescription. As Kiesler (1966) has observed, we have operated according to the therapist uniformity myth – i.e., as if psychotherapists were generally equivalent and that in evaluating treatments it mattered rather little who the therapists were. The highly infrequent occurrence in research reports of specification in any detail of the therapists utilized is testimony to the widespread nature of this uniformity myth. But, as Bergin and Strupp (1972) propose, there is reason to believe that therapists are far from interchangeable. They differ in their theoretical and procedural preferences, training, and experience, in their age, race, and sex, and on such dimensions as professional-nonprofessional, A-B type, and so forth. Many of these therapist characteristics, examined in recent outcome-related process studies, have been identified as outcome relevant. They clearly deserve their place in the treatment-patient-therapist triad necessary for optimal prescriptiveness.

PRESCRIPTION BUILDING

We and others have thus proposed that outcome-enhancing therapeutic prescriptions jointly reflect, for a given patient, a tailored selection of patient, therapist, and treatment characteristics. How may such optimal prescriptions be formulated? Several approaches to prescription building have been proposed and utilized.

Trial and Error

Woody (1971) correctly observes that much of the psychotherapeutic pre-scribing that is currently done is of a trial-and-error nature. While such an implicit strategy is the most rudimentary and least efficient approach to prescriptiveness, it clearly is superior in its potential for enhanced therapeutic outcomes than the nonprescriptive one-true-light strategem. Trial-and-error prescribing requires a degree of therapist openness and procedural eclecticism, but effectively ignores the empirical research that is available relevant to optimal prescribing. In effect, the trial-and-error prescriber is his own "pre-scription desk reference," a state not likely to enhance our profession's ability to formulate and utilize effective therapeutic prescriptions.

In practice, a trial-and-error orientation to prescriptiveness not infrequently is inadequate in yet one other way. The phrase "trial and error" connotes a tentative act (the "trial") whose results are objectively observed. Should the trial not succeed (an "error"), the failure purportedly functions as feedback suggesting (a) not repeating the initial trial again and again, and (b) how to shape subsequent trials more effectively toward one's goal. In reality, the "error" or failure of one's trial is often ignored or misperceived so that the initial trial continues indefinitely. More in terms of our present concerns, the psychotherapy initially prescribed is offered again and again in the face of either disconfirming evidence regarding its effectiveness or, more likely, no outcome evidence. This is the not uncommon functional autonomy tendency in our field — the tendency to confuse hypothesis with conclusion. The seriousness of this failure of feedback is not only the repetition of inadequate psychotherapeutic prescriptions but their everwidening implementation. Reis-man (1971) notes that Freud was

> ... most specific about formulating criteria for the use of psychoanalysis. He saw his method as the treatment par excellence for hysterical and obsessional neurosis, but for other disorders he had less enthusiasm than his followers ... However, every limitation connotes a temptation, and no sooner were the boundaries of psycho-therapy drawn than tests were made of their inviolability ... Perhaps all too quickly the qualifications about the characteristics of the suitable client for psychotherapy were punctured and collapsed. (pp. 63-68)

Semi-Prescriptions

The one-true-light assumption is not surrendered easily. Many of its holders, seeing certain types of patients remaining unimproved despite their partici-pation in the given psychotherapy, have concluded that their preferred ther-apy is still the one true light; either the patient must be altered to fit the treatment or the patient is not the right kind for that form of treatment. In its most extreme form, the therapist may pronounce the "untreatability" of the patient. Freud, again unlike many of his followers advocated the position that "... psychological theories of therapy must come to a point where they will make it possible to select the therapy which is good for a patient and not the patient who is good for a therapy" (Rapaport, 1959, p. 144). Yet, even this proposition is an overstatement in light of research indicating that relatively minor and brief interventions designed to realign the patient's preparedness for therapy can at times enhance the prescriptive potency of psychotherapeutic treatments. In these instances the "goodness" of a patient for a particular treatment is induced through specific procedures explicitly designed to change the patient in ways that maximize responsiveness to the treatment. The psychotherapy research group at Johns Hopkins (Hoehn-Saric *et al.,* 1964), basing their efforts on Orne and Wender's (1968) socialization interview, "made the patient fit the therapy" by means of having him participate in a Role Induction Interview. This is a session in which likely patient resistances, respective patient and therapist role obligations and expectations, and common therapeutic events and difficulties are described, examined, and anticipated. The positive relevance of this procedure for therapeutic outcome has been reported by other investigators as well (Sloane *et al.,* 1970; Strupp & Bloxom, 1971).

Our own research efforts, seeking to enhance the "psychotherapeutic attraction" of resistive and semi-resistive patients, provide a second example of seeking to make the patient fit the (unchanged) treatment. In these investigations (Goldstein, 1971), social psychological laboratory methods for increasing the attraction of one individual to another were extrapolated to psychotherapeutic contexts and examined for their relationship-enhancing potency. The procedures thus utilized included various structuring interventions, manipulations of therapist status or patient candidacy-stage effort, modeling, matching, use of conformity pressure, and combinations of these and related techniques. As seems true for role induction, attraction-enhancing techniques proved effective as a semi-prescriptive strategy. Of clear relevance to the differential treatments theme of this book, it is noteworthy that while attraction-enhancement was almost uniformly successful across enhancement procedures for our several samples of middle-class patients, these same procedures were almost singularly unsuccessful with patients of lower socioeconomic status.

Negotiated Prescriptions

Semi-prescriptions and prescriptions derived from trial and error both place the full responsibility for prescription building upon the therapist. Blocher (1968) proposes, and we strongly concur, that therapist and patient purposefully engage in the prescription-building process together. Approximations to such negotiated prescriptiveness already exist in those therapeutic approaches emphasizing a therapeutic contract (Homme, *et al.,* 1970; Kanfer & Phillips, 1970; Sulzer, 1962), mutuality of therapist and patient role expectations

(Goldstein, 1962; Lennard & Bernstein, 1960), and pre-therapy trial sessions (Bach, 1954). We would push this notion even further, and urge a full and extended therapist-patient exchange of preferences and options. The outcome-relevant value of active patient participation in the prescription-building process is dramatically illustrated by the investigation conducted by Devine and Fernald (1973) in which patients assigned to their preferred treatment approach changed significantly more than did those randomly assigned to the same array of treatments or those assigned to a nonpreferred approach.

New Treatment Prescriptions

In lieu of trying out existing therapeutic approaches, as in trial-and-error prescribing, or having patients either select (negotiated prescriptions) or conform to (semi-prescriptions) such existing prescriptions, we may advantageously utilize existing information about treatments, patients, and therapists to construct new prescriptive psychotherapies. We noted earlier that our own attempt to make the lower-class patient fit (verbal, insight-oriented) treatment procedures largely failed. We then turned to a "new treatment" prescriptive strategy and asked how we might, instead, construct a treatment approach to fit such patients. Drawing heavily upon developmental and sociological research on social class-linked child-rearing practices, personality development, language codes, psychopathology, and stress-reducing styles, we proposed that a treatment approach tailored to the typical lower-class patient would be brief, authoritatively administered, have a behavioral emphasis, involve conformity to concrete example and role-taking training, and emphasize the development and reinforcement of an array of interpersonal and personal coping and mastery skills. We have reflected these treatment characteristics in an approach we have labeled Structured Learning Therapy, consisting of modeling, role playing, social reinforcement, and transfer training. Patients are exposed to a hierarchically arranged series of videotapes or films depicting an array of effective behavioral implementations of the skill behavior in which they are deficient (modeling), are given extended opportunity, encouragement, and guidance in behaviorally rehearsing or practicing these series of skill behaviors (role playing), are provided with approval, praise, or reward as their role play behaviors increasingly approximate that of the model (social reinforcement), and the foregoing procedures are implemented in such a manner that generalization from training setting to real-life is maximized (transfer training). Our empirical tests to date of Structured Learning Therapy provide consistent, if beginning, evidence of its prescriptive value for lower-class patients (Goldstein, 1973).

Beyond its value as an illustration of a new treatment prescription, the development of Structured Learning Therapy suggests two additional concerns relevant to prescription building. Grinker (1969) has championed the value of drawing upon an interdisciplinary research base when formulating psychotherapeutic prescriptions. In a manner reminiscent of the fable of a blind man describing an elephant, he urges that we see beyond our preferred assumptions and collaborate with colleagues holding different preferences in our efforts to truly perceive the patient and his therapeutic needs. Not only are the analysts and psychopharmacologists well advised to collaborate, as Grinker proposes, but, we would add, prescriptive collaboration between the several disciplines *within* psychology (all of which are concerned with behavior change) can and has had positive outcome-relevant benefit in psychotherapy.

We reported above our beginning success in developing a prescriptive psychotherapy for the lower-class patient. But "lower-class" is but a single prescriptive basis, and one which no doubt masks as many prescription-relevant between-patient differences as it illuminates. We must, therefore, view such prescriptive successes as tentative and temporary. Our efforts must focus upon building progressively more differential and idiosyncratic treatment approaches. To do so, it is appropriate that we follow a process of incremental prescription building.

Incremental Prescription Building

Bergin and Strupp (1972) have urged an incremental prescriptive strategy, one in which partial or tentative prescriptions are replicated, combined, and empirically examined in such a manner that one can ascertain whether the percent of outcome variance accounted for is, as predicted, progressively increasing. Klett and Moseley (1963) champion a similar incremental strategy. They propose a prescription-building process in which (a) active treatment ingredients are identified, (b) their weighting vis-à-vis outcome variance is determined, (c) ingredients are combined into new sets and combinations, and (d) the new prescriptive combinations are offered, evaluated, reweighted, and so forth. Magaro (1969) has proposed a prescriptive schema in which both patient social class and level of premorbid personality functioning are reflected in the treatment procedures and personnel utilized. Were we to add, in our use of Structured Learning Therapy, the recommendations regarding type (occupation) of personnel he proposes, we would be implementing an incremental prescription-building strategy. We would be progressing still further along such incremental lines if, in addition, we tested McLachlan's (1972) notion that such treatment personnel be of the same Conceptual Level as the patients they are treating.

In the incremental building and evaluation of such therapeutic prescriptions, it is vital that the development and validation of both "false positive" and "false negative" prescriptions be avoided. False positive prescriptions — those that appear effective but are not — may result from failure to differentiate specific from nonspecific active ingredients. Primal screaming may appear to "work" and henceforth be prescribed, when more adequate research scrutiny might have revealed that the patient changes indentified were more parsimoniously attributable to "just" such nonspecific effects as relationship, expectancy, or attentional phenomena. False positive prescriptions may also result from need-determined confusion of hypothesis and conclusion, when attachment to one's theory overrides one's evidence.

False negative prescriptions, those that do not appear effective but that are, may readily follow from violation of any of the uniformity myths described by Kiesler (1966). The assumption that all patients in one's sample are the same or effectively interchangeable can, and probably will, mask evidence regarding for which sub-samples within this larger sample the treatment is effective. Parallel concerns exist regarding therapist samples. Patient and therapist samples displaying within-sample homogeneity on prescription-relevant dimensions are requisite for avoidance of false negative prescriptions. Weak outcome measures and failure to specify in advance the amount and type of changes expected are other likely sources of support for false negative prescriptions.

Prescriptive Levels – A Research Hierarchy

A great deal more outcome-related process research identifying therapeutic ingredients, and much more study of the therapeutic impact of prescriptively combined selections of these ingredients is a vital necessity. To aid in this investigative-prescriptive endeavor, we wish to propose a schema or hierarchy that may be utilized heuristically to both view and generate the needed prescriptive inquiry. This schema hierarchically arranges types of investigations by number and type of prescriptive variables systematically examined or differentiated.

At the lowest level of prescriptive differentiation, the Nondifferential prescription, an approach to psychotherapy (Type 1A) *or* a kind of psychotherapist (Type 1B), is specified for a type of patient. Such prescriptions are either declarations or demonstrations that a given set of therapeutic procedures or a given type of psychotherapist is of therapeutic benefit for a given type of patient. For example, Wolman's (1966) declaration regarding the usefulness of interactional procedures with schizophrenic patients, and Atthowe and Krasner's (1968) demonstration of the usefulness of contingent reinforcment procedures with similar patients are both Nondifferential prescriptions (Type 1A). Neither paper seeks comparisons with other types of treatments, nor does either seek to examine the effectiveness of its recommended procedures with other types of patients. Further, in both instances treater characteristics are neither varied nor, for the most part, even specified. These are straightforward proclamations (Wolman) or empirical demonstrations (Atthowe & Krasner) that psychotherapy A "works" for patients X. Such

Prescriptive Psychotherapies: A Research Hierarchy

Level 1. Nondifferential
> Type 1A: Psychotherapy A for patients X
> Type 1B: Psychotherapist 1 for patients X

Level 2. Unidifferential
> Type 2A: Psychotherapy A versus psychotherapy B for patients X
> Type 2B: Psychotherapist 1 versus psychotherapist 2 for patients X
> Type 2C: Psychotherapy A for patients X versus patients Y

Level 3. Bidifferential
> Type 3A: Psychotherapy A Versus psychotherapy B for patients X versus patients Y
> Type 3B: Psychotherapist 1 versus psychotherapist 2 for patients X versus patients Y

Level 4. Tridifferential
> Type 4A: Psychotherapy A versus psychotherapy B for patients X versus patients Y with psychotherapist 1 versus psychotherapist 2

articles are very common in the psychotherapy literature. Rather than describing the patient in psychopathological terms (as above), age, socioeconomic status, cultural background, and a wide array of other demographic, personality, and behavioral characteristics may be utilized.

A second type of Nondifferential prescription (Type 1B), similarly fails to vary or block on any of the three prescriptive components – therapy, patient, or therapist. A therapist type is specified and recommended for a given type of patient. Contrasting or inappropriate therapist types are not indicated, patients for whom the specified therapist is viewed as inappropriate are not differentiated, and no delineation of treatment procedures is concomitantly proposed. Brody's (1970) description of Freud's caseload, and McMahon and Shore's (1968) paper on therapist behaviors vis-à-vis low-income patients are two examples of a Nondifferential prescription, Type 1B. In addition, these two articles are also illustrations of two rather common means by which Nondifferential prescriptions of this type are communicated in the professional literature. Brody's article may be viewed as an example of "prescription by discipleship" – i.e., this is what the "master" does or did and thus, by clear implication, one should follow suit. McMahon and Shore prescribe, in contrast, by "negative example." By a detailed specification of the therapist qualities and behaviors deemed *in*appropriate for a given patient type, the converse is prescribed by implication.

Nondifferential prescriptions delimit or differentiate only by implication, but they are more valuable for prescriptive purposes than is the totally nonprescriptive one-true-light position by which psychotherapy A "works" not just for a given type of patient but for all or most types of patients. In an incremental or building-block approach to prescription building, the Nondifferential prescription is the first step. But our science of psychotherapy research and our art of psychotherapeutic practice both demand firmer foundation. Less rudimentary prescriptive questions must be addressed.

Somewhat more heuristic prescriptive concerns are raised and answered at the Unidifferential level of prescriptive research. Unlike the Nondifferential (in which, for example, a therapy is viewed as useful for a given type of patient), the Unidifferential prescription provides an important additional piece of information. In Type 2A, beyond specification that a psychotherapy is effective for a given type of patient, we are also informed as to which psychotherapy or psychotherapies are *not* of apparent effectiveness with the given patient population. Feinsilver and Gunderson (1972) provide just such Unidifferential information in their review of research on psychotherapy for schizophrenia. Schill and his associates (1974) do so in a highly rigorous manner for persons with public speaking anxiety.

The Type 2B Unidifferential prescription focuses on the therapist's contribution. Beyond the Nondifferential information that highly empathic (Truax, 1963) and B-type (McNair *et al.*, 1962) therapists are typically helpful to neurotic patients, we are also provided the important prescriptive findings that low empathy and A-type therapists are often not.

In a third type of Unidifferential prescriptive study (Type 2C), the treatment offered is held constant, but the types of patients for whom it is provided are systematically varied. MacCulloch and Feldman (1967) provide such a study, involving three sub-types of homosexual patients; Cole, Branch, and Allison (1962) do so with patients differentiated by social class.

Bidifferential prescriptive research systematically varies two of the three essential components of the "proper" outcome question — therapy, therapist, and patient. For example, Weinman, Gelbart, Wallace, and Post (1972) compare three treatment approaches for schizophrenic sub-samples differentiated by age. Love, Kaswan, and Bugental (1972) analogously vary treatments by socioeconomic levels. It will be instructive for the reader to compare these two Bidifferential studies with, respectively, the Unidifferential reports of Feinsilver and Gunderson (1972) and Cole, Branch, and Allison (1962), which were addressed to similar populations, but were not experimentally varied. It will become quite clear in doing so that the incremental prescriptive information in moving from Unidifferential to Bidifferential research is both investigatively significant and clinically of considerable importance. Feinsilver and Gunderson instruct us about treatments of likely use and not of likely use with groups of patients called "schizophrenic," but Weinman and his associates lead us to conclude that our prescription must also vary with the schizophrenic patient's age. Cole, Branch, and Allison, correctly report that the treatment represented in their study will or will not be likely to yeild results depending on patient social class, but Love, Kaswan, and Bugental tell us we can offer differential treatments as a function of social class.

Similarly useful clinical information is yielded by Type 3B Bidifferential research. Yamamoto, James, Bloombaum, and Hatten (1967) inform us that the patient's race combines with the therapist's ethnicity to influence treatment outcome. McLachlan (1972), working bidifferentially in a very different domain, provides outcome-relevant evidence regarding the importance of matching therapist and patient on Conceptual Level. We applaud these Bidifferential research efforts. They are significant clinical and investigative contributions. Yet, they are expensive investigations — in time, effort, and money. The expense, difficulty, and potential payoff of factorial psychotherapy research grows many fold when we consider the next level of prescriptive investigation — the Tridifferential, i.e., treatments X patients X therapists.

Tridifferential prescriptive research, *none of which to our knowledge has actually been conducted,* is the experimental attempt to answer the ultimate prescriptive questions: which treatment, for which patient, by which therapist. Tridifferential answers will be best obtained by Tridifferential research, and such research is to be most strongly encouraged. Tridifferential answers can be approximated by carefully sequenced studies in a research program consisting of primarily Bidifferential investigations. A few existing investigations, technically Bidifferential in design, have approximated Tridifferential answers on a *post hoc* basis. DiLoreto's (1971) investigation compared the effectiveness of three treatments (Systematic Desensitization, Rational-Emotive and Client-Centered) with two types of patients (anxious introverts and anxious extroverts). Therapist dimensions were not varied; thus, no specific therapist effects, main or interaction, were predicted. *Post hoc* analyses revealed, however, that certain therapists were indeed more effective than others with one type of patient sampled or the other. To have blocked on therapists would have required a more elaborate and expensive experimental design than the already admirably ambitious project DiLoreto did undertake. Nevertheless, not having blocked or otherwise manipulated therapist dimensions in this study clearly curtailed the prescriptive information it provides.

Three other approximations to a Tridifferential prescription may be briefly noted. As in DiLoreto's (1971) study, each actually manipulated only two of the three dimensions necessary for optimal prescriptiveness. Each sought to approximate such prescriptiveness, however, via *post hoc* analysis involving the given third variable involved. Stephens and Astrup (1965) conducted a retrospective analysis of treatment (insulin coma therapy versus no insulin coma therapy) by patient (process schizophrenic versus reactive schizophrenic) by therapist type (A or B). Blumberg (1972) manipulated treatment (leading versus following psychotherapy) and patient (high dogmatic versus low dogmatic) variables, and carefully chose as therapists persons judged to be consistent in their lifestyle with a leading or following orientation. Miller, Barrett, Hampe, and Noble (1972) compared Systematic Desensitization and traditional, verbal psychotherapy, each implemented by an experienced or inexperienced psychotherapist. Their *post hoc* analysis revealed that, in addition to these treatment and therapist manipulations, the age of their patients was relevant to psychotherapeutic outcome. In none of these studies were all three prescriptive dimensions manipulated. In none, therefore, were three-way interactions tested; and thus, in none were Tridifferential prescriptions forthcoming. Such prescriptions, it may be reemphasized, are the major stepping stones toward effective and enduring psychotherapeutic outcomes. Several of our clinical and research-oriented colleagues, as articles in the next section of this book will underscore, have also urged upon us the value of a prescriptive orientation in general and Tridifferential psychotherapy studies in particular. We seek in this book to join them in this viewpoint and elaborate its basis further. We wish to conclude this commentary on the hope that psychotherapy researchers will indeed operationalize such an investigative philosophy, thus augmenting the potential prescriptiveness of psychotherapeutic practice.

PART II

Prescription Development

Commentary: Viewpoints on Prescription

Our own views regarding the value and development of prescriptive psychotherapies have been presented. We have also suggested a schema for both conceptualizing and generating investigations that may yield progressively more useful psychotherapeutic prescriptions. In Part II we wish the relevant views of others to be heard. Issues bearing upon the prescriptive process are many and varied; they warrant thoughtful consideration.

The role of diagnosis, broadly defined, can and should be a central one in the development and utilization of prescriptive psychotherapies — in contrast to its frequent treatment-irrelevant status. Breger's paper is one thoughtful specification of this role, as he emphasizes the desirability of curtailing routine and broadly applied pre-treatment testing and a shift instead to selective testing implemented to answer specific treatment-relevant questions. His is a reasoned plea for prescriptively *useful* psychological testing. Goldfried and Pomeranz are of a similar mind. Diagnosis, they hold, must be oriented toward identification of specific treatment targets or outcome goals, and toward selecting the most appropriate treatment procedures for those targets. In their view, diagnosis and treatment must be mutually relevant. Woody espouses this prescriptive stance even more forcefully. For him, diagnosis *determines* treatment — a view we unequivocally endorse. His "psychobehavioral" diagnostic orientation leads to the gathering of information about the patient's reinforcement history and social learning contingencies as a means of deriving an initial treatment approach for *that* patient. This prescription is held tentatively in Woody's schema, and revised in an ongoing manner as its effects are observed. The prescriptive use of diagnostic information fits easily into a behavior modification orientation and should theoretically also fit well in a psychodynamic-medical model orientation. As noted earlier, it has not; diagnosis and treatment have assumed largely independent roles. Schlesinger, however, convincingly demonstrates that this need not be the case. Working from a psychodynamic viewpoint, he too calls for marked specification in the diagnostic process, both in detail and in relevance to treatment. Using the examples of supportive and expressive treatment approaches, he clearly makes evident how diagnosis *can* logically determine treatment.

The focus of these four articles, as noted, is upon diagnosis. Chief among the major points of each is the therapeutic benefit likely to follow from the prescriptive use of assessment data. Focusing on psychotherapy more than antecedent diagnosis, the next three articles take essentially a concurring view. Magaro, anticipating the major conclusion of the present book, urges the development of psychotherapeutic prescriptions that jointly reflect and optimally match therapy, therapist, and patient variables. Beyond this, his illustrative examples are seminal, and have already begun to prove empirically to be highly effective clinical prescriptions. Lazarus, reflecting his belief in judicious therapeutic eclecticism, wisely calls for a "personalistic psychotherapy," tailoring treatments to patients. Like Woody, he urges continued therapist openness and flexibility — rewriting the patient's prescription whenever and as often as necessary. Jacobson, Strickler, and Morley provide yet another affirmative view. They distinguish between generic and individual approaches to crisis-stress resolution. Generic approaches are stimulus-determined and focus on selecting and instituting treatments with a patient as a function of the type of stressor (e.g., death of a loved one, vocational or marital failure, etc.) rather than based upon the patient's individual dynamics. Individual approaches, in contrast, take the interpersonal and psychodynamic world of the person in crisis as the point of departure for determining the treatment to be offered. The dichotomy is a gross but meaningful one, particularly because the authors offer beginning prescriptive notions regarding when each type of approach may best be offered.

Regarding psychotherapeutic prescriptiveness, therefore, there is much theoretical agreement and much behavioral dissent. How is the prescriptive goal to be made more of a reality? How are an array of more adequate psychotherapeutic prescriptions to be determined? Paul's paper provides initial context for the primary answers to these questions. He deals well with the major issues of concern in psychotherapy outcome research, speaking to problems of design, criteria, variable selection and the like, comprehensively and with clarity. Pokorny and Klett add to Paul's presentation, as they speak with sophistication to a large number of central methodological concerns relevant to prescription determination. Both papers elaborate our view that outcome-relevant process studies yield the initial ingredients from which effective prescriptions are made. How such ingredients are optimally combined, and how such prescriptions are empirically validated are issues to which Kiesler addresses himself in the two articles of his we have included. Avoidance of the uniformity myths he describes, and reflection in the design of our prescription development studies of his grid model are major methodological steps toward the tasks of prescription development and verification.

The articles which follow, therefore, present a full array of issues and viewpoints relevant to the empirical development and clinical utilization of prescriptive psychotherapies. As a group, they will serve to both inform and set the stage for the remainder of this book, in which, currently useful clinical prescriptions are presented and considered in depth.

Diagnostic Considerations

1

Psychological Testing: Treatment and Research Implications*

LOUIS BREGER

Psychological testing has long been the unique speciality of the clinical psychologist, a fact that stems from the particular history of the field. Recent developments bring out a number of conflicts between the assumptions of this traditional emphasis and clinical practice. For example, Meehl (1960) has reported that only 17% of psychotherapists ($N = 168$ drawn from a "wide spectrum of orientations") believe that the prior knowledge contributed by testing is of much value to them. While this change in emphasis has come about first at the level of practice, the recent conference on training in clinical psychology (Hoch, Ross, & Winder, 1966) indicated that a reappraisal of the role of psychological testing in teaching and clinical training programs is also in progress. In these and other ways, it seems apparent that conflict exists between the traditional emphasis on testing and current practices. An examination of the history of this conflict and of the issues involved may allow us to break free of certain outmoded assumptions and practices.

Testing should be oriented in two broad directions: first, toward the practical question of what to do about persons and their problems—what might be called treatment in the most general sense—second, toward the comprehension of the nature of problems and effects of treatment—a function which might be labeled research or theoretical understanding. Traditional models of testing have been tied to the concepts of diagnosis and selection, both of which may prove largely inappropriate to much of the data that the clinical psychologist is now faced with and, more particularly, will be faced with in the future. Similarly, a good deal of the traditional research in the testing area (e.g., the innumerable Rorschach studies or the vast literature with intelligence tests directed at controversies over IQ constancy and the like) has not led to significant advances in theoretical understanding. To anticipate, it will be argued that assessment, built around the clinical-therapeutic interview, provides a more appropriate model for practice with that large group of persons referred for personality "diagnosis." First, let us consider a common

---

*From *Journal of Consulting and Clinical Psychology*, 1968, **32**, 176–181. Copyright 1968, by the American Psychological Association. Reprinted by permission.

justification for testing, that it constitutes an essential part of the clinical psychologist's "role."

TESTING AS PART OF THE PSYCHOLOGIST'S PROFESSIONAL ROLE

Deciding how best to help persons can be a very stress-producing affair, particularly when the state of understanding about persons, problems, and treatments is so far from complete. Clinical psychologists, along with their psychiatric and social-work colleagues, are, nevertheless, expected to function as experts in dealing with the persons and problems that face them in mental hospitals, outpatient clinics, counseling centers, and the like. Since it is almost impossible for anyone to continually question everything in his day-to-day functioning, psychologists and others react to this stressful state of affairs by falling back on some generally defined professional role which dictates in what areas they are experts, what kind of activities they will perform, what kind of language they will speak, how their relationships with other professionals will be structured, and other similar considerations. This is inevitable, though the pressure for it is probably greater in situations where there is much uncertainty about how to function ("treat" patients) and about who can function best. In this respect, we find psychiatrists falling back on certain historically established aspects of the physician role. (Physicians treat the sick—hence, they are the ones who must treat the "mentally ill"; physicians have the final responsibility—hence, they must be in charge of the ward or the "psychiatric team.") Similarly, we find clinical psychologists relying on certain historically established role characteristics in defining their functions and their areas of expertness vis-à-vis other professionals.

Psychological testing becomes especially valued in this regard because it is an area in which the psychologist is the unquestioned expert, as contrasted with an activity such as interviewing, where he must compete with psychiatrists, social workers, and others. Thus, testing becomes a key activity in defining the clinical psychologist's role in a way that gives him a sense of expertise in a distinctly outlined area with its own jargon, research literature, and special prerogatives.

Certainly not all, or even most, clinical psychologists use psychological testing solely as a rationalization for their lesser status or to gain security by reliance on a clearly defined set of routines, but these factors do enter to some degree in the functioning of many. More to the point is the inappropriateness of professional role considerations as a justification for psychological testing. To say that psychologists should test because this is their professional role makes little sense; it is like saying that barbers should bleed people because this is their professional role or that psychiatrists should give lobotomies because this is their role. Obviously this is a line of reasoning that can be used to perpetuate any existing form of practice, no matter how inappropriate or harmful. Psychological testing, like any other technique, must be evaluated in terms of the adequacy of its basic assumptions, its helpfulness to persons seeking treatment, and its contributions to actual decision making about patients, problems, and treatments. It makes little sense for the psychologist to perpetuate his role as tester in a state hospital where all patients receive the same treatment (or lack of treatment), regardless of what the psychological tests reveal, or in a situation where the individuals making decisions about treatment do not read the psychological report until after they have made their decisions. Testing may also be inappropriate when sources of information that may be more directly related to the decisions to be made can be quickly obtained (e.g., age, job history, length and number of previous hospitalizations).

HISTORICAL ANTECEDENTS

Beginning with Freud and continuing through the variety of psychotherapies that have branched out from psychoanalysis, there has been a merger of diagnosis with treatment. The psychoanalytic method of therapy is the method of personality "diagnosis." Sullivan's psychiatric interview is both "diagnosis" and "treatment." (Roger's client-centered approach, arising outside the medical framework, has never stressed the need for "diagnosis" before treatment.) The notion of separating treatment and diagnosis derives from different historical sources, as Gill, Newman, and Redlich (1954) point out, and cannot be justified within the frameworks of the major therapies themselves. Two such historical influences may be discerned: (*a*) a belief in the necessity of diagnosing patients before treating them, essentially a reassertion, following the psychodynamic trend begun by Freud, of the medical identification of psychiatry*; and (*b*) a belief in the value of accurate "selection," derived from the mental testing movement within psychology.

The medical diagnostic position is identified with workers such as Schafer (1948) and Rapaport (1954), who used tests to generate descriptions of personality or psychological functioning. Their identification with medical psychoanalysis has led many in this tradition to advocate complete psychological assessment as a part of the comprehensive diagnostic work-up. But, as Szasz (1965) points out, such a commitment to "diagnosis" is logically inconsistent with the basic premises of psychoanalytic therapy.

The belief in the value of selection springs from the mental testing movement, so prominent in clinical psychology's past, as typified by work with the

---

*A parallel reassertion is represented by the insistence of the orthodox psychoanalytic institutes that their candidates have medical training despite the almost wholly nonmedical nature of both psychoanalytic training and therapy (see Eissler, 1965).

MMPI and the value placed on accurate prediction (whether clinical or actuarial). The confluence of these traditions has reinforced a belief in the value of testing prior to treatment, a belief which begs the central questions concerning test usefulness and validity.

Testing, whether personality descriptive or selection oriented, is wasteful and may even be harmful insofar as it is separated from, and makes no practical contribution to, treatment. Many persons are most in need of, as well as most receptive to, treatment when they make their initial contact with a treating agency. A diagnostic enterprise that is separated from treatment may function as a road-block at this stage. Commitments to "diagnosis" before treatment or to "selection" both reinforce the fixed position or status of existing treatments. This is inappropriate in a field where little solid knowledge about the relationship between patient-treatment interactions exists. These commitments further the illusion that once a patient is diagnosed or selected, differential treatment will be forthcoming. An honest look at clinical practice reveals that in most instances differential treatment does not follow from differential categorization based on psychological tests. The main reason that testing is not integrally related to treatment is that the central implicit assumption underlying testing— that one will know what to do with the patient, how to "treat" him, once he has been "diagnosed" or assessed—is not true. The basic question of what sort of treatments (insight psychotherapy, group psychotherapy, family therapy, help in getting a divorce, help in changing jobs, etc.) work with what sort of people and with what effects or outcomes remains the central unanswered research question in the clinical assessment area. These points may be illuminated by a consideration of their implications for treatment and research.

TREATMENT

The following discussion is directed at those persons who voluntarily seek psychological help. Their disturbances may range from mild adjustment problems to severe psychosis, and their attitudes towards treatment may be resolute or conflicted; yet in a basic sense these voluntary patients differ from persons who are referred because someone other than themselves—whether parent, friend, or social agency—has decided that they have "psychological problems." Voluntary patients compose the bulk of the population which applies to outpatient · clinics, counseling centers, private practitioners, and community mental health programs. What is done with such persons at the time of their initial contact is frequently of great importance. Erikson (1964) directs his attention to what he terms "the problem of the lost momentum of initial commitment." He states:

> Hospitalized patients, having been committed, are often ready to commit themselves. They expect "to go to work," both on themselves and on whatever task they

may be asked to do. But too often they are met by a laborious process of diagnosis and initiation which emphasizes the absolute distance of patienthood from active life. Thus literally, "insult is added to injury" in that the uprooted one, already considered expendable or abnormal by his previous group of affiliations, finds himself categorized and judged by those who were expected to show him the way through a meaningful moratorium. Many a man acquires the irreversible identity of being a lifelong patient and client not on the basis of what he "is," but on the basis of what is first done about him. (p. 97)

The importance of not obstructing the individual's initial attempts to seek help holds equally with the less disturbed nonhospitalized person. Since psychological testing, like history taking and other diagnostic procedures, may obstruct the individual's initial help-seeking attempts, if and when one does test one should have very good reasons for doing so. Most clinician-testers would probably agree that the taking of tests themselves is of no great help to the patient; in fact the process may be harmful insofar as it reinforces his expectations of expert or magical cure and structures the future patient-therapist relationship in an inappropriate way. And as was pointed out above, when one tests during the initial contact, the opportunity to initiate treatment, whether psychotherapy or whatever, at the precise time when the patient is most receptive may be lost.

What reasons can be advanced in favor of testing? Essentially, the reasons are: first, testing can provide valuable information which aids in the decision about what kind of treatment is most appropriate; second, the information from testing is useful to the therapist if and when treatment is begun. Consider the following examples: (*a*) A patient may be tested to determine if he has sufficient resources (ego-strength) and assets to warrant psychoanalytic treatment, as opposed to brief less intensive psychotherapy*; (*b*) a patient may be tested to determine if he could be more suitably treated as an in or outpatient.

Examples of how testing could provide useful information to the therapist are: (*a*) Tests can detect psychotic or suicidal potential that might not become apparent to the therapist for some time and, hence, alert him; (*b*) it might be argued that the therapist is generally aided by prior knowledge of personality dynamics.

Each of these reasons raises its own important questions. First, can the testing procedures actually indicate which sorts of personalities are suitable for which sorts of treatment? Second, is the personality data supplied by testing useful in treatment? Clear-cut answers do not exist for either of these important questions at this time. In fact, the question of patient-treatment

---

*Such considerations are very likely to be irrelevant in most clinics where staff availability is the overriding concern.

interaction, what sorts of treatments have effects with what sorts of patients, should be the central research concern of anyone working with this material. Unfortunately, a commitment to diagnosis before treatment leads many to bypass this crucial issue.

Assuming that the patient somehow gets placed in treatment, whether group psychotherapy, individual psychotherapy, or whatever, one may again ask whether a knowledge of history and diagnosis is helpful in treatment. Again, there is no clear-cut answer; there are advantages and disadvantages. First, a foreknowledge of personality dynamics may alert the therapist to key conflict areas, key defensive operations, and the like and, hence, increase his sensitivity in responding to these areas. On the other hand, the same fore-knowledge may give the therapist a set for certain areas or topics which leads him to overlook or miss the importance of other things the patient is saying. Another consideration regards the effect of foreknowledge on the therapist's conception of himself—does it make him feel like an expert with secret wisdom to impart? If so, how does this affect his relationship with the patient? Many of the difficulties that stem from the untenable assumptions underlying diagnosis and assessment as prerequisites for treatment disappear when treatment is seen primarily as something which the patient himself must seek out and become involved in. Intake or first contact with voluntary patients may be viewed as the initial phase of treatment in which therapist and patient together explore the patient's difficulties and desires. The therapist acts as a therapist, giving the patient an opportunity to sample, first-hand, therapy as a way of coping with his problems. On the basis of this sample, the patient and therapist can work toward a decision about further treatment. Approaching the initial contact in this way is consistent with the assumptions of a variety of therapies—psychoanalytic, Sullivanian, Rogerian, etc. Furthermore, it makes good sense in terms of the assessment literature on predicting performance in complex situations. Experience here has shown that the best predictions stem from situations that most closely approximate the criterion situation itself. The best way for both therapist and patient to reach a decision on how the latter will perform in psychotherapy (or whether he wants to try it further) is to sample this criterion situation.

It should be stressed that the question of whether knowledge about personality dynamics is useful for treatment is a very open one that may ultimately depend on the kind of treatment, the kind of personality, and future improvements in both treatment techniques and testing instruments. For the present, it would seem that there are many ways in which testing is unrelated to treatment and may hinder it as well as help. One wonders whether many psychologists resort to tests rather than a direct engagement of the patient in an intake interview, which may be both diagnosis and treatment, for irrelevant professional role considerations. Hopefully, psychologists are beyond the point where they need feel they are infringing on the prerogatives of psychiatry when they interview rather than test. After all, what is medical about an interview?

An altogether different set of problems is presented by the chronic institutionalized populations found in many large state and veterans hospitals. Here, the basic treatment goal is to get the patient to the point where he can maintain a minimal level of functioning outside the hospital. In most cases, little in the way of internal psychological change can be accomplished, and treatment becomes oriented primarily to changing the syndrome of institutionalization. Programs in which the patients are formed into semiautonomous groups where they are forced to take charge of their own fates seem much more effective than many traditional forms of treatment (Fairweather, 1964). More recent modifications in this social-psychological approach to treatment include the establishment of patient-managed work centers in the community to facilitate the patient's reintegration in society. Traditional assessment and psychological testing activities have little use in these programs; rather, the psychologist turns his attention to the creation of experimental social groups and the evaluation of their effects.

RESEARCH

From the preceding discussion it should be clear that it is the use of tests in the clinical setting that is being considered and not their use for a variety of other research purposes (e.g., work in personality, child development, studies of stress, and the like). Still, within the clinical framework a number of research questions remain. The previous discussion indicated that psychological testing, like other diagnostic procedures, may obstruct the person's initial effort to do something about his difficulties. In fact, the actual effects of psychological tests on the person's subsequent response to treatment may be directly investigated. In a related form of research, Frank (1965) and his co-workers (Frank et al., 1959; Frank et al., 1963) have been studying the interaction of patient expectations and response to treatment. They find that patients with the most accurate expectations (i.e., those who were told what to expect in terms of their own and the therapist's behavior, including typical therapy phenomena such as resistance) exhibited the most favorable responses to the therapy. Insofar as testing and other diagnostic activities foster erroneous expectations (which they may do when no differential treatment follows diagnosis or when the therapist never "tells" the person what deep knowledge he has gleaned from the tests), they may be antitherapeutic.

While many persons voluntarily seek what amounts to therapy, there are others who voluntarily seek diagnosis or assessment. Along with these is a sizable group who are referred by others, including young children referred by parents or schools, cases of possible organic involvement, and similar problems. In all these cases, clinical assessment using psychological tests may be quite appropriate. In fact, because they lend themselves to standardized administration and scoring and, hence, may be more readily objectified, tests are superior to the interview for these purposes. Continuing research into the validity of tests for such specific assessment work is, of course, a necessity. There has been a tendency within the field towards identification with single instruments such as the Rorschach or with single approaches such as projective techniques, which really makes little sense when the goal should be the development of valid assessment procedures with respect to some specific goal such as identifying types of organic pathology. One would expect a process of on-going validation to result in the continual modification of the specific tests used in such a procedure. The fact that this has rarely taken place is probably the result of the confounding of two contradictory purposes—the "diagnosis of personality" and the assessment of specific problems such as organic brain damage. While the latter represents a legitimate use of tests in the clinical setting—it may be justified on both clinical and scientific grounds—the former is an unjustified carry-over of certain historical assumptions.

Perhaps, by recognizing these different purposes, clinical psychologists may give up, with a clear conscience, the testing of persons who voluntarily seek psychological help and, instead, use tests in those cases where they may make a valid contribution to specific decisions. Such a shift in emphasis has already occurred at the level of practice, but without a clear rationale the clinical psychologist is likely to feel guilty about not fulfilling his professional role. This guilt then tends to perpetuate the traditional emphasis on testing in training programs, an emphasis that may take training time away from more important skills. It is skills such as the sensitive use of the initial contact as both treatment and assessment and the continuing research refinement of assessment procedures with respect to specific and answerable diagnostic questions that seem more suited to the future roles of the clinical psychologist.

REFERENCES

Eissler, K. R. *Medical orthodoxy and the future of psychoanalysis.* New York: International Universities Press, 1965.

Erikson, E. Identity and uprootedness in our time. In E. Erikson (Ed.), *Insight and responsibility.* New York: Norton, 1964.

Fairweather, G. W. (Ed.) *Social psychology in treating mental illness: An experimental approach.* New York: Wiley, 1964.

Frank, J. D. Discussion of H. J. Eysenck, "The effects of psychotherapy." *International Journal of Psychiatry,* 1965, **1**, 288–290.

Frank, J. D., Gliedman, L. H., Imber, S. D., Stone, A. R., & Nash, E. H. Patient's expectancies and relearning as factors determining improvement in psychotherapy. *American Journal of Psychiatry,* 1959, **115**, 961–968.

Frank, J. D., Nash, E. H., Stone, A. R., & Imber, S. D. Immediate and long-term symptomatic course of psychiatric outpatients. *American Journal of Psychiatry,* 1963, **120,** 429–439.

Gill, M., Newman, R., & Redlich, F. C. *The initial interview in psychiatric practice.* New York: International Universities Press, 1954.

Hoch, E. L., Ross, A. O., & Winder, C. L. Conference on the professional preparation of clinical psychologists: A summary. *American Psychologist,* 1966, **21** 42–51.

Meehl, P. E. The cognitive activity of the clinician. *American Psychologist,* 1960, **15,** 19–27.

Rapaport, D. The theoretical implications of diagnostic testing proceedures. In R. P. Knight & C. R. Friedman (Eds.), *Psychoanalytic psychiatry and psychology.* New York: International Universities Press, 1954.

Schafer, R. *The clinical application of psychological tests.* New York: International Universities Press, 1948.

Szasz, T. S. *The ethics of psychoanalysis.* New York: Basic Books, 1965.

2

Role of Assessment in Behavior Modification*

MARVIN R. GOLDFRIED AND DAVID M. POMERANZ

Within the past decade, a group of investigators has brought into focus a number of techniques useful in dealing with clinical problems. These techniques, usually classified under the title "behavior therapy" or "behavior modification" have tentatively demonstrated their worth for a wide variety of behavior malfunctions (Bandura, 1961; Davison, in press; Franks, in press; Goldstein, Heller, & Sechrest, 1966; Grossberg, 1964; Kalish, 1965; Krasner & Ullmann, 1965; Paul, 1966; Ullmann & Krasner, 1965). At present, the techniques are in the process of refinement and change, and it is the hope of workers in this area eventually to develop a group of procedures which will be maximally effective in changing various forms of behavior which may be incapacitating to the individual.

Investigation is proceeding in several directions simultaneously. The therapeutic techniques themselves are being constantly modified, new approaches are being developed, new applications are being found, and numerous evaluations of the appropriateness and effectiveness of these techniques are being undertaken. All of these efforts will no doubt contribute to the classification and refinement of the major techniques and will provide the therapist-clinician with effective instruments for altering and maladaptive behavior.

Although research and investigation is proceeding at a rapid pace in the general area of behavior modification, one topic which has been conspicuously neglected by behavior therapists is that of assessment. By assessment we do not solely mean the measurement or other determination of the personality structure of the individual who is the object of some therapeutic endeavor. In using the term assessment, we are implying the identification and measurement of a broad spectrum of relevant factors which are necessary to ensure the best possible alteration of a particular individual's maladaptive behavior. Indeed, our thesis is that assessment procedures represent a *most crucial and significant* step in the effective application of behavior therapy.

---

*From *Psychological Reports,* 1968, **23,** 75–87. Reprinted by permission. The authors would like to thank Thomas J. D'Zurilla, Gerald C. Davison, and Anita Powers Goldfried for their many helpful comments on an earlier draft of this paper.

Any attempt to explain the relative lack of attention given to assessment for behavior therapy must of necessity be speculative. Perhaps the striking success achieved with certain procedures—such as systematic desensitization—has served to narrow the clinical and research interests to problems dealing with the refinement of specific therapeutic techniques (Lang, in press). We would maintain, however, that the absence of attention currently being paid to assessment in behavior modification more likely stems from the fact that assessment is not a very "reinforcing" activity. Although this may be the case for a large number of nonbehavioral clinicians, it is particularly true for behavior therapists. Consequently, before describing the specific role of assessment in behavior therapy, we would like to discuss some of the issues regarding clinical assessment which may have contributed to the relative absence of work in this area.

ISSUES AND PROBLEMS REGARDING ASSESSMENT

Over the years, the general area of assessment—but particularly as it has related to psychotherapy—has been fraught with many unresolved problems and issues. It is not our purpose here to review systematically the past and current status of assessment and measurement. Our primary interest, instead, is to point to those issues which, in a sense, may have served as setting events for the behavior therapists' relative avoidance of the area of assessment. Some of the factors which we believe to be relevant include: (1) the professional status of those engaged in assessment activities, (2) the conceptualization of personality which has typically been associated with assessment, and (3) the traditional relationship between assessment and therapy.

Professional Status of Assessment

In the history of clinical psychology, the assessment role of the psychologist has undergone some very distinct changes. Initially, the function of a psychologist in a clinical setting was that of a "mental tester" or psychometrician. With the onset of the Second World War, the need for therapists prompted the addition of therapeutic activities to the psychologist's role. Clinical psychology consequently moved one rung up the ladder of professional status.

Following the Second World War, more and more graduate schools included training in therapy as part of their clinical program, and the role functions of the clinical psychologist became more firmly defined as consisting of assessment *and* therapy (Raimy, 1950). Paralleling the biologists' observation that ontogeny recapitulates phylogeny, clinical psychology witnessed certain interesting intra-professional changes. Although the defined role of the clinical psychologist involved both assessment and therapy, most of the assessment and testing functions were gradually taken over by junior staff members or, if they were readily available, clinical trainees. Although not always overtly labeled, therapy became the more esteemed and rewarding way to spend one's professional time.

In reviewing the history of clinical psychology, it appears that the clinician's attitude toward testing and assessment has been influenced by inter- and intra-professional issues where, more often than not, assessment has been viewed as merely an occupational stepping-stone in the professional advancement of clinical psychology as a whole, as well as in the professional career of any given psychologist.

Traditional Conceptualization of Personality

A significant issue related to the behavior therapist's avoidance of assessment is the traditional conceptualization of personality on which most assessment techniques have been based. The units for understanding human behavior employed by most personality theorists have generally been dispositional in nature. Concepts such as "instincts," "needs," "drives," and "traits" have been the ones most frequently utilized in thinking about personality structure, with these variables having been "assumed to operate as motivational determinants of behavior across varied stimulus situations" (Wallace, 1967, p. 57). This general approach to understanding the determinants of human behavior, namely, emphasizing dynamics, needs, expectations, and underlying motivational forces, has been referred to by Murray (1938) as representing the *centralistic* orientation in the study of man. We would agree with Wallace, however, who criticizes this approach not only on the grounds that it is conceptually naive, but also that it often leads us into blind alleys in our attempts to predict and change human behavior.

Perhaps the most important reason why behavior therapists have neglected the area of assessment, therefore, lies in their partial or total rejection of the centralistic orientation underlying the procedures themselves. Operating within the broad framework of learning theory and general experimental research, behavior therapists have not been concerned with conceptualizing personality in any traditional sense. Rejecting the traditional formulations of personality, some behavior therapists have focused entirely on the role of extra-individual factors in the determination of human behavior. They have placed great stress on the importance of the stimulus configuration of the environment, and many of the techniques subsumed under the rubric of behavior modification involve the alteration of the surrounding environment in order to produce change in an individual's behavior. The fact that this emphasis on external determinants has resulted in the relative neglect of intra-individual variables is a point we shall discuss later in the paper.

Traditional Relationship Between Assessment and Therapy

As we have noted above, the term assessment has traditionally been used to denote a set of operations delineating a relatively stable set of dispositional variables which would allow for the explanation and prediction of behavior. Dispositional concepts were presumed to be useful not only in describing personality structure but also in the application of certain procedures which could alter the personality structure and thus produce behavior change. In other words, the questions the centralistically oriented clinician has typically asked himself are: "What is there about the *client's* developmental history and personality structure which is causing him to have certain problems, and what aspects of his *personality* should be altered in order to eliminate or minimize these problems?"

Although this connection between assessment and therapy seems to be a logical one, assessment procedures have in fact been used minimally or not at all by the clinician as therapist (Kelly, 1961; Meehl, 1960; Sundberg & Tyler, 1962). It is certainly possible that some therapists have been reluctant to utilize assessment methods because of their doubts regarding the validity of the instruments themselves. Although the validity of various assessment procedures may legitimately be questioned (Goldfried & Stricker, in press; Jackson & Messick, 1958; Little & Shneidman, 1959; Meehl, 1954; Zubin, Eron, & Schumer, 1965), the more relevant issue for the separation of assessment from therapy seems to be more closely related to *utility* than validity (Garfield, 1966; Rotter, 1954). As we see it, the two most significant potential clinical uses of assessment material for therapy are (a) to delineate those target areas where change should take place and (b) to offer some information about the specific therapeutic technique which would be best suited for bringing about such change with this particular individual. In practice, assessment procedures have served neither of these two purposes in traditional therapy.

In his incisive analysis of traditional approaches to therapy, London (1964) has accurately observed that, regardless of the problems or symptoms which may have brought a client to treatment, the goal of insight therapy remains constant—self-understanding and the search for meaning. In line with the centralistic approach, this certainly would be a logical step in bringing about behavioral change. More often than not, the theoretical orientation of the therapist determines what issues are crucial for self-understanding. Thus, the psychoanalytically oriented therapist would argue that the dynamics which must be dealt with in therapy are relatively universal; little in the way of any initial assessment is needed to delineate them. Nondirective therapists (Rogers, 1951) have gone even further by claiming that prior knowledge of conflict areas or focal problems is not only inappropriate but often detrimental to the effective progression of therapy.*

In the case of the second possible use of assessment procedures—to suggest the appropriate therapeutic technique—we find even less utilization by therapists. The probable reason for this is simply that in most cases, the specific technique used with any given client has tended to be more a function of the *therapist's orientation* than of the client's problem (cf. London, 1964). It is not at all uncommon to observe that therapists, having been trained according to a given therapeutic "school," invariably utilize the same therapeutic procedure—perhaps with some minor variations—for the full range of clients and problem areas.

Although there seems to be some logical need for assessment prior to therapy, this strategy has been lacking in the past. In the practice of traditional, insight-oriented psychotherapy, we would tend to agree that the need for detailed and comprehensive assessment information prior to the treatment itself may exist only minimally—if at all. From the viewpoint of the more contemporary, behaviorally oriented attempts to understand and change human behavior, on the other hand, the development and utilization of appropriate assessment techniques is crucial.

BEHAVIOR MODIFICATION TECHNIQUES AND ASSESSMENT

The popularity of the behavior modification movement in clinical psychology is increasingly evident. One of the main reasons for this popularity is that it offers to the clinician an array of highly specific and seemingly effective techniques. Unfortunately, this has led many to view behavior modification as representing a "new school" of therapy. We would hold that it is neither a school nor is it new. In the first place, it is an eclectic selection of techniques, many of which have been in existence for some time. More important, behavior modification represents more a general *orientation* to therapy than it does any specific set of techniques. The orientation taken by this new group of "behavioral clinicians" is the view that any laws or principles which have been derived from research have possible applications for behavioral change in the clinical situation. Basic to this approach is the obvious desire to keep clinical practice firmly based on empirical findings. Although behavior modification in the clinical setting is most frequently identified with the application of findings from learning studies, the results from experimentation on persuasion, social influence, placebo effect, attitude change, and other topics relevant to the modification of human behavior are equally appropriate (Goldstein *et al.*, 1966).

---

*In a later paper, Rogers (1957) has facetiously stated that assessment information might be useful but only by offering the therapist a certain measure of security and assurance.

Several unfounded and misdirected criticisms of the simplistic nature of behavior modification have come from individuals unsympathetic to this orientation (Strupp, 1967; Weitzman, 1967). Of greater significance and concern to us, however, is that criticisms have also been leveled by behavior therapists themselves—criticisms which particularly point to the clinical naivete often reflected in the application of behavior modification procedures (Davison, in press; Lazarus, 1965; Meyer & Crisp, 1966). These criticisms apply not so much to the behavior modification technique per se as they do to the inadequacy of the assessment procedures employed. The two general areas in which this inadequacy is most evident are in (a) the assessment of the most crucial *targets* (behavioral as well as environmental) for modification and (b) the selection of the most appropriate and effective *behavior modification technique.*

In both case studies and research in behavior modification, one often sees gross oversimplification reflected in the conceptualization of the behavior or situation which is seen as being in need of modification. For example, the emergence of what appears to be "symptom substitution" after the application of behavior therapy techniques may be viewed as an instance where the inappropriate target behavior was modified. Modification of maladaptive, anxiety-reducing behavior could very well result in the appearance of another maladaptive response, fairly high in the person's behavior repertoire, which may persist because of its ability to reduce anxiety (Lazarus, 1965). An example of the inappropriate selection of the specific behavior modification procedure is most dramatically seen in those cases where the client ends up being even more disturbed after the treatment. For example, even though there are instances in which aversive conditioning has proven to be quite successful (Eysenck, 1964; Ullmann & Krasner, 1965), there are several cases reported in the literature where it has failed miserably (Beech, 1960; Thorpe & Schmidt, 1963) apparently because it was the inappropriate procedure to use in these particular cases.

It is becoming increasingly evident that a more detailed, sophisticated approach to assessment for behavior therapy is currently needed. The need for assessment to delineate relevant "targets" toward which change should be directed, as well as a means of determining which of the several behavior modification procedures would be most appropriate and effective, is discussed in the following sections.

Conceptualization of "Targets" for Change

Within the past decade, clinical psychologists have begun to change their orientation in the study of human behavior. Although once highly centralistic, clinicians and personality theorists alike are moving increasingly in the direction of recognizing the significant role of the *concurrent environment* as an elicitor and reinforcer of human behavior (Kanfer & Saslow, 1965; Rotter, 1960; Sells, 1963; Wallace, 1967). This conceptualization is certainly nothing new; personality theorists spoke about the importance of environmental determinants some years back (Lewin, 1939; Murphy, 1947). What *is* new and exciting, however, is that this conceptualization of human behavior is now beginning to receive serious attention by clinicians in their approach to behavior change.

While this increasing emphasis on the role of environmental variables in determining behavior is a welcome one, the exclusion of all inferential concepts and the refusal to consider mediating factors, is an untenable orientation which severely limits the clinician in his conceptualizations and therapeutic endeavors. A completely environmentalistic, noninferential orientation to the study of human behavior—which Murray (1938) has referred to as the *peripheralistic* approach—does as much violence to the data as does an entirely centralistic orientation. Most contemporary behaviorists have indeed progressed beyond the simple and naive approach of conceptualizing behavior merely in terms of overt, molar responses, and have developed mediational constructs in terms of which unobservable events can be construed (Hebb, 1960). The application of general principles of behavior to internal, unobservable events has resulted in valuable theoretical constructs such as "higher mental processes" (Dollard & Miller, 1950), "symbolic processes" (Mowrer, 1960), "implicit responses" (Staats & Staats, 1963), and "coverants" (Homme, 1965), which enable the theorist and clinician to conceptualize more complex human behavior.

In an intriguing discussion of personality assessment, Wallace (1967) offers what appears to be a compromise between a centralistic and peripheralistic approach in describing an abilities conceptualization of personality. In place of the notion that human behavior can be accounted for by certain learned and innate dispositional characteristics of the individual, complex human behavior may be viewed in the same way that more specific human abilities have been typically conceptualized. Thus, Wallace uses the term *response capability* to refer to the extent to which certain responses or behavioral tendencies exist within the person's repertoire. *Response performance,* on the other hand, which refers to the likelihood that the individual will manifest these behavioral tendencies, is determined not only by the extent to which the person is capable of behaving in a given way but also by those environmental factors which might tend to elicit and/or reinforce this way of behaving.

In assessing the target behaviors which are in need of modification for any given client, it would indeed be simplistic to view behavior as referring to only that which is directly observable. Despite the broadened conceptualization of behavior which has recently become associated with behaviorism, gross oversimplification is often reflected in the selection of target behaviors in case studies and research in behavior modification.* Some behavior therapists fail to recognize that the most appropriate targets for behavior modification often involve cognitions as well as overt behaviors. Although we would not deny the fact that thoughts and feelings can sometimes be modified by changing the individual's overt behavior, quite often they should be target behaviors for direct modification themselves. Further, although the modification of conse-quent events is often effective in eliminating maladaptive behavior, the impor-tance of changes in the situational antecedents should not be overlooked.

We would agree with Szasz (1961) that the general goal of therapy should be the elimination of the individual's problems in living. Clearly, these prob-lems in living may be primarily a function of the individual's behavioral abilities or deficits, his current environmental situation, but more likely some combination of the two (cf. Wallace, 1967). Consequently, in the selection of the "target" in need of modification, the clinician should choose from: (a) the relevant antecedent, situational events which may have elicited the maladap-tive behavior, (b) the mediational responses and cues which, because of the individual's previous learning experiences, have become associated with these situational events, (c) the observable, maladaptive behavior itself, and (d) the consequent changes in the environmental situation, including the reactions of others to this maladaptive behavior. The decision as to which aspect of this environmental-mediational-behavioral complex is most relevant in any case should be determined by which, if effectively manipulated, is most likely to alter the client's maladaptive behavior. An illustration of the use of this paradigm in a case study is presented later in the paper.

Selection of Appropriate Behavior Modification Procedures

In addition to using assessment procedures to determine the target for change, assessment is essential in the selection of the therapeutic technique most appropriate for any given case. Unlike most traditional therapists who tend to follow therapeutic schools, the behaviorally oriented clinician finds himself faced with the task of having to choose from a wide range of possible procedures, each of which seems to have had some success in the modification of human problems (Bandura, 1961; Goldstein *et al.,* 1966; Kalish, 1965; Krasner & Ullmann, 1965; Ullmann & Krasner, 1965). The behaviorally oriented clinician must decide whether the most appropriate approach to take with any given client should involve such techniques as systematic desensi-tization, assertive training, aversive conditioning, role-playing techniques, mod-eling procedures, *in vivo* desensitization, or any one of a variety of other approaches (cf. Wolpe & Lazarus, 1966). The selection of any given procedure may be in part a function of the target behavior or situational determinant in need of modification. With further investigation of each of the therapeutic

---

*For specific illustrations of this point, the reader is referred to Davison (in press).

procedures, however, it has become clear that *other variables* may play a significant role as well.

In order to determine which would be the most appropriate therapeutic procedure to employ in any given case, we need to explore the specific variables related to effective application of each of the several behavior modification procedures. As an example, let us take the use of modeling procedures, since some empirical data exist relevant to this technique. Under what conditions would modeling be an effective procedure to employ clinically? To begin with, research findings by Bandura and his associates (Bandura, 1965; Bandura & Walters, 1963) indicate that modeling is particularly relevant in those instances where, due to inadequate social learning, certain desired behavior patterns are low in the individual's repertoire. Modeling procedures have additionally proven to be relevant in those instances where avoidance responses need to be eliminated (Bandura, Grusec & Menlove, 1967). Apart from delineating these particular target behaviors, however, any assessment procedure would also have to focus on *other* client and environmental variables relevant to the effective application of modeling. We have already spoken of the importance of assessing environmental and client variables in determining the relevant targets for modification. Our interest in these variables now lies in making a decision as to whether or not our therapeutic procedure is the most appropriate one to use in this particular situation.

In the case of modeling procedures, the assessment would have to provide information about such characteristics of the client as his arousal level, his self-esteem, and his degree of dependency, as well as data on the nature of the concurrent environmental situation, such as the availability of the appropriate models and the likelihood of the client's behavior being followed by positive consequences (cf. Bandura, 1965; Goldstein *et al.,* 1966). In contrast to the information available for the use of modeling procedures, our knowledge of the assessment variables relevant for each of the other behavior modification techniques is practically nonexistent.

The issues which have been discussed above regarding the importance of assessment for behavior modification may perhaps be brought into a clearer focus by the use of an illustrative case.

Illustrative Case

Consider the hypothetical case of a 50-yr.-old man who comes to therapy because he has difficulty in leaving his house. The situation has reached the point where merely comtemplating getting out of bed results in such anxiety that most of his time is spent in a prone position and he therefore must be constantly looked after by his wife. Further questioning reveals that his most salient fear is having a heart attack, which he states is the reason for remaining at home and in bed. Upon carrying the assessment further—this time evaluating the nature of his current life situation—it is found that this man has recently been promoted in his job to a position where he now has the responsibility for supervising a large staff. Prior to this promotion, he led a fairly normal life and his fears of having a heart attack were nonexistent.

Other assessment procedures reveal that the client has always had the tendency to become anxious in unfamiliar situations, and he is the type of person who would prefer to have other people look after and care for him. Additionally, questioning his wife reveals that she does not find the current situation entirely noxious; rather, she feels important and needed now that she has to care for her husband, and she lavishes much attention and affection on him in his incapacitated state.

Prior to the delineation of the appropriate target for modification, the clinician must conceptualize the data more systematically. As we have noted above, a formulation of the case should focus on: (a) the relevant environmental antecedents, (b) the significant mediational responses and cues, (c) the observable maladaptive behavior itself, and (d) the consequent environmental changes.

Using this paradigm, a formulation of this case might be as follows: the change in this individual's work situation elicited a number of mediational (labeling) responses (e.g., this is a situation requiring direction and supervision of others, judgments must be made about other people's performance, inadequate work of others reflects negatively on a supervisor, etc.). Because of this particular individual's previous learning experiences, these responses, associated with a change in job status, elicit anxiety. Among the many manifestations of this anxiety reaction is an increase in heart rate. Because of the client's mislabeling of this state of increased arousal, i.e., he associates the increased activity of the heart in a man of his age and position with the possibility of having a heart attack, he becomes concerned with thoughts that this might be happening to him. These thoughts serve as mediating responses which tend to elicit additional anxiety, thus adding to his distressed condition. Remaining at home and confined to bed, which belong to a class of behaviors relatively high in his behavioral repertoire, serve as successful avoidance responses which keep him out of the situation which initially elicited the anxiety; it is also appropriate behavior for a person who might be having a heart attack. His behavior elicits attention and care from his wife, providing additional reinforcement for the maladaptive behavior.

Following the translation of the data into conceptual terms, the clinician is then faced with the task of selecting the most relevent target for change. The most salient target in this case—the *observable, maladaptive behavior* of staying at home and remaining in bed—does not appear to be the most appropriate for direct modification. We have conceptualized this behavior as an avoidance response, where the stimuli eliciting the anxiety continue to be present. The direct alteration of this overt behavior without any change in the mediating anxiety could very well result in the manifestation of other avoidance responses lower in the client's repertoire. In considering possible modifications in the *current life situation,* we also encounter difficulties. Although a change in the situation which was *antecedent to* the appearance of this maladaptive behavior—his promotion at work—might successfully eliminate the problem, it would also result in a financial and status loss for this individual; the modification of other targets which would eliminate the problem and yet avoid these other negative consequences would be preferable. Modification of the *consequent* aspect of the client's current life situation—the attention he is receiving from his wife—would only be focusing on the additional reinforcers and not on the stimuli which are concurrently eliciting the avoidance response.

Having considered the observable maladaptive behavior and the current life situation as possible areas for modification, we would now turn to the *mediational responses.* The client's distorted labeling of the physiological cues which were a concomitant of the anxiety reaction seems to be of only secondary importance. Antecedent to this inappropriate labeling are the anxiety responses elicited by those situations requiring him to supervise and make decisions about others. It is his fear of functioning in this type of situation which seems to have resulted in a chain of internal and external maladaptive response. It, therefore, appears that the most crucial area toward which any therapeutic endeavors should be directed would be the client's anxiety regarding decision-making processes in the supervision of others.

Following the selection of the most crucial target for modification, some decision must be made in the choice of the most appropriate treatment procedure; it is here where assessment is most inadequate. The assessment of the target makes the task of selecting the appropriate therapeutic procedure less difficult, although certainly not clear-cut. Indeed, what we often find is that the assessment enables us *to eliminate* certain therapeutic techniques more than it does to indicate which would be most appropriate. In the case of our hypothetical client, the determination of whether or not to employ systematic desensitization, modeling techniques, implosive therapy, or perhaps assertive training in the reduction of his anxiety regarding decision-making, cannot easily be made on the basis of any currently existing assessment information. Although it may well be that one particular approach to anxiety-reduction would be most effective with this client in his particular life situation, we currently have little information about which variables would be relevant in making this choice. At best, we can only speculate about the variables (e.g., imaginal ability, level of anxiety, ability to relax, suggestibility, the reactions of others, etc.) pertinent to the successful application of the above-mentioned techniques.

Although it may be possible to use. clinical intuition and experience as an aid in determining what seems to be the most appropriate behavior modification technique, the typical clinical procedure currently involves selecting a few seemingly relevant techniques and then trying each in turn until one hopefully proves effective. A better strategy would be a thorough "criterion analysis" of behavior modification, with the goal being the determination of those predictive or assessment variables needed in the selection of the most effective treatment in any given case. Such a goal can best be achieved by means of systematic research efforts directed toward discovering these individual and environmental variables.

In a recent paper concerning psychotherapy, Paul (1967) has stated that the relevant research questions to be asked are as follows: *"What* treatment, by *whom,* is most effective for *this* individual with *that* specific problem, and under *which* set of circumstances?"* (p. 111). It is toward the goal of *answering* these questions that the future study of assessment for behavior modification should be directed.

REFERENCES

Bandura, A. Psychotherapy as a learning process. *Psychological Bulletin,* 1961, **58,** 143–159.

Bandura, A. Behavioral modifications through modeling procedures. In L. Krasner & L. P. Ullmann (Eds.), *Research in behavior modification.* New York: Holt, Rinehart, & Winston, 1965, 310–340.

Bandura, A., Grusec, J. E., & Menlove, F. Vicarious extinction of avoidance behavior. *Journal of Personality and Social Psychology,* 1967, **5,** 16–23.

Bandura, A., & Walters, R. H. *Social learning and personality development.* New York: Holt, Rinehart, & Winston, 1963.

Beech, H. R. The symptomatic treatment of writer's cramp. In H. J. Eysenck (Ed.), *Behavior therapy and the neuroses.* New York: Pergamon Press, 1960, 349–372.

Davison, G. C. Appraisal of behavior modification techniquies with adults in institutional settings. In C. M. Franks (Ed.), *Assessment and status of the behavior therapies and associated developments.* New York: McGraw-Hill, in press.

Dollard, J., & Miller, N. E. *Personality and psychotherapy.* New York: McGraw-Hill, 1950.

Eysenck, H. J. (Ed.) *Experiments in behaviour therapy.* New York: Macmillan, 1964.

Franks, C. M. (Ed.) *Assessment and status of the behavior therapies and associated developments.* New York: McGraw-Hill, in press.

Garfield, S. L. Clinical psychology and the search for identity. *American Psychologist,* 1966, **21,** 353–362.

Goldfried, M. R., & Stricker, G. *Clinical and research applications of the Rorschach.* Englewood Cliffs, N. J.: Prentice-Hall, in press.

Goldstein, A. P., Heller, K., & Sechrest, L. B. *Psychotherapy and the psychology of behavior change.* New York: Wiley, 1966.

Grossberg, J. M. Behavior therapy: A review. *Psychological Bulletin,* 1964, **62,** 73–88.

Hebb, D. O. The American revolution. *American Psychologist,* 1960, **15,** 735–745.

Homme, L. E. Perspectives in psychology: XXIV. Control of coverants, the operants of the mind. *Psychological Record,* 1965, **15,** 501–511.

Jackson, D. N., & Messick, S. Content and style in personality assessment. *Psychological Bulletin*, 1958, **55**, 243–252.

Kalish, H. I. Behavior therapy. In B. B. Wolman (Ed.), *Handbook of clinical psychology*. New York: McGraw-Hill, 1965, 1230–1253.

Kanfer, F. H., & Saslow, G. Behavioral analysis: An alternative to diagnostic classification. *Archives of General Psychiatry*, 1965, **12**, 529–538.

Kelly, E. L. Clinical psychology–1960; a report of survey findings. *Newsletter, Division of Clinical Psychology of the APA*, 1961, **14**, 1–11.

Krasner, L., & Ullmann, L. P. (Eds.) *Research in behavior modification*. New York: Holt, Rinehart, & Winston, 1965.

Lang, P. J. The mechanics of desensitization and the laboratory study of human fear. In C. M. Franks (Ed.), *Assessment and status of the behavior therapies and associated developments*. New York: McGraw-Hill, in press.

Lazarus, A. A. Behavior therapy, incomplete treatment, and symptom substitution. *Journal of Nervous and Mental Disease*, 1965, **140**, 80–96.

Lewin, K. Field theory and experiment in social psychology: Concepts and methods. *American Journal of Sociology*, 1939, **44**, 868–896.

Little, K. B., & Shneidman, E. S. Congruences among interpretations of psychological test and anamnestic data. *Psychological Monographs*, 1959, **73**, No. 6 (Whole No. 476).

London, P. *The modes and morals of psychotherapy*. New York: Holt, Rinehart, & Winston, 1964.

Meehl, P. E. *Clinical versus statistical prediction*. Minneapolis: University of Minnesota Press, 1954.

Meehl, P. E. The cognitive activity of the clinician. *American Psychologist*, 1960, **15**, 19–27.

Meyer, V., & Crisp, A. H. Some problems of behavior therapy. *British Journal of Psychiatry*, 1966, **112**, 367–382.

Mowrer, O. H. *Learning theory and the symbolic processes*. New York: Wiley, 1960.

Murphy, G. *Personality: A biosocial approach to its origins and structures*. New York: Harper & Row, 1947.

Murray, H. A. *Explorations in personality*. New York: Oxford University Press, 1938.

Paul, G. L. *Insight versus desensitization in psychotherapy*. Stanford: Stanford University Press, 1966.

Paul, G. L. Strategy of outcome research in psychotherapy. *Journal of Consulting Psychology*, 1967, **31**, 109–119.

Raimy, V. C. (Ed.) *Training in clinical psychology*. Englewood Cliffs, N. J.: Prentice-Hall, 1950.

Rogers, C. R. *Client-centered therapy*. Boston: Houghton-Mifflin, 1951.

Rogers, C. R. The necessary and sufficient conditions of therapeutic personality change. *Journal of Consulting Psychology*, 1957, **21**, 95–103.

Rotter, J. B. *Social learning and clinical psychology*. Englewood Cliffs, N. J.: Prentice-Hall, 1954.

Rotter, J. B. Some implications of a social learning theory for the prediction of goal directed behavior from testing situations. *Psychological Review*, 1960, **67**, 301–316.

Sells, S. B. (Ed.) *Stimulus determinants of behavior*. New York: Ronald, 1963.

Staats, A. W., & Staats, C. K. *Complex human behavior*. New York: Holt, Rinehart, & Winston, 1963.

Strupp, H. H. What is psychotherapy? *Contemporary Psychology*, 1967, **12**, 41–42.

Sundberg, N. D., & Tyler, L. E. *Clinical psychology*. New York: Appleton-Century-Crofts, 1962.

Szasz, T. S. *The myth of mental illness*. New York: Hoeber, 1961.

Thorpe, J. G., & Schmidt, E. Therapeutic failure in a case of aversion therapy. *Behavior Research and Therapy,* 1963, **1,** 293–296.

Ullmann, L. P., & Krasner, L. (Eds.) *Case studies in behavior modification.* New York: Holt, Rinehart, & Winston, 1965.

Wallace, J. What units shall we employ? Allport's question revisited. *Journal of Consulting Psychology,* 1967, **31,** 56–64.

Weitzman, B. Behavior therapy and psychotherapy. *Psychological Review,* 1967, **74,** 300–317.

Wolpe, J., & Lazarus, A. A. *Behavior therapy techniques.* Oxford: Pergamon Press, 1966.

Zubin, J., Eron, L. D., & Schumer, F. *An experimental approach to projective techniques.* New York: Wiley, 1965.

3

Issues in Application*

R. H. WOODY

The foregoing chapters have described the theoretical and technical bases for psychobehavioral counseling and therapy. As is true with so many areas of science, there is a potential for difficulty when the theoretical and technical aspects are translated into applied services. Some of these potential sources of difficulty can be predicted and prepared for, but others cannot.

This chapter focuses on several of the key issues in the process of achieving effective application of the integrated insight-behavioral approach to counseling and therapy. Specifically, consideration will be given to: *psychobehavioral diagnosis,* that is, the process of making psychological assessments and behavioral analyses that are meaningful to a behaviorally oriented form of counseling psychotherapy; the *selection of behavioral techniques* that will fit into the psychobehavioral frame of reference and that will be optimally tailored to the specific problem and the client being dealt with; *personal-social counseling and therapy,* that is, applying the psychobehavioral orientation to problems that influence the client's personal-social functioning; *educational counseling and consultation,* that is, helping clients deal more effectively with learning tasks via direct contact (counseling), and indirect service through other professionals (consultation with classroom teachers); *vocational guidance and counseling,* which employs behavioral techniques yet still retains vocational-development theories and the guidance-counseling relationship, *group counseling and therapy,* which emphasizes conditioning techniques in order to facilitate the group processes; *community service,* which is directed toward confronting societal problems through psychobehaviorism; and the *influence of the setting.*

We have examined the theory, the techniques, and the research documentation. This chapter moves on to the application of the theory and techniques in a practical clinical setting.

---

*From R. H. Woody, *Psychobehavioral counseling and therapy: Integrating behavioral and insight techniques,* pp. 117–128, © 1971. Reprinted by permission of Prentice-Hall, Inc. Englewood Cliffs, New Jersey.

PSYCHOBEHAVIORAL DIAGNOSIS

"Diagnosis" generally is defined as measuring (i.e., estimating) and describing a person's current functioning, deducing what past functionings were and what the etiology for the present problems might be, making a prognosis about the future, and setting forth a treatment plan. The central purpose of any diagnosis is to define the nature of the problem and to determine what requires treatment.

Psychodynamic diagnosis involves assessing the client's assets and liabilities, the strength and nature of defenses, and the strength and vulnerability of the ego (just to name a few of the primary dimensions). Behaviorists take a much different view of diagnosis, directing their attention to inferring the reinforcing contingencies or contingent stimuli in the past and present life of the client. The difference between the two conceptualizations of diagnosis reintroduces the differing concepts of the nature of problems to be treated and underscores a different concept of what the client needs to have treated. Or, as was illustrated by the symptom versus underlying neurotic conflict controversy, the behavior therapist would probably be likely to accept a client's statements regarding the nature of the problem in a literal manner (whether it be an interview comment or an item receiving a self-report preference on a standardized test) and would deal with the manifest problem, whereas the insight counselor-therapist would want to delve into the implicit problem, i.e., that which is, in a sense, out of the client's awareness. The psychobehavioal frame of reference, however, adds a third conceptualization for diagnosis: analysis of the client's reinforcement history and social-learning contingencies, i.e., specifying the reinforcing contingencies or contingent stimuli in a behavioral manner, thereby providing supplemental data for the psychodynamically oriented diagnosis.

Parenthetically, it should be noted that theoretical approaches to insight counseling and psychotherapy vary greatly in the amount of emphasis placed on diagnosis. For example, the client-centered therapist would probably give scant attention to diagnosis, whereas a psychoanalytically oriented therapist would give a great deal. As has been reflected in the evolution of client-centered therapy, the value placed on diagnosis (or any facet of treatment for that matter) by any one theoretical school is subject to shifts—and at this time that seems like a scientifically healthy attribute. Moreover, as is true with so many theoretical-versus-practical comparisons, it seems probable that practitioners espousing the same theoretical approach differ significantly amongst themselves. In addition to theoretical differences, the amount of emphasis placed on diagnosis is also subject to the types of clients. In general, the counselor-therapist working with so called "normals," such as in a college counseling center, would probably rely on diagnostic data much less than would the counselor-therapist working with more disturbed clients, such as in a mental health clinic or hospital.

The two diagnostic steps of making a prognosis and setting forth a treatment plan require that consideration be given to various possible treatment approaches. This means, in a sense, making a prognosis for each feasible treatment mode or technique and selecting the approach that seems to hold the most promise (recognizing, of course, that the treatment plan should be under constant appraisal and subject to modification at any time).

In actual practice, however, the diagnostic process all too often does not fulfill the multifaceted composition. Some diagnosticians stop with the first step, measuring and describing the current functioning. This seems to occur most often when the diagnosis is being made in conjunction with another professional. Perhaps the assumption is that the other one will carry out the remaining steps, but the result is often an incomplete diagnostic process.

When a fragmented diagnosis occurs, there is frequently an over-reliance on psychometric data. The psychological tests are useful only for describing current functioning and offering a diagnostic classification. The diagnostic classification or categorization is supposedly a means for communicating the uniqueness of the client so that professionals subsequently involved with the client can have a clearcut frame of reference as to what his characteristics are. But not even a psychiatric classification carries direct considerations of what should be done; certainly a diagnostic label provides little, if any, mainline revelations about the client as a unique human being, and it fails to yeild treatment ideas that are tailored to that one individual client.

Psychobehavioral diagnosis holds as its primary goal the derivation of a treatment approach. Granted, the other steps of diagnosis are potentially of value (even inferring etiology and making a psychiatric classification), but the real value for the counseling-therapy process comes from understanding the client's characteristics and reaction styles so that they can be translated into usable guidelines for treatment. Deriving the treatment approach might well involve the use of psychological tests, including intelligence, aptitude, perceptual, achievement, and personality measures. (Actually, any instrument that provides idiosyncratic data, which might also mean a nomothetic comparison through sample norms, can be used.)

Behaviorists believe that the use of the test data should go beyond a metrical analysis: there must also be a behavioral analysis or a behavioral diagnosis. In other words, there is an analysis of reinforcement contingencies. In accord with behavioral science, Greenspoon and Gersten (1967) note that "the behavior on any psychological test should be lawful" (p. 849), and because "the behavior therapist must resort to trial-and-error procedures to determine a contingent stimulus that may be effective with a particular patient" (p. 849), psychological tests should be used, but should be analyzed for contingencies or contingent stimuli. This means that a behavioral analysis of standard psychological test data is made to determine what kinds of reinforcers influence the client; understanding these would lead to the establishment of behavioral modification procedures that would be most likely to help the client, because they are tailored to his idiosyncratic characteristics.

In the process of behavioral analysis, the psychobehavioral diagnostician would go through the regular behavioristic diagnostic approach, perhaps even following a trait-and-factor model, but he would also subjectively analyze the responses to infer reinforcement contingencies. Greenspoon and Gersten (1967) suggest that the data be grouped into four classes of contingencies or contingent stimuli: positive verbal, negative verbal, positive nonverbal, and negative nonverbal. In other words, responses to test items that reflected verbal factors, e.g., reinforcing words, would be placed in the appropriate positive or negative verbal categories, while actions or events would be placed into the appropriate positive or negative nonverbal categories. These grouped materials would then be used to infer how behavioral modification contingencies should be scheduled to eliminate the problem being treated.

Almost any psychological test can yield material that can be analyzed for use in behavioral modification, but there are also instruments designed particularly for such use. Wolpe and Lazarus (1966) constructed a Life History Questionnaire that helps the counselor-therapist infer social learning contingencies from the client's behavioral history; Wolpe and Lang (1964) created a Fear Survey Schedule that taps a client's disturbed reactions to a variety of stimuli; and Willoughby (1934) developed a Neuroticism Schedule that is widely used by behavior therapists to gather information regarding neurotic reactions to commonly encountered situations. Wolpe (1969) presents and discusses several of these instruments for behavior therapy. For those behavioral techniques that involve suggestibility, such as clinicial hypnosis and perhaps systematic desensitization, scales have been constructed by London (1962), Shor and Orne (1962), and Weitzenhoffer and Hilgard (1959, 1962). It should be emphasized, however, that unspecialized instruments, including the Wechsler and Stanford-Binet intelligence tests and ink blot and thematic projective instruments (to name but a few), can yield material that will reveal reinforcement contingencies, particularly those of a social nature.

There have been few published descriptions of behavioral diagnosis. One of the seemingly best elaborations of behavioral diagnostic processes has been offered by Kanfer and Saslow (1969). In approaching the topic, they issue the reminder that behavior therapy:

> does not rest upon the assumption that (1) insight is a *sine qua non* of psychotherapy, (2) changes in thoughts or ideas inevitably lead to ultimate changes in actions, (3) verbal therapeutic sessions serve as replications of and equivalents for actual life situations, and (4) a symptom can be removed only by uprooting its cause or origin. In the absence of these assumptions it becomes unnecessary to

conceptualize behavior disorder in etiological terms, in psychodynamic terms, or in terms of a specifiable disease process. (p. 428)

For a behavioral analysis, they state:

> The compilation of data under as many of the headings as are relevant should yield a good basis for decisions about the areas in which intervention is needed, the particular targets of the intervention, the treatment methods to be used, and the series of goals at which treatment should aim. (p. 430)

They indicate that the methods for data collection can be quite traditional, such as via interviewing, observations, and psychological tests. The point is, of course, that the functional analysis of these data should take on a behavioral posture.

At this stage, the basic problem is how to actually conduct an analysis of the data in behavioral terms. Kanfer and Saslow (1969) set forth the following guidelines for a behavioral analytic approach:

1. A detailed description of the particular behavioral excesses or deficits which represent the patient's complaints, and of the behavioral assets which may be available for utilization in a treatment program.

2. A clarification of the problem situation in which the variables are sought that maintain the patient's current problem behaviors. Attention is also given to the consequences of psychiatric intervention on the current adjustment balance of the patient in his social environment.

3. A motivational analysis which attempts to survey the various incentives and aversive conditions representing the dominant motivational factors in the patient.

4. A developmental analysis suggests consideration of biological, sociological, and behavioral changes in the patient's history which may have relevance for his present complaint and for a treatment program.

5. An analysis of self-control, which provides assessment of the patient's capacity for participation in a treatment program and of the conditions which may be necessary to control behaviors with untoward social consequences.

6. An analysis of social relationships which provide the basis for assessing social resources in the patient's environment which have affected his current behavior and may play a role in the therapeutic program.

7. An analysis of the social-cultural-physical environment to assess the degree of congruence between the patient's present milieu, his behavioral repertoire, and the type of therapeutic goals which the therapist can establish. (pp. 443–444)

While these guidelines give much needed guidance, it must be pointed out that behavioral analysis, just like its psychodynamic counterpart, is unrelentingly dependent upon the diagnostician's expertise at making clinical judgements from the data obtained.

Psychobehavioral diagnosis, therefore, fully utilizes established assessment procedures, including psychological tests. However, emphasis is given to making the data useful, that is, translating it into treatment techniques; and when behavioral modification procedures are employed, the contingencies or contingent stimuli that have special applicability to the particular client must be identified. This requires a behavioral analysis.

SELECTION OF BEHAVIORAL TECHNIQUES

After he makes the psychobehavioral diagnosis or analysis, the counselor-therapist selects a technical approach. It would be convenient if a well-defined set of guidelines for the selection of techniques could be offered. In view, however, of the lack of research on the matter and the idiosyncratic reactions of clients to a given technique, it would be ill-advised to set forth a restrictive system. It is possible, however, to clarify the parameters of the selection process.

Behavior therapists presume to operate on algorithms, i.e., they employ rules of procedure that lead to the solving of a problem. In the rationale for behavior therapy, it is implicit that the proper application of conditioning will produce a predictable change in behavior. This would lead one to assume that, given a specified behavior, the conditioning procedure could almost be mechanically determined, but thus far, human nature being what it is, such cut-and-dried technical prescriptions are not tenable.

There is seemingly a simplicity within behavior therapy, such as would be reflected in the delineation of the reinforcement contingencies or contingent stimuli and would presumably be operational in fitting techniques to specified contingencies or stimuli. But this simplicity is contradicted by actual practice. As Klein, Dittmann, Parloff, and Gill state (1969):

> Many people suppose that the therapist begins by clearly and systematically defining the patient's problems in terms of manageable hierarchies and then selects appropriate responses to be strengthened or weakened. We found little support for this conception of behavior therapy diagnosis in our observations. Indeed the selection of problems to be worked on often seemed quite arbitrary and inferential. We were frankly surprised to find the presenting symptomatic complaint was often sidestepped for what the therapist intuitively considered to be more basic issues. Most surprising to us, the basis for this selection seemed often to be what others would call dynamic considerations. (p. 261)

This statement, aside from the support it offers to the psychobehavioral assertion that the use of behavioral techniques will be complemented by the use of insight or dynamic techniques, exemplifies how subjectivity affects the behavioral diagnosis, especially the decision of which problem should be treated, and it suggests consequently that the selection of techniques may be equally subject to the clinical judgment of the counselor-therapist.

Behavior therapists do not, in general, acknowledge this subjectivity; nonetheless they remain vague aboutt the process of selecting techniques. Analysis of Wolpe and Lazarus' (1966) description of their procedure suggests that: if a client has a marked degree of social inadequacy, this might well receive immediate (initial?) treatment, probably by assertive training; subsequently other sources of anxiety, guilt, and depression would be explored and dealt with therapeutically, probably by anxiety-reduction techniques. They state:

> In general it is expedient to give therapeutic priority to the patient's most pressing current problem. ... In cases that display particularly distressing and debilitating reactions, one tries to subdue these reactions as rapidly as possible. (p. 28)

They go on to point out that behavior therapy cannot be "rigid behavioral engineering" (but this position is not shared by certain other behaviorists). The unfortunate thing is that for all practical purposes, the matter of selection of techniques in behavior therapy is left to nebulous generalizations about tailoring the treatment to the needs and the characteristics of the client (and one might wonder if "and of the therapist" should receive similar emphasis) and the selection process is left to the professional expertise of the behavior therapist.

Relatedly, it is lamentable that the assessment of whether a behavioral technique is producing desirable results is left to the judgment of the therapist, and often his judgments are based on circumstantial evidence:

> Because behavior treatment is posited as highly specific, it follows that success depends on the patient's exact and close cooperation with the therapist's instructions. It is therefore very important for the therapist to test this cooperation repeatedly during treatment. The therapist must also constantly assess the patient's progress on hierarchy dimensions. With the possible exception of role-playing, the therapist is dependent in this evaluation upon the patient's report both of progress outside treatment and of events within the sessions themselves. Since there are no independent procedures for evaluating or verifying his report, the patient has considerable leeway to bias his report in order to please, frustrate, or otherwise manipulate the therapist, or to meet some personal expectation. And the form of much of the feedback from the patient (i.e., lifting his finger if he feels an increase in anxiety during desensitization or doing nothing if he does not) gives the therapist very few cues for distinguishing valid from invalid reports. Thus the therapist must use considerable intuition to assess progress and correct the treatment plan. This all serves to highlight a very basic discrepancy between the theoretical orientation of

behavior therapy and its actual practice. (Klein, Dittmann, Parloff, and Gill, 1969, p. 262)

It seems evident that assessing the suitability or success level of a technique within the behavior-therapy model for practice has at least the potential for fostering erroneous judgments. One way of alleviating the probability of judgmental errors would be to incorporate insight-related measures, but of course this would violate the pure behavioral stance, would require acceptance of validity for psychodynamic theoretical principles and assessment instruments, and would require an eclectic theoretical posture, such as is afforded by the psychobehavioral frame of reference.

The state of affairs, then, is that while there have been some attempts to determine which techniques work best for which disorder or problem, there is no empirically based set of rules for technique selection. This leaves the individual counselor-therapist with the task, fraught with the potential for judgmental error, of gleaning technical data from published research accounts. Other alternatives would seem to be the reliance on trial-and-error attempts, and the use of a gradually built repertoire of clinical experience, both behavioral and nonbehavioral. Obviously, none of these alternatives represents a thoroughly acceptable professional operational mode.

There have been few published attempts at matching techniques with problems to be treated. This is undoubtedly because of two clinical facts: first, clients have idiosyncratic reactions to techniques, i.e., there are subtle differences among clients with what seems to be the same problem; and second, one clinician might obtain successful results with one technique whereas another, because of personal-professional differences in preferences and skills, might not, and would have to turn to another technique.

Surveying the major published sources on behavior therapy, one finds, however, that gross matchings are possible. These matchings are derived fairly readily by perusing the research and clinical examples presented under each type of disorder or problem. To take one example, Eysenck and Rachman (1965) suggest the following groupings of problem areas and techniques: *anxiety states* (e.g., phobias, social anxiety, and pervasive or free-floating anxiety) are primarily treated by systematic densensitization; *hysterical disorders* may be treated by avoidance conditioning and operant conditioning, which involve such specific techniques as systematic desensitization, induced abreactions, negative·practice, and aversive therapy; *psychomotor disturbances* (e.g., tics, tremors, writer's cramp, and spasms), which are essentially hysterical disorders, may be treated by a variety of conditioning techniques, such as avoidance conditioning, aversive therapy, systematic desensitization, relaxation exercises, and negative practice; *obsessional-compulsive disorders* may be treated by avoidance conditioning, aversive therapy, clinical suggestion (i.e., systematic psychomotor or vocal inhibition), systematic densensitization, assertive training, and satiation or negative practice; and *sex disorders* (e.g., impotence, frigidity, voyeurism, fetishism, exhibitionism, homosexuality, and transvestism) may be treated by aversive therapy and systematic desensitization, with emphasis on the use of sexual responses and assertive responses.

A somewhat encyclopedia-like source for matching a technique with a problem has been provided by Yates (1970). He offers his analysis of what techniques are suitable for specific abnormalities; he presents chapters according to behavior problem, and the reader can easily extract techniques; and he sets forth a table (see p. 71 of his book) that connects numerous abnormalities with behavioral techniques. Basically, it is comparable to the ideas derived from Eysenck and Rachman (1965), but seemingly more up-to-date and more comprehensive (if the objective is to have a reference source).

The foregoing should not be viewed as a comprehensive set of problems-techniques matchings; it is merely one subjectively established set essentially from one source. Further, it is important to acknowledge that, in addition to the previously cited restrictions placed on problems-techniques matching by idiosyncratic reactions of clients and the personal-professional differences among clinicians, professionals vary in theri criteria for what they believe is adequate documentation for substantiating that a particular technique is successful when used with a certain problem area. To take a specific example, the interpretation of the efficacy for negative practice presented in Chapter 2 of this book seems, in some ways, to differ from (i.e., be less positive than) the interpretation for the same technique presented by Eysenck and Rachman (1965). Either might be considered accurate, depending upon the evaluation criteria.

With this admittedly less-than-desirable, but realistic, state of affairs, the following seem like appropriate steps that each counselor-therapist should take to assure that his technique selection is as academically astute as is possible, and is better than trial-and-error pot-shots. First, assuming that a psycho-behavioral diagnosis has provided him with relevant data, the counselor-therapist should weigh the client's clinical information composite against more global composites illustrated by published research and clinical accounts. This would, of course, require a review of what documentation there is for the use of a given technique with a certain problematic condition, and this is the point at which the individualized interpretation of the strength of the documentation must occur, i.e., whether documentation is adequate enough to allow for an assumption of efficacy. Second, having weighed the client's characteristics against the technical documentation, the counselor-therapist must introduce his own personal-professional characteristics, giving consideration to the matter of how his unique set of preferences, skills, and attributes will influence the outcome of the use of a particular technique. Third, each feasible technique should be subjected to a prognostication for effects. And fourth, following application, every technique should be constantly assessed, with accommodations for change being possible. From this sequence of activities, the counselor-therapist will evolve his own set of (potentially transitory) algorithms.

To some behavioral scientists, the foregoing recommendations should only be offered with extreme apologies. But to the practicing clinician, who must make daily judgments that are admittedly subjective, these recommendations seem to provide the basis for at least tentative guidelines. (Note the discussion in Chapter 6 on the scientist-versus-practitioner controversy—the categories are not, of course, mutually exclusive.)

Obviously, this approach offers no concrete rules for selection and implementation, but one rule can be explicitly stated: *when using either an insight or behavioral technique, the counselor-therapist should constantly be assessing its effects and should continually be prepared to make alterations in his technical intervention.* The result of technique selection, although perhaps regrettable from a purist point of view, is unquestionably dependent upon the clinical judgment of the counselor-therapist. Perhaps some day a computer, programed to receive data about the client and the counselor-therapist, will be able to make recommendations for techniques. While this possibility is offered somewhat facetiously, it should be acknowledged that this may not be far from reality. For example, Veldman (1967) has programed a computer so that data from sentence-completion tests (administered to college freshmen) can be fed in and the computer will feed back "interview questions" appropriate to a particular student's set of test responses and which, if asked by the counselor, could provide diagnostic-interview clarity.

REFERENCES

Eysenck, H. J., & Rachman, S. *The causes and cures of neurosis.* San Diego, Calif.: Knapp, 1965.

Greenspoon, J., & Gersten, C. D. A new look at psychological testing: Psychological testing from the standpoint of a behaviorist. *American Psychologist,* 1967, **22**, 848–853.

Kanfer, F. H., & Saslow, G. Behavioral diagnosis. In C. M. Franks (Ed.), *Behavior therapy: Appraisal and status.* New York: McGraw-Hill, 1969, 417–444.

Klein, Marjorie H., Dittmann, A. T., Parloff, M. B., & Gill, M. M. Behavior therapy: Observations and reflections. *Journal of Consulting and Clinical Psychology,* 1969, **33**, 259–266.

London, P. *The children's hypnotic susceptibility scale.* Palo Alto, Calif.: Consulting Psychologists Press, 1962.

Shor, R. E., & Orne, Emily C. *Harvard group scale of hypnotic susceptibility.* Palo Alto, Calif.: Consulting Psychologists Press, 1962.

Veldman, D. J. Computer-based sentence-completion interviews. *Journal of Counseling Psychology,* 1967, **14**, 153–157.

Weitzenhoffer, A. M., & Hilgard, E. R. *Stanford hypnotic susceptibility scale, form A and B.* Palo Alto, Calif.: Consulting Psychologists Press, 1959.

Weitzenhoffer, A. M., & Hilgard, E. R. *Stanford hypnotic susceptibility scale, form C.* Palo Alto, Calif.: Consulting Psychologists Press, 1962.

Willoughby, R. R. Norms for the Clark-Thurstone inventory. *Journal of Social Psychology,* 1934, **5,** 91–95.

Wolpe, J. *The practice of behavior therapy.* New York: Pergamon Press, 1969.

Wolpe, J., & Lang, P. J. A fear survey schedule for use in behavior therapy. *Behaviour Research and Therapy,* 1964, **2,** 27–30.

Wolpe, J., & Lazarus, A. A. *Behavior therapy techniques.* New York: Pergamon Press, 1966.

Yates, A. J. *Behavior therapy.* New York: J Wiley, 1970.

4

Diagnosis and Prescription for Psychotherapy*

HERBERT J. SCHLESINGER

It is one of the paradoxes of psychiatry that our relatively sophisticated understanding of mental illnesses in terms of personality structure and conflicts between unconscious motives and structures within the personality finds expression in a relatively crude nomenclature that offers only a few widely spaced categories to capture and summarize our understanding of patients. That it does so poorly is a source of continuing complaint. The model we have inherited from medicine holds that rational treatment depends on accurate diagnosis. But, at best, our diagnostic labels are only rough approximations of the state of affairs in the patient and hardly satisfy the condition of accurate diagnosis that might permit us to make an effective prescription for treatment. And, if diagnosis cannot guide treatment, why diagnose at all?

There is a school of thought about psychotherapy that denies the necessity of any sort of diagnosing as a preparation to treatment. I do not share this view, but if our understanding of diagnosis were really to be so corrupted as to be synonymous with diagnostic *labeling*, then I would have to agree about the uselessness of diagnosing for guiding treatment. However, labeling is *not* diagnosis and, as I hope to demonstrate, the understanding of a patient derived from his examination and history *can* provide a rational basis for guiding at least the initiation of treatment.

We have many more or less sophisticated notions about the ways persons can change or mature, can become relieved of symptoms or otherwise learn more efficient and more humane ways of living. We explain these changes in terms of theories of interpersonal relationships of psychotherapeutic process, of learning theory and the like. It is ironic, however, that just as the final common path of our subtle theories of personality may be a crude diagnostic label, a similar funneling may occur when prescribing psychological treatment. When we prescribe a course of treatment to accomplish such changes, we tend to resort to a nomenclature of treatment modalities that provides only a few widely spaced categories of psychological treatment—psychoanalysis, expressive psychotherapy, supportive-expressive psychotherapy and supportive psychotherapy—and, in most settings, the choices range only between expressive and supportive psychotherapy.

*From *Bulletin of the Menninger Clinic,* 1969, **33**, 269–278. Reprinted by permission.

Have we really nothing more to say to a psychotherapist-elect than that his efforts ought to be supportive or expressive? Are these really categories of treatment at all in the sense that psychoanalysis is supposed to be?* It is a waste of effort to examine a patient in depth only to have the range of therapeutics predefined by a two-fold classification. The time-honored terms, "supportive" and "expressive," do attempt a distinction that should be useful in describing or prescribing psychotherapy. But I believe they have come to be misapplied and, as used, no longer capture with any precision the distinctions they were coined to preserve.

One image evoked by "supportive psychotherapy" is of a therapist earnestly trying to talk with a patient about the details of everyday living, to suggest better ways of dealing with problems, to offer himself as someone to lean upon, but without specific ambitions to arrive at a point where the purpose of the treatment could be said to have been accomplished. He perhaps wishes to sustain a tentatively reconstituted schizophrenic patient in a marginal existence—a treatment in which "no movement is good movement." Like a good caricature, this image magnifies some part of the truth not beyond recognition and, even though it is a polar example of supportive psychotherapy, this prototype does exist and in large numbers.

For many patients such a concept of treatment is often entirely suitable—perhaps even exclusively suitable. My quarrel is not with the treatment I have sketched but with the name that is applied to it. It is called "supportive" because, I suppose, supporting the patient is its main purpose. But by arrogating the name "supportive" for a polar example of psychotherapy in which the purpose of supporting a patient is pursued in a particular way with particular techniques and with limited aspirations, we debase the term "supportive." We tend to obscure the fact that support is one of the essential purposes of all psychotherapy, and we use it to imply a specific *kind* of psychotherapy—which it is not.

It is, of course, characteristic of the concept "purpose" that it connotes an end achievable by more than one means. In psychotherapy the supportive purpose can be implemented in a variety of ways: (1) by the therapist's accepting silence; (2) by the simple gesture of offering a Kleenex to a crying patient; (3) by a quizzical look conveying "You know better than that" to a quite disturbed patient who is tempted for the moment to accept as realistic an autistic notion; or (4) by a forthright so-called "reality interpretation." These few acts and many others all subserve a conservative or supportive purpose in treatment. It is true that the conservative purpose needs to be

---

*I shall exclude the category, psychoanalysis, from my discussion. While psychoanalysis as a treatment method encompasses a wide range of techniques, structural elements and styles of procedure, it is by and large distinguishable from other forms of psychotherapy and has a theory that attempts to explain the personal changes which it brings about.

kept much more explicitly in the foreground of the therapist's attention in the treatment of certain patients, just as it is true that for others it hardly ever comes to the therapist's attention at all. I doubt, however, that in the latter instance it is also equally distant from the patient's awareness; those patients who impress us as likely candidates for expressive psychotherapy or psychoanalysis merely may be more fortunate than others in having the capacity to derive support from relationships with persons, institutions, things and ideals, including those that do not seem to offer such support in any explicit way. But support is there to be had by those who can make use of it, and it is probably true that those obtain support most successfully who do not seek it explicitly.

It would not be amiss on logical grounds to term that treatment "supportive" in which the psychotherapist must be ever mindful of the patient's need for support. But when used to denote a brand or type of psychotherapy this term has psychological pitfalls and may have unsought and even pernicious consequences. When "supportive" is used as a type-modifier of psychotherapy, some therapists understand that the term requires the *exclusive* use of certain explicit supportive techniques and prohibits the use of certain other techniques (notably content and even defense interpretations). The term suppresses the therapist's interest and alertness to (if not, indeed, rendering him fearful of) whole classes of content of the patient's communications not having explicit reference to the here and now of his experience. Supervisors of psychotherapy often hear a beginning psychotherapist report the painful gropings and musings of a patient who is struggling to master a painful conflict, and learn that the therapist is aware of at least some of the underlying meanings of the patient's difficulties. When the therapist is asked why he did not help the patient by interpreting the situation to him he answers, in the full confidence that it is an adequate response, "The patient is schizophrenic," or "The therapy is supportive." The prescription "supportive psychotherapy," like the label, "schizophrenia," has the potentiality for interfering with the proper treatment of a patient, limiting the achievements that the patient might make were he and his therapist unhampered by these restrictive designations.

But the term "supportive" has a place in the lexicon of psychotherapy even though not, in my opinion, as a category name. To use it as I have suggested, to denote one of the several interlocking purposes of all psychotherapy, suggests different connotations and imposes different requirements on the user. For instance, we would have to ask ourselves: In what sense (areas, instances, etc.) does this patient need support? More specifically, *what* in the patient needs support: (1) his sense of reality against the temptations of dereistic preoccupations, (2) his conscience against the temptations of corruption, (3) his frightened ego against the anxiety-inspired wish to banish all derivatives of a troublesome instinctual impulse or even against intense feelings of any kind? Or is it a fragile and remote impulse-derivative that needs support (*e.g.,* a tender, affectionate feeling against defenses that would stifle it), or perhaps it is the shaken patient who needs support against momentarily overwhelming outside pressures, or does his flagging motivation need support in order to continue treatment during a phase of uncomfortable resistance? Or is it the patient's self-esteem that needs support against the painful discovery of the infantile core of certain strivings?

The term "supportive" applies to each of these different situations, though the manner in which the support would be offered, if indeed it would have to be explicitly offered by the psychotherapist at all, is likely to be quite different in each. In the phrase "supportive psychotherapy," "support" usually implies either support for the ego against the pressure of threatening impulses (*i.e.,* support for the testing of reality) or support against unbearable external pressures.* But even in these more restricted senses, no specific technical implications can be derived from the term "supportive." The support that is needed can be provided in many ways, depending upon the therapist, the patient and the context. Thus, one must not only ask "Support what?" but also "Support *how*?" And this question, like the first, cannot be answered without intimate knowledge of the patient, the therapist and the context.

When "supportive" is used in the sense of bolstering the patient's testing of reality against the pressures of instinct, the term is often linked with or even replaced by the term "suppressive." This latter term, which is so rich in political connotations, is quite barren of specific technical psychotherapeutic implications. Like "supportive," "suppressive" characterizes all psychotherapy to some degree, though more euphonious, less tendentious terms may be used to describe the thinking and operations that could be arrayed under it. In brief, the whole issue of "dosing" interpretations so as not to force the patient's ego to cope with too much at any one time could be subsumed under this concept. Suppression is also accomplished by any expression of the therapist's interest in one rather than in another facet of a patient's communications.

For completeness' sake we must consider an additional question that a therapist should keep in mind about the term "supportive": Support *when*? What vicissitudes in the treatment, in the transference situation, in outside life circumstances, etc., increase or decrease the patient's need for support? Examples probably are not necessary here as they will come easily to your mind.

The therapist should also ask himself, When is support *un*necessary? After support, *then what*? This last is a misleading question, though it lends itself easily to apparently simple answers. The fallacy which this question contains is the implication that the terms supportive and expressive as applied to

---

*In this latter sense the term so dilutes the usual concept of psychotherapy that the task may be delegated to a less prestigeful person than a "doctor," and the process may be called "counseling."

psychotherapy are antithetical. One is led to think that one prescribes and does *either* supportive psychotherapy *or* expressive psychotherapy (or psycho-analysis, *i.e., very* expressive psychotherapy). But can one straddle the issue with the category "supportive-expressive" therapy, thinking that perhaps the apparent antithesis is resolved by this composite form? While this hyphenated term would seem at first glance to be a hybrid that might combine the best features of two ideal parents, it is in fact a most 'unnatural and ungainly offspring. In one usage it is a changeling creature, now like one parent and again like the other, switching its guise as expedience dictates. In another usage it begins like the one parent, and at some inflection point becomes like the other.* The trouble with these fanciful metaphors is that, if we accept that there "ain't no such animal" as supportive psychotherapy, then our conceptual hybrid is left in the embarrassing position of being the offspring of only one parent whose existence, at this point, I hope you are beginning to doubt as well.

When one examines the logic of the supportive-expressive antithesis, then the terms appear obviously incoordinate. They refer to different areas of discourse (since the one refers to a therapist's *purpose* in psychotherapy while the other refers, if somewhat vaguely, to a *means* and *style* of doing psycho-therapy) and can hardly be thought of as opposites or even as alternatives. A logical opposite to the term "expressive" might be "inexpressive," but I do not know of any therapist who would be willing to have his work so described. The term "suppressive," at least in some usages, seems conceptually coordinate with "expressive" and cannot be dismissed on *a priori* linguistic grounds. But when we consider that a psychotherapist may help a patient *suppress* something by encouraging the *expression* of something else, the clarity of the logical distinction is lost. Consequently, the term "suppressive" seems to me better thought of, like its kin "supportive," as a quite general part-purpose of all psychotherapy. Similarly "expressive," while really not of the same order, also characterizes all psychotherapy. A psychotherapy in which the patient is not helped to express something of the depth of himself would be quite unthinkable.

But you will insist that I am merely being perverse in hewing to the everyday senses of these terms while ignoring the technical connotations that they have long since acquired. They may be jargon, you will say, but they are useful jargon and convey to the initiated quite distinctive ideas that no other terms are now available to convey. I concede that in practice a poor tool may be better than none and that distinctions in the kind, style, method, etc. of

---

*I recognize that these situations do in fact arise in clinical practice, that these terms singly or in hybrid form do describe certain instances of psychotherapy. My objection, however, is to considering them as prototypes of treatment or as polar ideals, as examples to which all other instances of psychotherapy are supposed to conform in theory if not entirely in fact.

psychotherapy need to be made—indeed made as precisely as they can be made. It is just for these reasons that I attack the current usage. For the terms we now use, I believe, obscure distinctions that ought to be made and supply only a pair of pseudo-categories which permit discrimination only between polar examples. As for the contention that they are nevertheless useful terms to the initiated, I would reply that it is just such initiated persons who should learn to be more discriminating in describing psychotherapy. The initiated have learned to supply their own private footnotes to fill the gaps in understanding that the category names leave. In short, it is just the "initiated" who have the least need for these misleading terms; they have ways to get around them and their obscurities.

The young psychotherapist who receives a treatment prescription of supportive psychotherapy for a patient will understand that he is not expected to work miracles and can be fairly certain that the patient is not suitable for psychoanalysis. With only this prescription to guide him, however, the therapist-to-be would not know if the patient is too sick to risk a more ambitious treatment or not sick enough to warrant the investment of more time (and possibly a better qualified psychotherapist). The tendencies of certain patients to judge their worth, and the esteem in which we hold their illnesses in terms of the number of hours per week we devote to them (and to a lesser extent, I believe, by whom), are matched by a quite similar if less openly verbalized set of values among therapists. But whatever index to socio-psychiatric status the terms may provide, they can hardly be defended on the grounds that they offer a succinct and accurate guide to a psychotherapist about what he should or should not do, or even to convey to a third party an adequate description of what was or was not done to or with a patient. Yet a psychotherapy prescription should certainly meet these minimal criteria.*

If we are to do away with "supportive" and "expressive" as defining adjectives, how then should psychotherapy be described and prescribed? I do not propose to banish these terms completely, but rather to use them more precisely in describing psychotherapy and to cease using them as if they described different *kinds* of psychotherapy.

It is unreasonable to expect that any word or brief descriptive phrase could convey the information and conclusions from the patient's psychological

---

*Perhaps the riddle of why psychotherapists have become used to uninformative treatment prescriptions is that, unlike the field of medicine in which the diagnostic function is in general more prestigeful than the therapeutic function, in psychiatry the therapeutic function is at present the more prestigeful. For example, a patient may be examined by a junior staff person whose prescription for treatment might be carried out by a therapist who possesses greater training and skill than the diagnostician. Perhaps the brevity and unspecificity of treatment prescriptions reflect this potential disparity of status and the justifiable feeling that a more detailed prescription might be considered presumptuous

examination and history that should guide the treatment he is to be given. The usual sort of case summary or case abstract condenses the multiple overlapping points of view, historical and examinational, that have contributed to the understanding of the patient; but its primary purpose is to represent the several studies briefly but faithfully. It is not permitted the kind of selectivity and special emphasis that should characterize a treatment prescription. A treatment prescription should bear the same relationship to a case summary as a good map does to a guide book.

In the first place, a treatment prescription should serve as a guide in selecting a psychotherapist in terms of his level of skill, particular aptitudes and gender. In the second place, the prescription should serve to alert the psychotherapist-elect to the nature of the patient's problem in terms of the "language of control" (including likely pitfalls and sensitive areas, as well as his strengths and other factors that favor successful treatment) and help him to gauge the likely frequency of appoinments that will be needed.

The following example of a treatment prescription for a hypothetical case has been divorced from the case summary that it should logically follow. Therefore, I must ask you to assume that the examination has established that the patient is moderately ill and severely incapacitated by his illness, and that psychotherapy is the treatment modality of choice. Rather than a prescription of techniques to be followed, this reformed psychotherapy prescription offers a precis of the case from the point of view of treatment, a hierarchy of treatment objectives supported by the findings of the examination, a rationale for an approach to the treatment that could assist the psychotherapist in choosing at least an initial treatment strategy, and an appraisal of the hazards as well as the favorable factors both within the patient and in his environment that could influence the program of the treatment. The example is longer and more discursive than an actual one would need to be in order to make up for the absence of the supporting material that would normally be present.

PSYCHOTHERAPY PRESCRIPTION

1. Objectives

To help the patient resolve what he understands to be a conflict over whether to continue in a turbulent marriage and an uncomfortable job, a situation which appears to be merely the latest of repeated crises having the general form of a self-destructive and environmental-manipulating attempt at resolving an infantile conflict over autonomy versus dependency. While this problem has important pregenital roots, the most prominent obstacle to achieving a workable resolution at this time seems to be the patient's unsuccessful attempts a identify himself with his father whom he experiences as an unreasonable tyrant in whose value system the patient amounts to nothing.

The patient's mother is an inconstant, alcoholic woman who attempts to be protective of the patient in relation to his father but who also behaves quite seductively to the patient and explicitly would like to keep him close to her. The patient's promiscuity and other misbehavior seem to amount to efforts at repudiating the unconscious attraction that his mother holds for him and to neutralize the father's implicit threat to him as a competitor. The patient seems capable of resolving the current aspects of this conflict on the basis of his glimmering awareness both of his father's actual weakness and dependence on the patient and that the patient's own value system has at least as much validity as his father's. The patient should be helped to express his deep-seated resentment and fear of his father and to understand the way in which he has allowed himself to be used as a pawn in their disturbed relationship. It seems likely that such a resolution could be favored if the patient would have an opportunity to identify himself transiently with a consistent and tolerant therapist in the course of working on his difficulties in current life terms.

2. Recommendations

The recommendation to attempt a resolution in current-life terms is based in part on the patient's intense investment in his current difficulties and the degree to which the present situation seems to recapitulate and contain much of the patient's pattern of difficulties of his infantile past. More important, there are contraindications to encouraging regression in the course of psychotherapy because of the ease of stimulating a latent homoerotic (passive feminine) attitude toward the father against which the patient is too weakly defended and in the face of which paranoid symptoms are a likely danger. The patient has already experienced episodes of acute panic in which flight, in the form of wild promiscuity, has been resorted to seemingly in an effort to avoid disintegration. It is expected that periods of hospitalization may be necessary in the course of outpatient psychotherapy when the temptation to flee from mounting anxiety becomes too great. In the hospital as well as out the patient should be encouraged to be active, to work at a job that taxes his abilities and be helped to perform at the highest level of which he is capable.

3. Selection of a Therapist

Attributes of the patient that should condition the selection of a therapist and may influence the course of treatment include the patient's analytic and creative intelligence with, paradoxically, a distrust of intellectualizing and his keen sensitivity to the least indication of insincerity in others, matched by a difficulty in trusting others. The patient loves and practices the outdoor life and has a broad romantic streak in his make-up, idealizing feats of daring and mastery over the forces of nature. The patient has also demonstrated an ingrained sense of decency and fair play that stops somewhere short of application in his relations with women. This inconsistency in himself only vaguely disturbs the patient at present. Lastly, the patient has a fine sense of humor. A therapist-to-be will have to make an instantly good impression on the patient, and will have to be able to match wits with him, at least at the beginning of treatment. He will also have to be able to keep his equanimity and sense of humor in the face of the patient's almost certain efforts to test his sincerity and patience with misbehavior. Because of the patient's focal problem with his father and his feelings of contempt for women it seems likely that the initial course of treatment would go more smoothly if the therapist were male.

4. Structural Elements

At the close of the examination the patient and his family were advised that we recommend psychotherapy and that one-hour interviews two to three times per week for a period we estimate to be one to three years would be involved. They accepted these recommendations and the fee which was quoted to them. The patient is ready to begin treatment at any time. While his initial hostility to the idea that his troubles might have psychological roots within him has abated, he retains much skepticism about the potential helpfulness of psychotherapy.

SUMMARY

I have tried to show that the usual dichotomy, "supportive" versus "expressive," used in prescribing psychotherapy is inadequate and that a useful prescription must be much more explicit about what needs to be supported and when and why, and what needs expression and why. A thoroughgoing psychiatric examination can yield information that is indispensable in deciding upon a program of psychotherapy, if the information is properly organized in the form of a prescription.

Therapeutic Considerations

5

A Prescriptive Treatment Model Based Upon Social Class and Premorbid Adjustment*

PETER A. MAGARO

In the past few years, there has been a change from the medical concept of a patient as a carrier of a disease to the concept of a student engaged in various forms of social learning (Levinson & Gallagher, 1964). The hospital treatment approach has reflected this change by shifting from a custodial-medical model which theoretically emphasized the intervention into the organic or psychological structure to a sociopsychological model which attempts to control the effects of the disease by the exercise of "non-diseased" structures (Cumming & Cumming, 1962). Although the older custodial model attempted therapies the usual treatment was an isolation of the disorder through what could be considered as an incarceration of the patient. Milieu therapy has been the main hospital treatment approach stemming from the sociopsychological model and has emphasized the determining effect of the environment in controlling psychotic behavior. It attempts to reduce symptomatic behavior by modifying or accentuating environmental conditions in order to create an opportunity for the emerging of previously practiced social behavior or for the teaching of new, more adaptive skills. There is an attempt to change stimulus elements in the patient's surroundings at the physical or the authority-structure level to permit an experimentation with a greater range of past or new responses than would have been permitted in the more restrictive custodial situation.

There are variations in specific milieu therapy programs just as there are variations in any method of modifying behavior; however, the variation in types of milieu therapy programs does not seem to depend upon a consideration of patient characteristics. There seems to be a general agreement that the main goal of a milieu therapy approach is increasing the decision-making

*From *Psychotherapy: Theory, Research and Practice,* 1969, **6**, 57–70. Reprinted by permission.

power of the patient. Since there are many levels in the life of a patient where he can exercise his autonomy, milieu therapy cannot be defined as a specific set of ward practices, but is best seen as an "attitude" of transferring responsibility from staff to patients. The problem seems to be that the area of concentration for a particular program or the methods that are utilized are not determined or seemingly influenced by patient characteristics but rather by the values or style of the local practitioner.

The change in treatment attitudes and goals from the custodial to the milieu therapy approach has been considered the third revolution in the field of mental health (Hobbs, 1964). The connotation of this new technique has been characterized as liberal, humanitarian, and progressive, etc., that is, a connotation of "good," while the custodial approach has been considered as authoritative, rigid, old-fashioned, etc., that is, a connotation of "bad" (Zolik *et al.,* 1966). The acceptance of the sociopsychological model has therefore entailed discarding most aspects of its predecessor and protagonist, the medical model, and in some respects can be viewed as "throwing out the baby with the bathwater."

The sociopsychological model which neglects intrapsychic determinants produces little concern for individual differences. It tends to fit all disorders into the one category of hospitalized patient. Treatment in the medical model traditionally involved the sequential process of diagnosis and prescription. Diagnosis served the purpose of discrimination among classes of disorders and prescription attempted to differentially treat according to the initial discrimination. The current approach in its zeal to negate the medical concept of a disease has also negated the process of discrimination and prescription. The sociopsychological approach seems to be applied as indiscriminately in the present as the older custodial approach was applied in the past. There seems to be little attempt to empirically examine the efficiency of the present approach as compared to other approaches, nor to specify the patient characteristics most related to improvement under each treatment model.

An example of the neglect of patient characteristics in the application of a milieu therapy program is the lack of an attempt to understand the effects of a sociopsychological approach upon different social classes. Although a clearly defined lower social class without change and modification of its members does not exist, there are low income, poverty-stricken, and blue-collar individuals in the society who comprise the majority of our hospitalized population and for whom the traditional orthodox treatment approaches do not apply (Riessman *et al.,* 1964). It seems probable that when considering a milieu therapy approach which regards patient characteristics as having no weight in determining treatment effectiveness, that the patient characteristics may, in fact, produce a negative treatment effect. That is, when deciding to apply a milieu therapy approach to a lower-class patient, one may be prescribing the least applicable treatment to the patient, although it may be the most applicable to the treater. In other terms, treatment effectiveness, E, is considered to be a function of the interaction of a particular treatment, T, and the appropriate patient characteristic, C. $E = T \times C$. Although there are many characteristics which vary on continuums in a population, treatment is effective (+) when the particular treatment is matched with an appropriate characteristic. Treatment effectiveness is negative (−) when the particular treatment is related to the characteristic in a detrimental manner. Treatment effectiveness is zero when the treatment is not related to the characteristic. For example, E may be positive when applying psychoanalysis to insightful intelligent individuals; it may be zero when applying it to action-oriented non-introspective individuals; and it may be negative when applying it to poorly defended passive schizophrenics. In somatic terms penicillin may be positive when applying it to an infection, zero when applying it to a person without an infection, and possibly negative when applying it to someone allergic to penicillin. In each case, the patient characteristics are different and positive treatment effectiveness is the matching of the appropriate characteristics to that particular treatment. The treatment can usually be defined in operational terms. The problem becomes finding that patient dimension which responds positively to the treatment. This can only be done empirically through testing each treatment with different patient characteristics. The present paper raises the question of whether the current milieu treatment approach is resulting in negative treatment effectiveness due to it not considering patient characteristics.

The middle-class patient may find the current sociopsychological procedures conducive to his needs in that it allows practicing old skills. Consequently, the current treatment approach, as so briefly described here, may be quite effective for this patient. The lower-class patient possibly may not find such treatment as beneficial due to not having the necessary acceptable behavior to repeat and consequently cannot exhibit what is considered "improved" behavior. There is also the possibility that he may consider the present treatment goals as an imposition upon his personal value system and refuse to cooperate with the middle-class treater. In either case, the result may be that the psychotic behavior of the lower-class patient may increase relative to the treater-defined healthy behavior or even to the previously adaptive, non-psychotic lower-class behavior. In our formula terms, milieu therapy × middle class = positive treatment effectiveness, $T_1 \times C_1 = + E$; however, milieu therapy × lower-class = negative treatment effectiveness, $T_1 \times C_2 = - E$. Since the great majority of patients are lower class, especially in the state hospital, overall treatment effectiveness would be negative.

Until recently, social class has been generally neglected in the treatment of mental disorders and still has not been considered in the application of a milieu therapy approach even though the relationship between the treated prevalence of mental illness and social class has been widely recognized

(Hollingshead & Redlich, 1958; Miller & Mishler, 1959). The upper, middle, and lower-middle classes are under-represented in a hospital patient population, while the lower class is over-represented with twice as many patients as might be expected on the basis of their number in the community (Miller & Mishler, 1959). It is more relevant to note that this disproportionate distribution increases when type of mental illness is considered.

The lower the social class, the greater the incidence of treated psychosis; and, inversely, the higher the social class, the greater the incidence of neurosis, (Hollingshead & Redlich, 1958). This is especially true for schizophrenia (Dohrenwend & Dohrenwend, 1967; Mishler & Scotch, 1963). This relationship may be partly due to the lower class having only a state hospital available for treatment and the hospital is predisposed to diagnose a patient as psychotic while higher classes have private hospitals, clinics, and private practices available which tends toward assigning more neurotic diagnoses (Haase, 1964).

Besides the factor of diagnosis, there seem to be aspects of lower-class life that contribute to the prevalence of psychosis. One aspect is the availability of contact with others, which is related to the incidence of psychosis. Gruenberg (1954a) found that in Syracuse the apartment areas have higher rates of psychosis than one-family dwellings. Other studies also found the incidence of schizophrenia related to the central and socio-economically depressed sections of the city (Burgess, 1955, Faris & Dunham, 1939). These findings have supported Durkheim's concept of "anomie" or of a sense of identity which develops from living in an environment without human contact. This is characteristic of lower-class life and suggests the role of social class as a determinant of psychosis.

From these often-reported results, one would expect that treatment would focus on the conditions and values of the lower-class culture as they could be utilized in treatment. This is not the case, and in fact, the lower class is one patient grouping which has been discriminated against in terms of the types of treatment administered as well as being neglected in terms of the theories of mental illness and the criteria of mental health, (Riessman *et al.,* 1964). In terms of treatment, the higher the social class background of a patient, the better the treatment (Kohn, 1963). This is reflected in the middle-class patient being treated by more qualified personnel, being treated more often and spending more time with the treater in interactive types of therapies. The lower-class patients more often receive somatic or custodial types of treatment since they are not considered to benefit from the "sophisticated psychotherapies" (Brill & Storrow, 1960; Schaffer & Myers, 1954). Such discrimination occurs in clinics in which the economic factor is eliminated. This fact has led Hollingshead and Redlich (1958) to state: "To use a metaphor, private hospitals are designed for the 'carriage trade' but they are supported by the 'shock box'."

In the theories of mental illness and the criteria of mental health, social class seems to again play an essential or even a determining role. In the late thirties an affinity was noted between the Protestant ethic and the concept of mental health as found in the mental hygiene literature (Davis, 1938). In the late fifties, this same relationship was found again, leading to the conclusion that the present mental health movement is unwittingly propagating a middle-class ethic under the guise of an authoritative scientific knowledge of the defining conditions of mental health (Gursslen *et al.*, 1959–1960). Under the guise of authoritative scientific knowledge the mental health movement can be viewed as an enforcement and propagation of middle-class values. Valued methods of treatment are designed for use between people who belong to the same class and share in common a large number of associations (Ruesch, 1963). Lower-class patients are seen as having different strategies for receiving information, conceptualizing and responding to the environment which tends to determine the quality and quantity of their treatment (Riessman *et al.*, 1964). In contrast to their minority position in the theory and practice of mental illness, the lower class comprises the vast majority of our severe treatment problems especially in our public institutions.

The state hospital is considered to be charged with the responsibility of treating the segment of society which does not have other resources. Since the great majority of our mental health "treaters" in the state hospital are of middle-class origin and maintain the middle-class Protestant ethic and its derived conception of mental health, their resultant treatment procedures tend to have goals which reflect such values. The treatment goals are aimed toward changing behavior to meet middle-class standards rather than adapting their treatment goals to the attitudes and skills of a foreign lower-class culture. These treatment goals are imposed on the lower-class patient who does not share or possibly even comprehend such a foreign behavior system. The socio-psychological treatment model mostly utilized in the state hospital is considered to be democratic; however, it is authoritarian in enforcing "healthy" middle-class behavior.

An examination of middle-class values shows definite relations to the goals of the current milieu therapy approach. The present culture has been described as group oriented, deriving exemplary conduct from peer group norms rather than from authoritarian dictates. A positive social value is placed on *responsibility to others, the importance of work, control of emotion, planning ahead, problem-solving,* and *participation in community and group activities.* These same values are the present milieu therapy treatment goals (Gursslen *et al.*, 1959–1960). For example the Cumming and Cumming (1962) approach to milieu therapy emphasizes the executive ego to *control emotions, take on responsibility*, and engage in *problem-solving* through patient-government. The value of *work* is an essential part of the treatment program developed by Jones (1953), which emphasizes the patient being given freedom to *plan ahead* and execute physical changes in the environment. A milieu therapy program also delegates the power of granting privileges to the patients so that *group participation* is essential for benefits and even a basic adaptation to the ward. It can, therefore, be inferred that the goals of the present treatment model reflect the present middle-class concern with group pressures and the importance of environmental conditions in determining behavior. In short, the current treatment philosophy seems to concentrate on imposing a micro-middle-class society with the staff's middle-class values onto the patient culture and demanding that all patient benefits be derived through acceptance of these "treatment goals."

The first step in examining the relationship of social class as well as other diagnostic dimensions to different prescribed treatments is to assess the characteristics which are most descriptive of the hospitalized patient. Thus, the first purpose of the present paper is demographic in terms of describing a state hospital population. The second purpose is prognostic in terms of isolating the patient characteristics which are most related to chronicity in a milieu therapy treatment situation. The third purpose is to propose a treatment model which may utilize aspects of the custodial and sociological models to permit greater treatment effectiveness by prescribing treatment for specific diagnostic categories especially those of social class and premorbid adjustment. The general intent of the present paper is to consider the problem of diagnosis and prescription in treating hospitalized patients. It is not thought that the proposed diagnostic system is the most effective, but it could be the empirical beginning of a prescriptive approach and serve as an illustration of how such an approach can increase treatment efficiency.

DESCRIPTIONS AND DISCUSSION OF PATIENT CHARACTERISTICS

The following discussion will be augmented by data derived from a sample drawn over a six-month period of 161 male patients, mainly veterans, in a state mental hospital which was extensively applying a milieu therapy approach. The patients of this sample are more characteristic of the chronic population since patients who entered and left the hospital in a short period of time could not be tested and patients on geriatrics and medical-surgical wards were excluded. Data were primarily derived from the case history folders. However, when information was not available in the folder, interviews were utilized to complete the data forms.

The first column in Table 1 provides the means or percentages for each factor for all patients. The second and third columns in Table 1 indicate the means and percentages of the demographic variables of patients who were discharged (59%) and those who were not discharged (41%) respectively. Discharge data encompass a one-year period from initial assessment and include patients transferred to other institutions (mainly veteran hospitals) as well as those discharged into the community. Of the 50% who left the

Table 1. Means and Percentages of Patient Characteristics in Sample (N = 161)

	I Total Patient Group	II Still Hospitalized	III Left Hospital	
	100%	41%	59%	
			Discharged	Transferred
			62%	42%
Means				
Age (years)	41.15	43.71	38.60	
Phillips Score	15.32	18.00	12.65	
Education (years)	10.00	9.87	10.34	
Hollingshead Score	54.10	59.72	48.48	
Birth Order	2.90	2.98	2.83	
Number of Siblings	3.53	3.22	3.84	
Previous Hospitalization Time (mos)	135.67	133.47	2.20	
Total Hospitalization Time (mos)	182.34	162.68	19.66	
Medication (mgs per day)	249.65	269.19	230.12	
Percentages				
RACE:				
White	73	78	68	
Negro	25	18	32	
RELIGION:				
Protestant	54	51	57	
Catholic	37	38	36	
Jewish	3	6	0	
No Information	6	0	3	
MARITAL STATUS:				
Single	55	68	43	
Married	14	9	19	
Divorced	14	12	17	
Separated	12	4	19	
No Information or Other	5	7	2	
URBAN	75	72	79	
RURAL	13	14	12	
SHOCK THERAPY:				
Yes	24	30	18	
No	65	54	75	
No Information	11	16	7	
CURRENT DIAGNOSIS:				
Undifferentiated Schizophrenic	48	49	47	
Paranoid	13	16	11	
Catatonic	4	4	4	
Depressive	4	5	3	
Other	23	13	34	
No Information	8	13	1	
ADMITTING DIAGNOSIS:				
Undifferentiated Schizophrenic	37	39	35	
Paranoid	19	22	16	
Catatonic	4	3	5	
Depressive	4	9	0	
Other	25	12	39	
No Information	10	15	5	

hospital, 60% were discharged into the community and 40% were transferred to other institutions, mainly veteran hospitals. The comparison of the group which left and the group which remained is not considered to represent those who have benefited from a milieu therapy approach and consequently have been discharged, and those who have not benefited. It is mainly in comparison of those "selected" to remain and those selected to leave for a combination of social, administrative, and treatment reasons.

Considering the large percentage of transfers in the present sample, the percentage of patients leaving the hospital (59%) is similar to the 66% spontaneous recovery rate with hospitalized neurotics (Eysenck, 1961 p. 710) and to other reports with psychotics (Freeman & Simmons, 1963; Kelly, 1965) including a study of Melazo-Polynesian aborigines which has 65.6% discharge after a year (Rin & Lin, 1962).

Age

The high average age of hospitalized patients (in our sample 41 years) implies a time in life when there is usually an adjustment to a particular life style and little expectation of changing economic or social position. The greater preponderance of psychosis in the middle-age bracket has also been reported with psychosis being the only disorder to increase with age (Pasamanick *et al.,* 1959). The age of the discharged patient is lower than the patient who remains in the hospital. As often reported the younger the age of the patient, the better the prognosis regardless of treatment conditions (Israel & Johnson, 1956).

Education and Occupation

The average education of hospitalized patients (in our sample ten years) is usually substantially below the high school education level. Kornhauser (1962) in a study of mental health of factory workers found for a middle-age group that mental health was inversely related to education and this effect was additive to the relation between mental health and occupation. Although occupational mental health differences persist apart from the influence of education (Kornhauser, 1964), the middle-aged hospitalized male (poor mental health) does persist in a lower occupation with fewer years of education. The lack of education certainly prohibits occupational mobility and its financial rewards. The occupational level of the group under study was 5.80 on the Hollingshead Scale which approximates the semi-skilled occupational level. It is not to be construed that the educational level is a causative factor in the occurrence of hospitalization, but rather that the social and psychological factors which led to little schooling have possibly also led to utilizing the state hospital as a social institution.

Medication and Shock Therapy

The amount of medication used in the sample should be viewed as a rough index due to the combining of different types; however, the vast majority of patients were on tranquilizers. Tranquilization along with milieu therapy is the customary hospitalized treatment and both methods seem to be indiscriminately applied. Amount of medication as well as having shock therapy seems to be more closely related to staying in the hospital than leaving. In the present results, the greater the somatic therapies, the greater the likelihood of remaining in the hospital. This may indicate that the patient who receives such treatment evidences greater disorganization and consequently receives a greater amount of treatment, or it may be hypothesized that the more severe the treatment the less likely the improvement.

Birth Order and Sibling Number

The present data indicate that the average patient is born 2.90 in a family of 3.53. Langner (1964) reports that lower-class patients report greater economic deprivation in childhood and are from more broken homes than high-class patients. This suggests that the large family background of the lower-class patient may be a situation where there is a great deal of group stress, parents having little time for children, and constant exposure to hostility toward authority (Myers & Roberts, 1959). Considering the lower-class patient's early adverse group experiences of condemnation and deprivation, the present milieu therapy stress on group interaction may elicit previously learned withdrawal avoidance behavior, or may encourage psychotic behavior rather than combat the stress of group interaction. Birth order and number of siblings do not seem related to discharge. The present patient group seems representative of the population in terms of race, religion, and urban-rural status. Pasamanick *et al.,* (1959) have also found that the incidence of mental disorders seems more closely related to socio-economic conditions than to race.

Diagnosis

A greater number of patients (48%) were diagnosed as chronic undifferentiated schizophrenics than any other diagnosis. There was an increase in the use of this diagnosis from the admitting to the current diagnosis which may indicate an increasing deterioration of the patient with longer hospitalization. The nonpsychotic group was next (23%), with little change in diagnosis after being in the hospital. Paranoids were the next largest group (15.6%) with a decrease in the use of the diagnosis from the admitting to current status (19% to 13%). The diagnostic results indicate that the large lower-class group exhibits more psychotic and especially more schizophrenic diagnoses. This result has also been found by Langner (1964).

The traits ascribed to schizophrenics resemble those of the lower class in regard to treatment. The needs of the schizophrenics are spoken of in terms of needing structure, being dependent, being passive, and not being able to satisfy needs except in a magical wish-fulfillment manner. These are similar to the lower-class expectations of treatment. The lower-class patient expects the treater to assume an active medical role while he remains passively dependent and he will terminate treatment when these conditions are not met (Overall & Aronson, 1963). The lower-class individual views the community structure as providing benefits which are outside of his realm of influence and rather foreign and distant. He, like the schizophrenic, feels rather impotent in instigating any change in the structure (Miller, 1964). Treatment is perceived as being part of this distant structure and fits his view of the disorder as a medical problem. The effect of viewing the problem as medical and assuming the passive role in treatment creates a different doctor-patient relationship than the interactive one shared by the middle-class patient and may lead to the lower-class patient's expectation of a more dominating or custodial treatment when he is hospitalized. The milieu therapy code of "you are responsible" may not seem to be "treatment" and something to be avoided while in the hospital.

Diagnosis is not related to leaving the hospital, but it is related to the method of leaving the hospital. Of the patients transferred to veteran hospitals 73% are schizophrenic while only 2% are non-schizophrenics. The hospital transfers 28%, retains 43%, and discharges to the community 29% of the schizophrenic population. The large movement from the hospital (59%) is therefore mainly due to transferring schizophrenics and discharging non-schizophrenics.

The population that remains contains 65% schizophrenics in our data. These have accumulated over a period of time. This same result is reported by Isreal and Johnson (1956) who found that 36% of diagnosed schizophrenics remain after a ten-year period and consequently consist of the majority group in the hospital. This group also comprises the group of schizophrenics who have 13.1 years average length of hospitalization although they are only 25% of the first admissions. In general the schizophrenic population, although it comprises a small percentage of first admissions, is the group which has the longest stay in the hospital, the least number of discharges to the community, and a large number of readmissions. As shown below, this result is more specifically due to poor premorbid adjustment schizophrenia. It would consequently seem that current social treatment methods are not having the same effect on this patient group as with non-schizophrenics, at least as measured in terms of discharge or readmission. In fact, recent recommendations for treatment have reacted to this condition by proposing that since we cannot modify the schizophrenic disorder, we should make provisions in the community for the patient to adjust at a maximum level, even if it is at the level of a therapeutic workshop (Kelly, 1965).

Premorbid Adjustment and Marital Status

The premorbid adjustment of our hospitalized group is poor, with only 14% currently married. Ties to the basic cohesive unit in the society are consequently minimal. In relation to discharge, the premorbid adjustment and marital status variable indicate that the better the premorbid social and sexual adjustment, the better the prognosis in that a good premorbid adjustment is related to discharge and a poor premorbid adjustment is related to remaining in the hospital. This is further support for the predictive validity of the Phillips Scale (Phillips, 1953). The practical reasons for this seem to be similar to those of the lower-class patient, such as a lack of family ties and poor occupational history (Zigler & Phillips, 1962). The social class and premorbid adjustment factors are somewhat independent, however, with the goods of each class representing an adequate social-sexual adjustment and the poors an inadequate social-sexual adjustment. Performance on laboratory tasks is determined by the two factors with schizophrenic premorbid adjustment mainly reflecting a sensitivity to censorious stimuli as possibly determined by specific childrearing experiences, and social class reflecting a possible acclimation to task-taking situations. The social class effect is most prominent in the normal and good premorbid adjustment groups and disappears in the poor premorbid group, suggesting that the effect of social class is relatively unimportant with the poor premorbid schizophrenic (Magaro, 1967).

The poor on the Phillips measure is equivalent to the older concept of the process schizophrenic while the good is equivalent to the reactive (Magaro, 1968). For the premorbidly poorly adjusted, previous attempts at social interaction have been minimal. The skills essential for social interaction are lacking or have not been practiced to any great extent. The few social contacts and lack of group relationships tend to characterize the patient as a loner without any ties to the community or to any smaller more intimate units which would permit an organizing situation and mutual dependency in the middle years. It would seem that any interpersonal contact could not be group oriented and have to be derived from other social institutions which would permit more distant separate relationships. One and possibly the only such institution where this can occur besides a prison is the state hospital. The state hospital can provide a situation where there is a cohesive unit with common ties but with no need for interpersonal relations. The state hospital also has a consistency in that it has its own culture where action can be projected into the future with a great deal of security (Goffman, 1961). Premorbid adjustment is related to length of hospitalization with a poor premorbid adjustment characterizing the majority of patients; consequently, this distinction should be of major interest in prescribing forms of treatment.

Social Class

Of the total number of patients in the first sample from which social class was available, 59% were from the lower social-economic class as contrasted with 15% from the middle and upper classes. Information was not available on 27% of the patients. In another later survey in which all patients on a unit were examined and consequently geriatric and short-term patients were taken into account, 86.4% were from the lower class. In regard to discharge, there was a trend for the patients that stayed in the hospital to be of lower social class than those who left, as indicated by their score on the Hollingshead.

Considering the age, education, and occupation level of the present sample, they could not be considered the upwardly mobile members of the community or in fact the lower-class group itself.

The middle-class male in our society may find some degree of security and consistency in middle age through a settled-on occupation, neighborhood, peer group, etc. Such consistency may not be available in the lower-class segment of the community. His job is most subject to lay-offs, there is not much opportunity for moving into a more secure occupational position due to his lack of skill and education, and possibly more important there is not the social structure in the lower-class neighborhood of apartments and tenements to provide the consistent off-work grouping found in the single-dwelling neighborhood. It is possible that the state hospital supplies the consistency and security of middle and old age for this population, whereas the middle-class group finds other institutions in the society.

Time Hospitalized

The data indicate that the average patient has had approximately 11 years total hospitalization before the present hospitalization and 15 years including the present hospitalization. This is a chronic group which has been institutionalized, with the administration of different forms of treatment over the years seemingly having little effect. Considering the above-mentioned past history of this group and its possible attempt to utilize the hospital as a place to escape the social economic struggle and conflict found in the community, chronicity may be viewed as an adaptive social condition rather than a psychic withdrawal. The chronic hospitalized patient is therefore not "hospitalized" in the passive sense of its being beyond his control, but he is actively manipulating staff to maintain his mental illness status.

Braginsky *et al.,* (1966) have labeled this type of activity impression management, which is an adopting of many tactics to actively manipulate the staff in order to remain hospitalized. This view is in contrast to considering the patient as a passive and ineffective pawn in the interplay of social or institutional forces, but rather it views the patient as needing the institution and expending effort to stay hospitalized as another would expend effort to maintain a position in the community and not be hospitalized. Hospitalization may, therefore, be an attempt to achieve social homeostasis in light of pessimistic opportunities for some relief in terms of economic freedom or interpersonal contact in the community. This condition is reminiscent of Gruenberg's (1954b) remark that social forces which produce high rates of psychosis are intimately connected with those which produce state mental hospitals. In the present context, it would be that the social conditions which isolate and inhibit a social class from sharing in the institutions provided for the older middle-class male will provide other institutions such as state hospitals to meet the lower-class needs. It is not that we neglect the poor in middle and old age, but their retirement plan may be supervised and planned in the realm of mental illness. The needs which are not met in the lower-class subcultures are provided by the state in old age. The incarceration of the lower-class old has the added advantage of providing a boogie man or a warning to the middle-class deviants of what can later occur when the middle-class values are not upheld. Obviously, there are psychological factors which produce hospitalization, and the social factor is only one part of the picture; however, it is being emphasized here because so little consideration is usually given this factor in the prescription of treatment.

In light of such an intertwining of class values and treatment goals, and the relative homogeneity of a lower social class and a poor premorbid adjustment in the hospitalized population, an attempt should be made to prescribe treatment according to these diagnostic categories. The custodial and the psychosocial approaches may both be effective modes of treatment if they are applied discriminately according to patient characteristics. Therefore, the following treatment model will prescribe either a custodial or a psychosociological approach depending upon the diagnostic classification of the patient in terms of social class and premorbid adjustment.

A PRESCRIPTIVE TREATMENT MODEL AND THE ROLE OF THE HOSPITAL

The role of the hospital can be viewed as having alternate goals: first, to allow adaptive behavior patterns to emerge which were dominant before the increased dominance of psychotic behavior; and, second, to teach new skills which are adaptive for the individual to his particular environment. The current milieu therapy approach seems to emphasize the emerging and teaching of social skills which would seem to have been an essential part of the middle-class repertoire. The custodial approach was probably detrimental to this patient in that it repressed such behavior. This treatment approach considered order as the prerequisite for a "good" custodial ward and consequently emphasized a minimal amount of social interaction and a maximum of passivity to an authoritative and sometimes punitive structure. Previous interpersonal behavior was possibly inhibited and the alternate psychotic or withdrawn institutional behavior was encouraged or positively reinforced. That is, the dominant middle-class interpersonal and social behavior was negatively reinforced and allowed the alternate positively reinforced psychotic behavior, which was probably dominant upon admission, to increase in its dominance.

The lower-class patient may be in the opposite situation. The custodial model may have encouraged previous adaptive pre-psychotic dominant behavior and discouraged psychotic behavior. The adaptive behavior may have consisted of being dominated by an authoritative structure, even when it was punitive, taking a passive view of his relation to the hospital in the form of the physician who is treating his sickness, and viewing social responsibility and interpersonal contact as dangerous as compared to being alone and following directions. A milieu therapy approach would expect him to exhibit interpersonal social behavior which is contrary to his past experiences and minimally practiced. In this case the competing psychotic behavior may be more probable than the expected social behavior and remain dominant, leading to longer hospitalization.

If the hospital is viewed as having a treatment model which inherently defines certain types of behavior to be correct, the defining and rewarding of the correct behavior by the hospital may increase nonpsychotic behavior of one social class, *i.e.* treatment, and increase the psychotic behavior of another social class, *i.e.* institutionalization. What would be considered treatment, therefore, would depend upon the matching of the hospital-defined healthy behavior and the social class group. Just as psychotherapy may diminish the severity of symptoms in the worst affected patients and may accentuate the range of symptoms in others (Lin & Standley, 1962), a milieu therapy approach may do the same by reinforcing the easily dominant social behavior of the middle-class group leading to patient improvement. At the same time, the hospital may punish the non-social, but adaptive behavior of the lower-class patient and consequently increase the psychotic or withdrawn behavior leading to chronicity. This reasoning suggests that chronicity is a social problem in terms of treatment matching class values and previous behavior patterns.

Another patient characteristic which was found to be related to extensive hospitalization was a poor premorbid adjustment. The good is discharged regardless of treatment conditions. It would, therefore, be expected that the most advantageous role of the hospital in the treatment of this patient would be to allow the previous dominant adjusted behavior to emerge. Such a role for the hospital would be custodial or what will be called "recovery" in order to avoid the punitive and other surplus meanings attached to custodial. The good premorbid adjustment group in each social class seems to have developed appropriate behavior to his class group while the poor usually has not. The goods of either class would be expected to improve in a non-intervening condition especially if the setting was social class-oriented in terms of the behavior which could emerge and be practiced. In effect, the hospital could utilize "time" and the emerging of class experience-expectant behavior to allow a return to the patient's previous level of organization. This would be an attempt to capitalize on the spontaneous remission factor by providing the patient an "escape" from pressures in order to reduce drive and allow the good premorbid dominant behavior to emerge and the alternative, psychotic regressive behavior to subside. The role of providing for the emergence of previous dominant behavior places the hospital in the position of an escape valve for the society. The individual who cannot tolerate particular class-oriented stresses can remove such stress by entering the hospital. Viewing the patient as one needing to reduce external societal drives makes intervention into the psychological systems of the good premorbid patient unnecessary.

It is therefore proposed that the entering wards of the hospital should be considered as recovery wards and oriented towards social conditions which elicit previously dominant responses of the good premorbid adjustment patient. In a sense, this suggests adapting a medical model in allowing the "disease" to run its course in that natural processes of the organism can combat the infection. This is only suggested for the good premorbid adjustment patient. The structure of the recovery ward would be class oriented. A middle-class good patient would enter a ward which expects previous social interaction patterns to emerge by emphasizing social activities, and simple decision-making in a milieu therapy approach. It would seem that possibly social workers would be the main program developers to organize group activity and maintain constant contact with the patient's family. The lower-class patient would enter a more authoritarian ward with less social activities and more structure. Occupational and industrial therapists could function as the main program developers for the lower-class ward to allow a practicing of former occupational skills.

In effect, the entering wards would attempt to recreate the past life experiences of the patient without the environmental stresses. The simulated aspects of the recovery wards would not permit the mortification and depersonalization so typical of the total institution (Goffman, 1961). The goal of the program would not be to teach, but to practice former premorbid behavior and increase its dominance. Living conditions, entertainment, recreational facilities, etc., should simulate the specific social class as much as possible. Patients who prefer other life styles than those reflected by the social class factor could be transferred to the other class-oriented ward. For example, the lower-class patient who is middle-class oriented would be originally classified as lower class in terms of occupation and education, but if he is upward mobile in terms of previous behavior patterns, he could be transferred to a more appropriate ward. The classification of patients on the basis of social class as determined by educational level and occupation would seem to be a fairly reliable measure, however, it may not be a valid indicator of a commonality of past interest and activities which the recovery wards would attempt to recreate. If it was found that the variation in regard to previous dominant behavior was too great for such measures, other past experience dimensions may be tapped. The goal of classification would be to place patients into ward settings which simulate situations requiring previous dominant interpersonal and social or asocial behavior to emerge. If other classificatory measures could be as reliably developed and demonstrate a greater validity in terms of grouping patients, they could be attempted. The present classification system of premorbid adjustment and social class is only one system which has a degree of simplicity and efficiency.

The poor premorbid adjustment patient would enter more active treatment wards in accord with our second goal of teaching new skills. Also the middle- and lower-class good who does not improve after a short period of time on the recovery ward would also be transferred to such wards. The intensive treatment approach of the teaching wards would attempt not only to modify psychological processes, but also combat the social processes of colonization (Goffman,1961). This is a reduction in the usual tension between the outside world and the hospital by a demonstration of the relative ease of hospital life compared to negative experiences in both lower- and middle-class life. There is a danger that increasing the benefits in the hospital by removing the aversive qualities in treatment programs may increase a colonization process. However, a transfer to the intensive treatment wards may increase the benefits of being discharged relative to the pressures exerted by the psychological pushing exerted by the intensive treatment staff. Magaro (1970) found that an intensive treatment team will discharge more chronics than a custodial team, which will discharge more acutes. The results suggested that the chronic could not tolerate treatment pressure from staff and left the hospital to avoid treatment since he could not withdraw or act institutionalized.

The intensive treatment wards also would be class oriented. The lower-class intensive treatment ward would be action oriented and concrete with an emphasis on modifying specific forms of behavior. A behavior modification program might be best utilized at this level, although certainly besides social class the degree of pathology would have to be considered. In fact, the social class distinction may drop-out at the poor premorbid level as it does on experimental or testing tasks (Magaro, 1967). In this case other dimensions may be more predictive of treatment effectiveness. Occupational skills could also be taught once the basic adaptive behavior patterns are learned. The middle-class intensive treatment ward could be socially oriented with the use of the psychotherapies including group and family therapies. A milieu approach could also be attempted with an emphasis on group processes and need systems as manifested in maladaptive behavior.

The intensive treatment ward would use the greatest concentration of professional staff and the greatest patient-staff ratio. The entering wards would require few staff and consequently allow staff concentration on the intensive treatment wards. The typical treatment institution, especially the state hospitals, is usually understaffed so that the proposed approach advocates more efficient use of staff depending upon the needs of the patient.

The traditional procedure of transferring patients from well-staffed intensive admitting treatment wards to poorly staffed custodial back wards, would be in effect reversed. The back wards would be teaching wards, the learning of new behavior, while the entering wards would be recovery, emerging behavior wards.

The aim of the proposed treatment approach is to be discriminative in offering types of treatment. The characteristics of the patient are the starting point to begin treatment, not the current treatment philosophy to which the patient has to adapt. The proposed model suggests that ward placement be based upon premorbid adjustment and social class. All goods would be assigned to recovery wards. Middle-class goods would enter a structured milieu program and lower-class goods would enter a structured occupational program. Within a short period of time, if there is no improvement, there would be a transfer to an intensive treatment ward. Lower- and middle-class poors would be immediately assigned to such wards. A behavior modification program may be applicable to the intensive ward of lower-class poor in that it would still maintain an authoritative structure with emphasis on concrete rewards. The middle-class intensive treatment ward would be more concerned with dynamics, social skills, and the talk-orientation of a less structured milieu program. If such a classification system proved not to be productive of improvement, other classification systems could be attempted. Since the wards would be separated and have defined treatment programs, data could be accumulated on the effectiveness of each treatment program in terms of patient characteristics. Whatever patient characteristics are found to be related to discharge under each program would then become the basis for future classification and prescription. The essence of the proposed model is not to allow current therapeutic models to become more important than the characteristics of the individual they were developed to treat.

It sometimes seems that the search for "the treatment" has pronounced a failure verdict upon any treatment before it could ever be adequately tested on the particular patients for whom it was developed. A therapeutic success is reported; it is immediately and indiscriminately applied; and naturally it fails. The rapid application and judgment of a therapeutic technique is like developing a drug to control a specific disease, administering it to all diseases and considering it a fraud when it fails. The present proposal is an attempt to return to a classification of the patient and prescribing treatment to as narrow a diagnostic category as possible in order to observe the relative effects of many treatments on each category.

REFERENCES

Braginsky, B. M., Grosse, M., & Ring, K. Controlling outcomes through impression-management. An experimental study of the manipulative tactics of mental patients. *Journal of Consulting Psychology*, 1966, **30**, 295–300.

Brill, N. Q., & Storrow, H. A. Social class and psychiatric treatment. *Archives of General Psychiatry*, 1960, **3**, 340–344.

Burgess, E. W. Mental health in modern society. In A. M. Rose (Ed.), *Mental health and mental disorder*. New York: Norton, 1955, 212.

Cumming, J., & Cumming, E. *Ego and Milieu*. New York: Atherton, 1962.

Davis, K. Mental hygiene and the class structure. *Psychiatry*, 1938, **1**, 55–65.

Dohrenwend, B. A., & Dohrenwend, B. P. Field studies of social factors in relation to three types of psychological disorders. *Journal of Abnormal Psychology*, 1967, **72**, 369–378.

Eysenck, H. J. The effects of psychotherapy. In H. J. Eysenck (Ed.), *Handbook of abnormal psychology*. New York: Basic Books, 1961, 697–725.

Faris, R. E., & Dunham, H. N. *Mental disorders in urban areas: An ecological study of schizophrenia and other psychoses*. Chicago: University of Chicago Press, 1939.

Freeman, H. E., & Simmons, O. G. *The mental patient comes home*. New York: Wiley, 1963.

Goffman, E. *Asylums*. Chicago: Aldine, 1961.

Gruenberg, E. M. Community conditions and psychosis of the elderly. *American Journal of Psychiatry*, 1954a, **110**, 888–896.

Gruenberg, E. M. The epidemiology of mental disease. *Scientific American*, 1954b.

Gursslen, O. R., Hunt, R. G., & Roach, J. L. Social class and the mental health movement. *Social Problems*, 1959–1960, **7**, 210–218.

Haase, W. The role of socioeconomic class in examiner bias. In F. Riessman, J. Cohen, & A. Pearl (Eds.), *Mental health of the poor*. Glencoe, N. Y.: The Free Press of Glencoe, 1964.

Hobbs, N. Mental health's third revolution. *American Journal of Orthopsychiatry*, 1964, **34**, 822–833.

Hollingshead, A. B. Two factor index of social position. Mimeographed copy, Yale University, 1960.

Hollingshead, A. B., & Redlich, F. C. *Social class and mental illness*. New York: Wiley, 1958.

Isreal, R. N. & Johnson, N. A. Discharge and readmission rate in 4,254 consecutive first admissions for schizophrenia. *American Journal of Psychiatry*, 1956, 112.

Jones, M. *The therapeutic community*. New York: Basic Books, 1953.

Kelly, F. E. Research in schizophrenia: Implication for social workers. *Social Work*, 1965, **10**, 32–44.

Kohn, M. L. Social class and parent-child relationships: An interpretation. *American Journal of Sociology*, 1963, **68**, 471–480.

Kornhauser, A. Toward an assessment of the mental health of factory workers: A Detroit study. In F. Riessman, J. Cohen, & A. Pearl (Eds.), *Mental health of the poor*. Glencoe, N. Y.: The Free Press of Glencoe, 1964, 49–56.

Langner, T. Comparison of experience and behavior of lower and higher status groups: Findings and hypotheses. In *Life stress and mental health.* Glencoe, N. Y.: The Free Press of Glencoe, 1964, 49–56.

Levinson, D. J., & Gallagher, E. B. *Patienthood in the mental hospital.* Boston: Houghton-Mifflin, 1964.

Lin, T., & Standley, C. C. The scope of epidemiology in psychiatry. *Public Health Papers,* **16,** World Health Organization, Geneva, 1962.

Magaro, P. A. Perceptual discrimination in schizophrenics as a function of censure, social class, and premorbid adjustment. *Journal of Abnormal Psychology,* 1967, **72,** 415–420.

Magaro, P. A. A reliability and validity study of the process-reactive self-report scale. *Journal of Consulting Psychology,* 1968, **32,** 482–485.

Magaro, P. A., & Giardina, P. Comparing custodial and democratic treatment programs. *Hospital and Community Psychiatry,* 1970, **21,** 118–119.

Miller, S. M., & Mishler, E. G. Social class, mental illness and American psychiatry: An expository review. *Milbank Memorial Fund Quarterly,* 1959, **37,** (2), 171–199.

Miller, S. M. The American lower classes: A typological approach. In F. Riessman, J. Cohen, & A. Pearl (Eds.), *Mental health of the poor.* Glencoe, N. Y.: The Free Press of Glencoe, 1964, 139–154.

Mishler, E. G., & Scotch, N. A. Sociocultural factors in the epidemiology of schizophrenia: A review. *Psychiatry,* 1963, **26,** 315–351.

Myers, J. K., & Roberts, B. H. *Family and class dynamics in mental illness.* New York: Wiley, 1959.

Overall, B., & Aronson, H. Expectations of psychotherapy in patients of lower socioeconomic class. *American Journal of Orthopsychiatry,* 1963, **33,** 421–430.

Pasamanick, B., Roberts, D. N., Lemkau, P. N., & Krueger, D. B. A summary of mental disease in an urban population: Prevalence of race and income. In II. Nussbaum (Ed.), *Epidemiology of mental disorders.* Washington, D. C.: American Association for the Advancement of Science, 1959.

Phillips, L. Case history data and prognosis in schizophrenia. *Journal of Nervous and Mental Disease,* 1953, **17,** 515–525.

Riesman, D., Glazer, N., & Denny, R. *The lonely crowd.* New Haven: Yale University Press, 1950.

Riessman, F., Cohen, J., & Pearl, A. *Mental health of the poor.* Glencoe, N. Y.: The Free Press of Glencoe, 1964.

Rin, H., & Lin, T. Mental illness among Formosan aborigines as compared with the Chinese in Taiwan. *Journal of Mental Science,* 1962, **108,** 134.

Ruesch, M. P. The disadvantaged child and the learning process. In A. H. Passon (Ed.), *Education in depressed areas.* New York: Columbia University Teacher's College, Bureau of Publications, 1963, 163–179.

Schaffer, L., Myers, J. K. Psychotherapy and social stratification: An empirical study of practice in a psychiatric outpatient clinic. *Psychiatry,* 1954, **17,** 83–93.

Zigler, E., & Phillips, L. Social competence and the process-reactive distinction in psychopathology. *Journal of Abnormal and Social Psychology,* 1962, **65,** 215–222.

Zolik, E. S., Lantz, E. M., & Busiel, G. J. The "new look" in mental hospital programs as reflected in patient return rates. Paper presented at the American Psychological Association Convention, New York, 1966.

6

Toward a Flexible, or Personalistic System of Psychotherapy*

A. A. LAZARUS

"Nothing is working out. My wife left me and I'm about to lose my job. I drink too much and I smoke too much. I'm a nervous wreck. For no good reason, I break out into sweats, tremble inside, and feel dizzy and tight in the head. Sometimes I think about killing myself. I'm getting nowhere. I don't even know who I am most of the time. Sometimes I get a weird feeling as if I'm watching myself doing things. At other times, my heart beats so fast that I get more and more frightened. I thought there was something wrong with my heart but my doctor said it checked out fine. But sometimes I wonder about that, especially when I have pains in the chest."

The above is not an uncommon clinical syndrome. The tendency in psychiatric circles would be to label it "anxiety hysteria" or perhaps "incipient psychosis," with or without additional tags like "minor melancholia," "depersonalization," "hyperventilation," or "hypochondriasis." But diagnostic labels give little indication of antecedent factors and provide equally few clues about therapeutic management. Besides, it is difficult to find close agreement among independent raters regardless of their respective diagnostic skills. Few would disagree, however, that irrespective of the right or wrong diagnostic label, it would be desirable to enable this unfortunate individual to "find himself" and to effect a genuinely happy marriage coupled with gratification from his work, fulfillment from life, and lasting freedom from the symptoms which plague him. How is this to be achieved? Should he be psychoanalyzed, psychosynthesized, leukotomized, hypnotized, tranquilized, or hospitalized? Despite the frequent lip service that is paid to individual differences, many psychotherapists tend to generalize, if not universalize, in a manner that is totally unsupported by the facts. Some therapists believe that people must solve their own problems and that any active intervention on the part of the therapist

*From A. A. Lazarus, *Behavior therapy and beyond.* New York: McGraw-Hill, 1971, pp. 31–47. Copyright © 1971 by McGraw-Hill Inc. used with permission of McGraw-Hill Book Company.

will inevitably prove antitherapeutic. These clinicians studiously avoid offering any advice, guidance, or even reassurance. At the opposite pole, other therapists feel that since they are "experts in living" and since psychotherapy is predominantly a reeducative experience, they can only earn their keep by actively manipulating, shaping, and reinforcing their patients' behavior.

Is there a "best" or "correct" way of achieving serenity in place of turmoil, and happiness instead of misery? Wedded by faith to a theory, some therapists insist that their way is really the only way of proceeding in psychotherapy. Thus, I have had colleagues inform me that in their estimation, "No cure is complete unless the patient has gained full insight into his incestuous wishes," or "Any treatment which does not include the vigorous expression of hate and anger is, at best, half-baked" and "Unless the entire family unit is brought in for readjustment, therapy is bound to be one-sided and incomplete." More recently, I have been informed that, "Any course of treatment which fails to include systematic desensitization is bound to leave the patient hypersensitive to innocuous stimuli."

The explicit assumption throughout this book is that the saying, "one man's meat is another man's poison" is particularly applicable to the field of psychotherapy. Another explicit assumption is that the "best" therapy is that which works for the individual. Consequently, it is considered extremely important to match each individual patient to the particular therapy and therapist appropriate for him. In this regard, the most essential ingredients for an effective psychotherapist are *flexibility* and *versatility*. This implies an ability to play many roles and to use many techniques in order to fit the therapy to the needs and idiosyncrasies of each patient. By contrast, therapists with pet theories or specially favored techniques usually manage, in their own minds at least, to fit their patient's problems within the confines of their particular brand of treatment.

For example, the fact that problem-focused interviews often succeed in breaking down vague and abstruse clinical problems into areas of specific hypersensitivity, has led some therapists (e.g., Wolpe, 1964, 1969) to believe that nearly all complex neuroses are merely clusters of phobialike responses. This rigid and oversimplified view of human functioning has the danger of omitting important conceptual problems which require treatment in their own right and at their own level (Lazarus, 1968). Consider the following clinical excerpt, by no means atypical, in which a problem-focused interview proceeded from simple phobia to complex problem in living.

THE "BRIDGE PHOBIA"

Patient: I have a fear of crossing bridges.

Therapist: Do you have any other fears or difficulties?

Patient: Only the complications arising from my fear of bridges.

Therapist: Well, in what way has it affected your life?

Patient: I had to quit an excellent job in Berkeley.

Therapist: Where do you live?

Patient: San Francisco.

Therapist: So why didn't you move to Berkeley?

Patient: I prefer living in the city.

Therapist: To get to this institute, you had to cross the Golden Gate.

Patient: Yes, I was seeing a doctor in San Francisco. He tried to desensitize me but it didn't help so he said I should see you because you know more about this kind of treatment. It's not so bad when I have my wife and kids with me. But even then, the Golden Gate, which is about one mile long, is my upper limit. I was wondering whether you ever consult in the city?

Therapist: No. But tell me, how long have you had this problem?

Patient: Oh, about four years, I'd say. It just happened suddenly. I was coming home from work and the Bay Bridge was awfully slow. I just suddenly panicked for no reason at all. I mean, nothing like this had ever happened to me before. I felt that I would crash into the other cars. Once I even had a feeling that the bridge would cave in.

Therapist: Let's get back to that first panic experience about four years ago. You said that you were coming home from work. Had anything happened at work?

Patient: Nothing unusual.

Therapist: Were you happy at work?

Patient: Sure! Huh! I was even due for promotion.

Therapist: What would that have entailed?

Patient: An extra $3,000 a year.

Therapist: I mean in the way of having to do different work.

Patient: Well, I would have been a supervisor. I would have had more than fifty men working under me.

Therapist: How did you feel about that?

Patient: What do you mean?

Therapist: I mean how did you feel about the added responsibility? Did you feel that you were up to it, that you could cope with it?

Patient: Gee! My wife was expecting our first kid. We both welcomed the extra money.

Therapist: So round about the time that you were about to become a father, you were to be promoted to supervisor. So you would face two new and challenging roles. You'd be a daddy at home and also big daddy at work. And this was when you began to panic on the bridge, and I guess you never did wind up as a supervisor.

Patient: No. I had to ask for a transfer to the city.

Therapist: Now, please think very carefully about this question. Have you ever been involved in any accident on or near a bridge, or have you ever witnessed any serious accident on or near a bridge?

Patient: Not that I can think of.

Therapist: Do you still work for the same company?

Patient: No. I got a better offer, more money, from another company in the city. I've been with them for almost 1½ years now.

Therapist: Are you earning more money or less money than you would have gotten in Berkeley?

Patient: About the same. But prices have gone up so it adds up to less.

Therapist: If you hadn't developed the bridge phobia and had become foreman in Berkeley at $3,000 more, where do you think you would be today?

Patient: Still in Berkeley.

Therapist: Still supervisor? More money?

Patient: Oh hell! Who knows? (laughs) Maybe I would have been vice-president.

Therapist: And what would that have entailed?

Patient: I'm only kidding. But actually it could have happened.

Therapy in this case was deflected away from his bridge phobia toward unraveling a history in which the patient, the youngest of five siblings, tended to accept his mother's evaluation that, unlike his brilliant older brothers, he would never amount to anything. Desensitization was in fact employed, but not in relation to bridges. A hierarchy of his mother's real or imagined pejorative statements was constructed, and the patient was immunized to these hurtful allegations. He was also trained in assertive behavior. As he gained confidence in his own capabilities, his bridge phobia vanished as suddenly as it had appeared.

Perhaps it can be argued that the patient's bridge phobia developed through a process of conditioning, which Rachman (1968, p. 27) regards as the basis of all phobias. A behaviorist with whom I discussed the case contended that the man was apprehensive about his future and that his anxieties *just happened by chance* to erupt while traveling on a bridge. He added that bridges thereupon became invested with high anxiety potential and that the patient's avoidance of bridges blocked the extinction of his fears. But what was he really avoiding? Bridges per se? And was the first anxiety attack on the bridge fortuitous? Did not his bridge phobia serve the function of preventing the full impact of his own uncertainties and shortcomings vis-à-vis his work, competence, obligations, and achievements? Why did the phobia disappear as soon as these basic anxieties were overcome? These questions reflect the inadequacies of peripheral S-R theories of learning as touched on in Chapter 1.

FINDING THE APPROPRIATE THERAPIST AND THERAPY

A large percentage of patients are most obligingly suggestible. Those who end up in the hands of Freudian therapists provide "evidence," especially during their dreams, of infantile sexuality; while Jungian analysands end up convincing their analysts of the existence of a racial unconscious. Patients who consult Wolpeans are almost invariably phobic and hypersensitive. In other words, when a therapist has a strong theoretical bias, no matter in what direction, he will inadvertently influence his patients to react in a manner which "proves" his own theoretical assumptions. This even holds true for very farfetched notions. For instance, a mystic and his clients with whom I was acquainted claimed that they each independently perceived the origin of their difficulties in acts performed during previous lives, and that these discoveries were independent of any overt suggestions from their "guru." The studies on verbal conditioning (Krasner, 1958; Krasner & Ullmann, 1965)—and more especially Truax's (1966) demonstration of the way in which a client-centered therapist like Carl Rogers unconsciously shaped and influenced, via selective reinforcement, his patient's perceptions—show how powerfully these subtle cues can influence behavior.

The trouble is that even therapists who lack any obvious charismatic qualities, but who are nonetheless capable of mobilizing some feelings of optimism in some of their patients, are likely to receive enough intermittent positive reinforcement to keep them behind their desks. These factors probably account for the proliferation of today's systems and schools of psychotherapy. The pundits of each system have vigorously lauded their own approach while denigrating all others. But claims for the overall superiority of any one system of psychotherapy—including behavior therapy—have not been scientifically verified. Even if one particular brand of therapy was shown to be superior to all others, it still might not cater to those individuals whose rehabilitation called for the use of certain methods practiced only by the generally less successful schools of therapy. For example, certain people may have such overriding needs to have their dreams interpreted or to sit in an orgone box that only sincere practitioners of these cults will make any headway with them (but not necessarily for reasons ascribed by the practitioners).

In line with the foregoing, those who practice psychotherapy, be they psychiatrists, psychologists, social workers, ministers of religion, teachers, nurses, counselors, or intelligent laymen, should be trained to (1) rapidly identify the patient's basic problems, (2) determine the seemingly best way *for that individual* of dispelling these problems, and (3) skillfully apply the necessary procedures or make the appropriate outside referral(s). This is obvious and straightforward enough, but unfortunately a good deal of psychotherapy practiced today seldom follows this logical sequence. Instead, problem identification is likely to depend almost exclusively upon the orientation of the therapist. We have already alluded to the one-sided views of some (not all) psychoanalysts, nondirective therapists, operant conditioners, and family therapists. The tendency to grasp a segment of the truth and to magnify it into the whole truth is not confined to the aforementioned camps.

In the light of all the contradictory theories and methods, just how should the sincere and dedicated clinician proceed? He cannot afford to suspend all action and judgment until advances in neurophysiology, biochemistry, and genetics provide many of the answers he so desperately needs today. Nor can he confine himself to the drawing boards of experimental psychology because the practicing clinician still has derived precious little therapeutic ammunition from laboratory studies. He can, however, draw upon several established principles and place his own findings and practices within a broad theoretical framework while constantly searching for new empirical data to increase his therapeutic effectiveness and test the soundness of his theories. Much of this book will be devoted to stepwise descriptions of methods and techniques, because in the hands of compassionate, candid, and flexible clinicians, the skillful application of appropriate techniques will often determine the difference between therapeutic failure and success. An explicit assumption is that genuine rapport and a good therapeutic relationship are usually necessary but often insufficient for profound and durable behavior change.

The points being stressed may be said to constitute a truly "personalistic psychotherapy." While taking cognizance of general principles (e.g., the Truax and Carkhuff [1967] findings that effective therapists display accurate empathy, warmth, and genuineness), one should remain on the lookout for individual exceptions to these general rules—e.g., those cases who react adversely to warmth or empathy and require a distant, impartial, and business-like interaction. As already mentioned, within this framework *flexibility* and *versatility* are the key ingredients of efficient and effective therapeutic interaction. Yates (1970, p. 380) in his scholarly book on the academics of behavior therapy stresses that "each abnormality of behavior represents a new problem so that each patient must be considered as a subject of experimental investigation in his own right."

Nearly all therapists must have seen cases who remained refractory to their own valiant psychotherapeutic efforts, and who derived no benefit from colleagues of similar or even different persuasions, but whose emotional suffering came to a sudden and oftentimes dramatic end upon discovering a chiropractor, or some other such person who manipulated their spine, or perhaps irrigated their colon, or prescribed some herbal mixtures. Our diagnostic interviews should enable us to determine whether the case under consideration is more likely to derive benefit from a brief spell of relaxation rather than a protracted regime of assertive training; whether prolonged free association would help more than rapid densensitization; or if a series of seances, some sessions with a Ouija board, or a course of yoga, or any combination of the foregoing plus several other procedures would be the answer.

This does not imply a random trial-and-error procedure where the "flexible clinician" prescribes anything from mineral baths to phenothiazines as his whims dictate. Well-conceived guiding principles and general theories about human behavior should enable the clinician to decide when and why certain therapists and therapies are to be favored. Let us consider some obvious cases in point:

EXAMPLE ONE: THE THERAPIST'S AGE AND APPEARANCE

Therapist: Mrs. Miller?

Patient: Yes?

Therapist: Hi! I'm Arnold Lazarus. Good to see you. Would you like to sit in that armchair or do you prefer this one over here?

Patient: This one will be just fine.

Therapist: Did you have any difficulty in finding this office?

Patient: No, your directions were very clear.

Therapist: Oh, good. Well, let me just take down some formal details and then we can look into your problems.

Patient: So you're Dr. Lazarus.

Therapist: Why do you say it like that?

Patient: Oh, I don't know. It's just that I expected you to look different. Umm! (laughs) You don't look like a psychologist.

Therapist: How do you think a psychologist should look?

Patient: (Laughs) Oh, I know it sounds stupid, but I expected to find a little old man with a gray beard.

Therapist: (Joking) Well, did you notice my gray hairs?

Patient: Oh, I know it's foolish . . . .

Therapist: Not at all. If you need someone who comes across to you in a special fatherly way, you may indeed be more comfortable and derive much more benefit from working with an older man than I, and it's very wise of you to raise this point at the very beginning. Let's look into it more closely . . . .

Comment

Some therapists may attempt to persuade this woman to remain in therapy with them in spite of, or because of, her learnings or prejudices. Issues of this nature warrant careful exploration. For some people, words spoken by a little old man with a long gray beard may have ten or twenty times the impact of identical utterances from younger men (even if they can lapse into heavy Viennese accents). If taken literally, this example may seem naive. The point being made is that it is important for therapists to assess their "reinforcement values" for individual clients and to try and remedy the situation when laboring at a disadvantage. Goldstein (1970) has provided many excellent studies on "relationship-enhancement" and indicates that therapists can structure initial sessions to augment therapeutic attractiveness.

A more precise example concerns the case of an experimental psychologist who reported that he found it incredibly simple to shape the verbal behavior of a group of female students. One of his colleagues failed to replicate these results. The disparate findings were accounted for in terms of possible differences in pretest expectancies, variations in intensity and timing of reinforcement contingencies, slight age differences between the samples, and so forth. Neither of them considered the obvious fact that the first experimenter was an extremely charming and handsome young man with high reinforcement potential for young girls whether he winked, whistled, or cackled, whereas his odd and pimply-faced counterpart required very potent techniques to compensate for his deficiencies in personality and appearance.

EXAMPLE TWO: THE REAL THING OR NOTHING

Therapist: I've studied all the questionnaires you filled out and would now like to discuss my impressions and give you some idea of the way in which I think we should proceed in therapy.

Patient: Some of the answers were quite confusing. What I'm saying is that I can't vouch for all my answers.

Therapist: That's okay. All I needed were some general trends. Let me tell you what I deduced from your answers. Generally, there seemed to be three main areas of, what should we call them...umm...emotional hypersensitivity. First you seem to be really up-tight about making it with women.

Patient: That's no surprise considering what I was telling you about my dear mother and sisters.

Therapist: Right. And that brings up the second factor. You have a lot of hostility towards your mother and older sisters, yet you have never expressed your grievances directly to any of them. In fact, they probably have no idea about the way you really feel about anyone or anything. Which ties into the third factor, and that is your general secrecy and lack of trust.

Patient: Well, I'd say you've hit it on the head, but I guess there's a good reason for all this . . . umm . . . .

Therapist: Sure, but I don't think we need spend too much time on discovering *why* you act and feel the way you do as much as *what* can be done to change it.

Patient: How do you mean?

Therapist: Well, do you know anything about techniques like desensitization, assertive training, and similar methods?

Patient: It sounds like *1984,* or maybe *Brave New World.*

Therapist: Many people get the wrong idea about these procedures. It's not a matter of brainwashing or any form of coercion. Let me give you an example. Just imagine as realistically as possible that you are at a party. Close your eyes and imagine this really vividly. Try and pretend that you are not in this office but project yourself right into the scene at the party. Try to see the people and hear the hum of conversation. Look around the room. Some folks are dancing. Get the picture?

Patient: Uh huh!

Therapist: Good. There's a pretty girl sitting by herself. Look at her. Now picture yourself deciding to go up to this pretty girl and ask her to dance. (pause of about five seconds) How does that make you feel?

Patient: Up-tight!

Therapist: Okay, suppose I first trained you in relaxation so you could picture many of these scenes without feeling anxious, you would soon find yourself actually doing these things in real life without getting up-tight.

Patient: Like I said, *1984*. Or maybe Pavlov's dogs. Look here, you told me to be honest. I can see how this would be great for some people, but I want to do this thing properly; you know, like go back to my childhood and try to get some real understanding and insight into myself.

Therapist: Well, sure. To go about this properly I'm going to need your full life history. We will need to look into all your meaningful and formative relationships and explore your attitudes and values . . . .

Patient: How about my dreams?

Comment

Further discussion revealed how much this patient was conditioned by the Freudian *Zeitgeist*. For him, therapy had to consist of a couch, free association, deep introspection, and dream interpretation. Any other approach was but a poor imitation of the genuine article. It is usually bad therapeutic practice to argue and to try and sell one's own therapeutic system in place of that which the patient believes can best help him. The patient in question was accordingly referred to a psychoanalyst. In my experience, patients who specifically ask for hypnosis or dream interpretation or any other special procedure should be treated by their self-prescribed procedures. The patient often knows best. If his method of choice proves unsuccessful, it clears the way for the therapist to reevaluate the case and to apply procedures which he considers more appropriate.

EXAMPLE THREE: YOU MUST RELAX

Therapist: Okay, let's go on to the relaxation now. Would you like to push the chair right back so you can let your whole body have support?

Patient: I'm still not sure what you said about the incident involving my sister's husband.

Therapist: Oh, I thought we had covered that one. I think you should ignore it at this stage.

Patient: Yes, I reckon it's the only thing I can do right now. Okay, I feel better about that.

Therapist: Fine. All right, now push the chair back and get comfortable . . . .

Patient: Did I mention that Marge sends you her love?

Therapist: Yes, thank you. You can get even more comfortable by sitting farther back in the chair.

Patient: Will we have time today to talk about something that involved me and my niece's maid?

Therapist: Sure. We only need to extend the relaxation from your arms to your facial area today. It will take about ten minutes.

Patient: I also want to get into that bit about my feelings towards Janice.

Therapist: Should we forget about the relaxation today and rather talk about the matters you have raised?

Patient: Well, if you say so.

Comment

Therapists who are overenthusiastic about their own favorite techniques are apt to keep pushing them at their patients despite their obvious resistance or reluctance. A less reticent patient might not have hedged but may have expressed her need to talk about her problems rather than practice relaxation exercises during that particular session. Or she may have expressed her antipathy towards relaxation procedures in general. Even when this occurs, some therapists make the error of insisting that relaxation be applied because they consider it unwise to allow patients to control or manipulate them. Yet, sometimes a distinct therapeutic gain may be derived from allowing the patient to be controlling or somewhat manipulative, especially when he is testing out newly formed assertive skills. Passive-aggressive forms of manipulation should usually be identified and discouraged, but a patient's refusal to relax or to role play, or to carry out an assignment, is often too hastily labeled "resistance" or "contrariness" when it is nothing of the sort. In keeping with the tenor of this book, it should be noted that contrary to Jacobson (1964) relaxation is not always effective in decreasing anxiety but may, on occasion, even heighten it (Lazarus, 1965).

EXAMPLE FOUR: LET'S FIRST TALK FOR A YEAR OR TWO

Therapist: Well, I would say that your anxiety seems to boil down into three main areas. First, you are overconcerned about your performance at work. Second, you really are in two minds about your love affair and need to settle it one way or the other. And third, you have a real "thing" about doctors, hospitals, and illness.

Patient: Holy cow! That's like summarizing *The Brothers Karamazov* in less than fifty words. Half a life-time of feelings and experiences neatly cut up into three slices, filed under three categories, in three compartments. And all this after knowing me and listening to me for less than two hours. Christ! Well, how's about adding a number four while we are at it, and that is how I feel that oversimplification not only misses the boat but does the other person and yourself a grave injustice. And for a number five, you now know that I'm an angry and aggressive bitch!

Therapist: You seem to be saying that I am unaware of how extremely complicated or complex people really are and that I have insulted you by identifying three main trends which seem to account for much of your tensions and anxieties.

Patient: It's not that as much as the fact that I feel you shouldn't leap to conclusions about people that you hardly know. I mean, a hell of a lot has happened to me in thirty-five years and it's obviously going to take time for me to sort it all out with you. I mean, if you made a one-two-three statement after knowing me for a year or two, I could more easily accept that you were basing your diagnosis on some extensive facts. But to almost suck it out of the air after less than two hours . . . .

Comment

One might be tempted to explain to this patient that just as one is not required to drain every pint of her blood in order to assess its chemical content, but that a 5 cc sample can often tell us all we need to know, it is not necessary to look into every facet of her "life stream" in order to draw plausible inferences about her feelings and behavior. But this patient seemed above all else to be expressing the need for a prolonged therapeutic relationship. As I was about to move to a different part of the country in less than six months, I discussed my further impressions with her and gave her the option of continuing to see me for another few months and then, if necessary, being referred elsewhere, or of consulting someone else from the start. Not surprisingly, she considered it unwise to be "shunted from pillar to post" and chose the latter. At an earlier stage of experience, I was so technique- and problem-oriented that I would probably have missed her need for a relationship per se, or what Schofield (1964) so aptly called "the purchase of friendship." Although I am generally impressed by the advantages of short-term and time-limited therapy (Phillips & Wiener, 1966), I have seen several cases who needed more than a year's therapy to develop sufficient trust in me before they could or would reveal highly charged emotional areas which had eluded all preliminary psychometric and diagnostic evaluations.

MATCHING PATIENT TO THERAPIST

The implicit theme throughout this chapter is that a therapist cannot adapt his therapy or himself to every patient. Sagacious referrals will continue to serve a crucial therapeutic function. The examples outlined above stress the need to fit the patient to the most well-suited therapist whose age, brand of therapy, utilization of techniques, and way of establishing rapport are all in keeping with the patient's needs and expectancies.

Considerable information about a person, apart from his chief complaints, is required before the best suited therapies and therapists can be found and properly matched to his idiosyncratic needs. We must know *when* deviant responses are elicited, by *what* they are maintained, and *how* they can best be eliminated. (Traditional psychotherapy seems to be too preoccupied with discovering *why* the person is as he is.) Effective therapy seems to require a well-balanced client- and problem-centered orientation. For instance, while most phobic sufferers can be expected to derive benefit from desensitization therapy, one needs to be on the alert for important exceptions to this rule.

Hoch (1955, p. 322) observed that "there is some relationship between the efficacy of psychotherapy and the patient's expectation of it, [his] 'ideal picture' about the therapist and also about the procedure to which ... [he] would like to respond." Similarly, Solovey and Michelin (1958, p. 1) have pointed out that "the individual who comes to consult, usually has his own mental representation of his disease, of the recovery he hopes to achieve, and often, even of the psychotherapeutic procedure he desires to have applied in his case." Conn (1968) observed that "when everything else failed, Stekel would purposely antagonize a patient. In almost every case the patient would leave in a huff and later have his glasses changed, visit a spa, or go to another doctor who would cure him. The patient would then call Stekel to report that another method of treatment had cured him."

In addition to adopting a flexible and personalistic system of psychotherapy, may I enter a plea for therapists to search continuously for new techniques in order to develop a large and effective repertoire for overcoming the anxieties, depressions, and other disruptive feelings and thoughts that mar the attainment of sustained well-being. Throughout this book, I hope to demonstrate that techniques, rather than theories, are the active means for achieving constructive therapeutic ends.

REFERENCES

Conn, J. H. Hypnosynthesis: Psychobiologic principles in the practice of dynamic psychotherapy utilizing hypnotic procedures. *The International Journal of Clinical and Experimental Hypnosis,* 1968, **16,** 1–25.

Goldstein, A. P. *Psychotherapeutic attraction.* New York: Pergamon Press, 1970.

Hoch, P. H. Aims and limitations of psychotherapy. *American Journal of Psychiatry,* 1955, **112,** 321–327.

Jacobson, E. *Anxiety and tension control: A psychobiologic approach.* Philadelphia: Lippincott, 1964.

Krasner, L. Studies of the conditioning of verbal behavior. *Psychological Bulletin,* 1958, **55,** 148–170.

Krasner, L., & Ullmann, L. P. (Eds.) *Research in behavior modification.* New York: Holt, 1965.

Lazarus, A. A. A preliminary report on the use of directed muscular activity in counterconditioning. *Behaviour Research and Therapy,* 1965, **2,** 301–303.

Lazarus, A. A. Behavior therapy and marriage counseling. *Journal of the American Society of Psychosomatic Dentistry and Medicine,* 1968, **15,** 49–56.

Phillips, E. L., & Wiener, D. N. *Short-term psychotherapy and structured behavior change.* New York: McGraw-Hill, 1966.

Rachman, S. *Phobias: Their nature and control.* Springfield, Ill.: Thomas, 1968.

Schofield, W. *Psychotherapy: The purchase of friendship.* Englewood Cliffs: Prentice-Hall, 1964.

Solovey, G., & Mielchin, A. Concerning the criterion of recovery. *Journal of Clinical and Experimental Hypnosis,* 1958, **6,** 1–9.

Truax, C. B. Reinforcement and non-reinforcement in Rogerian psychotherapy. *Journal of Abnormal and Social Psychology,* 1966, **71,** 1–9.

Truax, C. B., & Carkhuff, R. R. *Toward effective counseling and psychotherapy: Training and practice.* Chicago: Aldine, 1967.

Wolpe, J. Behavior therapy in complex neurotic states. *British Journal of Psychiatry,* 1964, **110,** 28–34.

Wolpe, J. For phobia: A hair of the hound. *Psychology Today,* 1969, **3,** 34–37.

Yates, A. J. *Behavior therapy.* New York: Wiley, 1970.

7

Generic and Individual Approaches to Crisis Intervention*

GERALD F. JACOBSON, MARTIN STRICKLER AND WILBUR E. MORLEY

In several recent papers,[1-6] my colleagues and I have reported on the program of the Benjamin Rush Center for Problems of Living, a division of the Los Angeles Psychiatric Service. The Los Angeles Psychiatric Service is a community-supported outpatient clinic, engaged in direct service to adults, training in psychiatry and the other mental health professions, research and community service.

The Benjamin Rush Center division of the Los Angeles Psychiatric Service was established in 1962. To date, upward of 2,000 individual patients have been seen in three and one-half years of operation. The characteristics of the Benjamin Rush Center are:

1. Service is available to any individual over 17½ years of age, or to any family, regardless of financial or diagnostic considerations. Fees are charged according to ability to pay.

2. Immediate treatment is offered—on the day the patient walks in, if possible—subject only to availability of staff.

3. Treatment deals with the immediate problem, or crisis, rather than with long-established modes of functioning.

4. Treatment is carried out by a team of psychiatrists, psychologists, and psychiatric social workers, under psychiatric direction. A psychiatric nurse serves as program coordinator.

The present paper is concerned with some theoretical issues inherent in crisis intervention.

THE NATURE OF CRISIS

As Caplan[7] defines it. "A crisis is provoked when a person faces an obstacle to important life goals that is, for a time, insurmountable through the utilization of customary methods of problem-solving. A period of disorganization ensues, a

---

*From *American Journal of Public Health*, 1968, **58**, 338–343. Reprinted by permission.

period of upset, during which many different abortive attempts at solution are made. Eventually some kind of adaptation is achieved which may or may not be in the best interests of that person or his fellows."

It should be noted that a complete characterization of any crisis must include references to social, intrapsychic and somatic factors, in other words to the biopsychosocial field. A crisis may result from change in any one area, and such a change may result in crisis processes involved in all areas.

Relevant to the social factor in crisis are role changes or other alterations in the interpersonal balance. Intrapsychic aspects are most readily conceptualized as referring to changes in a previously existing equilibrium within the psychic apparatus and involving unconscious as well as conscious processes. Somatic changes may also be significant in the instigation and or subsequent course of crisis as exemplified by the work of Lindemann[8] on the relation of pathologic grief to chronic psychosomatic illness.

There is a further distinction between the hazard or hazardous situation and the crisis proper. The hazard is that social intrapsychic or somatic change which in certain circumstances may result in a crisis. Examples of hazard are loss of significant relationships through death or separation, birth of premature or deformed children, or physical illness. A crisis results only if the individual experiencing the hazard does not have a previously developed coping mechanism available to deal with the hazard. Such coping techniques are acquired throughout life so that each individual must inevitably pass through a succession of crises, as he encounters new hazards. Each successfully mastered crisis in turn adds to his coping armamentarium. For this reason, crisis has been described as both a danger and an opportunity.

It follows that certain hazards uniformly result in crises whereas others may or may not do so. Examples of the former are the life crises described by Erickson, which occur as each person for the first time encounters a new stage in life as he progresses from birth through childhood, adult life, and into old age. Loss by death, or other means, of important other persons also invariably results in a new situation for which previous coping mechanisms could not be available, and requires a new crisis process before it can be resolved. On the other hand, the loss of employment or physical illness may or may not result in a crisis for any one person, depending on whether he is equipped to handle the situation within himself and in the external world by previously established methods.

The outcome of each crisis is of great significance for the individual. Any crisis may result in solutions which are in varying degrees adaptive or maladaptive. Adaptive solutions are reality-oriented, result in the acceptance of what is inevitable, in strengthening of interpersonal ties, in renewed intrapsychic equilibrium without neurotic or psychotic manifestation and, as mentioned, in the enrichment of the coping repertory. Maladaptive responses, on the other hand, are inappropriate to the reality situation, and may result in lasting interpersonal disturbances or in newly formed or exacerbated neurotic or psychotic syndromes. The implications for prevention are obvious.

There are a number of factors which influence the outcome of any given crisis, consisting not only of the objective nature of the hazard, i.e., the extent of the real threat to effective functioning, but of a number of other factors as well. These include experience with other crises encountered earlier, revival of memories and fantasies of loss or failure with associated fear and guilt, constitutional factors, cultural and socioeconomic prescriptions, and the amount and kind of support available in the environment during crisis. It is the last-named factor that leads us to considerations of crisis intervention.

CRISIS INTERVENTION

Crisis intervention may be defined as activites designed to influence the course of crisis so that a more adaptive outcome will result, including the ability to better cope with future crisis. If classified according to the means employed, crisis intervention may be divided into two major categories which may be designated as individual or generic. These two approaches are complementary. Both concepts have their roots in the growing literature on crisis and crisis intervention[9] but have not previously been explicitly formulated or differentiated from each other.

Generic Approach

Its central thesis is that for each crisis, such as bereavement, birth of premature children, divorce, and so on, there are certain identifiable patterns, some of which result in adaptive and others in maladaptive outcome. This approach is particularly well documented in the work of Lindemann[8] on bereavement. Lindemann found that a bereaved person goes through a well-defined process in adapting to the death of a relative, consisting of the so-called "grief work" which includes preoccupation with the image of the deceased person, usually in connection with the revival of memories of joint activities. While most persons grieve appropriately, some do not. Failure to complete the grief process is believed to be a potential cause of later psychiatric or psychosomatic illness. Work aimed at examinig distinct adaptive or maladaptive patterns with regard to another crisis, that of premature birth, has been described by Caplan, Mason, and Kaplan.[10]

There is no attempt to determine or assess the specific psychodynamics of the individual involved in the crisis. Rather, the focus is on the course that a particular *kind* of crisis characteristically follows and a corresponding treatment plan aimed toward adaptive resolution of the crisis.

Intervention consists of specific measures designed to be effective for the target group as a whole. Approaches include direct encouragement of adaptive behavior, general support, environmental manipulation, and anticipatory guidance. This broad approach to all members of a given group with relative disregard of individual differences permits a partial conceptual analogy to such public health measures as immunization and water fluoridation.

It is one of the merits of this conceptualization that it provides a rationale for a type of crisis intervention which may be carried out by persons not specifically trained in the mental health field, such as nonpsychiatric physicians, nurses, welfare workers, and so on. In brief, the generic approach emphasizes (1) specific situational and maturational events occurring to significant population groups, (2) intervention oriented to crises related to these specific events, and (3) intervention carried out by nonmental health professionals. An example of the generic approach follows.

Case Report

A public health nurse visited the home of a couple in their early 30's, both highschool teachers, who had one week earlier brought home their newborn and first baby. The baby boy was grossly deformed and diagnosed immediately by the obstetrician and pediatrician as almost certainly severely mentally impaired.

The nurse found the mother alone with the baby and in a highly lethargic and depressed state. The mother managed to communicate that she was "just waiting" for the State Hospital to contact her and take "it" into permanent placement. She was vague about any details of arranging the placement and indicated that she and her husband found it very hard to talk to each other. Before the baby's birth she felt that there was very good communication between them. Her mother called her frequently to caution her about getting involved with the baby and to remind her that the physician had told her in the hospital to handle the baby as little as possible, i.e., to just care for its physical needs so as not to get emotionally attached to the baby.

The nurse noted that the mother constantly referred to the baby as "it" and kept a physical distance from the baby's crib. She said to the mother, "Look, this is your baby. It came out of you and you have a right to hold it and cuddle it." Thereupon, the nurse picked up the baby and put it in the mother's trembling hands. The nurse stayed for another half-hour while the mother looked at and stroked the baby.

On the next visit, several days later, there was a dramatic change in the mother's appearance, for she was quite alert, active, and talkative. In response to the nurse's comments on this change, the mother said that a lot had happened since she had last seen her. She had been crying on and off for the first time since the baby's birth, had displayed anger at her husband's passivity in planning for the baby's hospitalization, and now they were talking to each other again. The husband had set up appointments with the State Hospital staff for conferences on the consideration of placement.

The nurse asked what caused such changes in such a short period. The mother stated that it started when the nurse put the baby into her arms and encouraged her to look at it and recognize that it was her baby. The nurse had been the only person who had not cautioned her about thinking of the baby as a "real living thing." Although she now feels the terrible pain of her disappointment and the loss over the prospect of giving up her baby, she herself feels more alive again.

The nurse encouraged her in this and in subsequent visits to talk about her feelings, her disappointment, shame, and guilt, as well as her sorrow about the impending loss of the baby.

This illustrates a case of preventive help where the individual diagnoses of the mother and father were not known or explored, but where the necessary grief work was permitted to emerge and take a healthier course. The training and experience of the public health nurse in crisis situations involving separations or loss were instrumental in her approach to this family.

There are some factors limiting the applicability of the generic approach. First, there are many types of crises for which patterns characteristic of adaptive and maladaptive solutions have not as yet been identified. Further, it appears very likely that among all persons experiencing a common crisis, some proportion will fail to respond to an approach based on the universal characteristics of the crisis, and will require assistance which takes their individual psychological processes into account. For this reason there exists a need for another approach to crisis resolution.

Individual Approach

This is the approach that we have found most helpful in conceptualizing much of our own work in crisis intervention, though we do make use of generic concepts also. The individual approach differs from the generic approach in its emphasis on the assessment by the professional person of the specific intrapsychic and interpersonal processes of the individual(s) in crisis, although this information may not be directly presented to the person. Professional efforts are directed toward the achievement of that solution which is optimal given the *unique* circumstances of the particular situation.

This approach differs from more extended psychotherapy in its lack of concern with long-established processes, except as they provide clues that aid in understanding the current crisis. The focus clearly is on why and how a previous equilibrium had been disturbed, and on the processes involved in the reaching of a new equilibrium. Another differentiation from much conventional therapy is the frequent inclusion in the individual process of family members or other important persons.

Unlike generic techniques, individual intervention requires a greater measure of understanding of psychological and psychosocial processes. It is most effectively carried out by individuals with preexisting skills in one of the mental health disciplines, who have undergone further training in the theory and practice of crisis intervention. In brief, the individual approach emphasizes (1) biopsychosocial events unique in the life of a given individual, (2) intervention directed to the individual, and (3) intervention carried out by mental health professionals. A clinical example of the individual approach follows.

Case Report

A 42-year-old woman came to the Benjamin Rush Center acutely anxious and depressed, following the first experience of sexual intercourse that had occurred in her lifetime. She was preoccupied with fears that her lover would abandon her, assured herself that he would contact her, but questioned the value of going on should he fail to do so. It was significant that the sexual experience had followed an automobile accident in which the patient's car had hit that of the friend from the rear. The friend had comforted the patient following this accident, and sexual relations ensued.

The patient's father had committed suicide when the patient was 12 years of age, an event for which the patient was totally unprepared. For a year the patient had totally denied the father's death to herself, yet had been in a very disturbed state, which had not been usual for her previously.

In her subsequent life, she functioned in superior fashion in her chosen occupational area, but her relations with men were casual and she avoided any significant emotional involvement. She had some concern that she might have "homosexual tendencies" because of this apparent lack of interest in men, but had had no homosexual experience. Within a year prior to the acute crisis she had returned to her native country and found that the marker designating her father's grave had been removed in accordance with local customs.

In the course of six visits, it was possible for both therapist and patient to become aware of the manner in which the current crisis was related to the earlier trauma of the father's suicide when the patient was age 12. Since that age, the patient had repressed much of her reaction to the loss of the father, and had developed a characterologic defense consisting of withdrawal from and partial identification with men.

When at last she began to reach out to men—motivated probably by both age-related factors and the reminder of the finality of the loss of the father, due to the removal of the gravestone—she chose a man with whom she became involved in the context of violence (the accident) and who, as it turned out, had no real interest in her, a fact which at first she staunchly denied, as she originally denied her father's death.

This patient was seen for six visits. Treatment was carried out by a resident psychiatrist under the supervision of one of the authors (Dr. Jacobson). The focus was on the current crisis, i.e., the problems relating to the sexual experience and subsequent "abandonment" by the boy friend. The patient was able to achieve insight into the realistically inappropriate nature of her response to this situation, which was either to deny the reality of the loss or to face overwhelming and chaotic feelings of anxiety and depression. The origins of this inappropriate reaction were identified as a chain of specific events beginning with the suicide of the father.

In the opinion of both therapist and supervisor the patient gained meaningful insight into the connections between her current plight and these earlier events.

In this particular case, it was our impression that the patient came to us at a fork in the road in her overall development, and that it is possible that her gain from crisis intervention may have gone beyond the mastery of the current situation with the boy friend, and may have included the beginnings of a working through of her long-established attitudes toward all men. Only time can tell whether such a result did in fact occur. What is known is that at the end of six visits and at follow-up, three months later, the patient was markedly improved. She showed no signs of acute crisis, but only an appropriate grief reaction over the years she had lost in withdrawing from men. She was making plans to build sounder relationships with men when she was last contacted. The boy friend had never called.

If the generic approach is in some way analogous to such public health measures as immunizations which can be broadly applied to large population groups, the individual approach is analogous to the diagnosis and treatment of a specific disorder in an individual patient. Both appear to have a significant place in comprehensive mental health programs, and both are economical in terms of use of manpower, and important in terms of prevention of long-term disability. Individual approaches, however, require far more skilled personnel, and should therefore be used selectively. Optimum use of individual intervention, in our opinion, would occur if generic crisis intervention were widely available, and care-takers practicing the generic approach could be trained to detect cases which do not appear to respond to the generic approach, and refer these cases to mental health specialists for individual treatment. Another valuable contribution that the individual approach could make consists of gaining additional experience in the natural history of crisis, which would then be used in training of nonmental health professionals using the generic approach.

SUMMARY

Generic and individual approaches to crisis intervention have been outlined and discussed in terms of similarities and differences of theory and practice, with special reference to the use of mental health and nonmental health personnel in crisis intervention.

REFERENCES

1. Jacobson, Gerald F. Crisis theory and treatment strategy: Some sociocultural and psychodynamic considerations. *Nerv. & Ment. Dis.,* 1965, **141,** 209–218.
2. Jacobson, G. F., Wilner, D. M., Morley, W. E., Schneider, S., Strickler, M., & Sommer, G. The scope and practice of an early-access brief treatment psychiatric center. *Am. J. Psychiat.,* 1965, **121,** 1176–1182.
3. Morley, W. E. Treatment of the patient in crisis. *Western Med.,* 1965, 3;77.
4. Paul, Louis. Treatment techniques in a walk-in clinic. *Hosp. D. Comm. Psychiat.,* 1966, **17,** 49–51.
5. Strickler, Martin. Applying crisis theory in a community clinic. *Social Casework,* March 1965.
6. Strickler, M., Bassin, E. G., Malbin, V., D. Jacobson, G. F. The community-based walk-in center: A new resource for groups under-represented in outpatient treatment facilities. *A.J.P.H.,* 1965, 55, 377.
7. Caplan, Gerald. An approach to community mental health. New York: Grune & Stratton, 1961.
8. Lindemann, Eric. Symptomatology and management of acute grief. *Am. J. of Psychiat.,* 1944, **101,** (2), 141.
9. Parad, Howard J. (Ed.) Crisis intervention: Selected readings. New York: Family Service Association of America.
10. Caplan, G., Mason, E. A., & Kaplan, D. M. Four studies of crisis in parents of prematures. *Community Ment. Health J.,* 1965, **1,** (2), 149–161.

Research Considerations

8

Some Myths of Psychotherapy Research and the Search for a Paradigm*

DONALD J. KIESLER

One of the unfortunate effects of the prolific and disorganized psychotherapy research literature is that a clear-cut, methodologically sophisticated, and sufficiently general paradigm which could guide investigations in the area has not emerged. Perhaps this is an unavoidable state of affairs in a new area of research. Yet a perusal of this literature indicates that most of the basic considerations necessary for a general paradigm have appeared, albeit in many cases parenthetically, at some place or another. But to date no one has attempted to integrate empirical findings and methodological concerns in a way that might lead to a useful research paradigm. This lack of integration of the paradigm ingredients has minimized their impact on investigators in the area. Moreover, concomitant with, and perhaps because of, the absence of a paradigm several myths have been perpetuated; and because of these myths, inadequate designs continue to appear.

This paper will first attempt to spell out in some detail several myths current in the area of psychotherapy research which continue to weaken research designs and confuse the interpretation of research findings. Secondly, it will attempt to present a minimal but general paradigm which takes into account current theoretical inadequacies and empirical learnings, and focuses on methodological considerations which can no longer continue to be ignored.

SOME MYTHS OF PSYCHOTHERAPY RESEARCH

We should be wary of pseudo-quantifications and methodological gimmicks which often tend to close off prematurely an area of inquiry and give rise to the illusion that a problem has been solved, whereas the exploration has barely begun. (Strupp, 1962, p. 470).

---

*Excerpt from *Psychological Bulletin*, 1966, **65**, 110–136. Copyright 1966 by the American Psychological Association. Reprinted by permission.

This first section is devoted to enumerating and refuting several misconceptions about psychotherapy research which have tenaciously persisted. These myths have served the unfortunate purposes of confusing the conceptualization of psychotherapy, hence impeding research progress; and of spreading pessimism regarding the utility of further research. Let us deal with these myths in turn.

The Uniformity Assumption Myths

This misconception was first labeled by Colby (1964) although it has been alluded to by several other authors (Gendlin, 1966; Gilbert, 1952; Kiesler, 1966; Rotter, 1960; Strupp, 1962; Winder, 1957). Colby only parenthetically mentioned the myth, and alluded to only one of its aspects, that regarding patients in psychotherapy research. This paper will extend its meaning to cover the psychotherapy treatment itself. The former is referred to as the Patient Uniformity Assumption, the latter the Therapist Uniformity Assumption.

Patient Uniformity Assumption. For Colby, the Uniformity Assumption refers to the belief that "patients at the start of treatment are more alike than they are different." This implicit assumption has led to a remarkably naive manner of choosing patients for psychotherapy research: patients are not selected, rather they pick themselves by a process of natural selection. In searching for patients for investigating psychotherapy, researchers have traditionally chosen available samples, such as any patient coming to a clinic over a certain period of time. In some cases patients are further divided into experimentals and controls. But, in most studies, all patients receive therapy, measures being taken pre and post in order to reflect its efficacy. In any case, the assumption has been made that by this procedure one obtains a relatively homogeneous group of patients differing little in terms of meaningful variables, and homogeneous simply because they all sought out psychotherapy (be it in a counseling service, outpatient clinic, mental health clinic, private practice, or what have you).

Far from being relatively homogeneous, patients coming to psychotherapy are almost surely quite heterogeneous—are actually much more different than they are alike. The assumption of homogeneity is unwarranted since on just about any measure one could devise (demographic, ability, personality, etc.) these patients would show a remarkable range of differences. This is apparent from clinical experience and from much of the evidence on initial patient characteristics that is available today. Because of these initial patient differences, no matter what the effect of psychotherapy in a particular study (be it phenomenally successful or a dismal failure), one can conclude very little if anything. At best, one can say something such as: for a sample of patients coming to this particular clinic over this particular period, psychotherapy performed by the clinic staff during that period on the average was either successful or unsuccessful. No meaningful conclusions regarding the types of patients for whom therapy was effective or ineffective are possible. This is inevitably the case since no patient variables crucially relevant for subsequent reactivity to psychotherapy have been isolated and controlled.

This Patient Uniformity Assumption hampered research in the area of schizophrenia for years. The assumption was that patients diagnosed as schizophrenic are more alike than different. Subsequent data showed very clearly that some schizophrenics were quite different from others, in fact more like normals than they were like other schizophrenics (Herron, 1962). In other words, extreme variability was the usual case when one lumped all patients diagnosed schizophrenic. It was only when this variability could be reliably reduced that useful research could begin to be done. The important empirical finding was that schizophrenic patients differed markedly with respect to the abruptness of onset of their disorder. Some could be reliably classified in terms of their case histories as "process" schizophrenics, those with a relatively long-term and gradual onset; while others had a quite short-term and abrupt onset, "reactive" schizophrenics. It was further discovered that the reactive schizophrenics had much better prognosis. But most importantly, the radical reduction in variability permitted by this operational distinction made possible for the first time research that could lead to replicable differences among process schizophrenics and other diagnostic groups.

Now, few would argue that for some patients psychotherapy is *not* effective. Clinical experience as well as research data point clearly to this conclusion. Many studies have shown patient differences evident at the beginning of psychotherapy which are crucially related to subsequent dropout or failure in therapy.* If psychotherapy is differentially effective depending on initial patient differences, as the evidence strongly suggests, then it seems clear that research should take these differences into account. This would imply the use of a design with at least two experimental groups, dichotomizing patients by one or more patient variables shown to relate to subsequent outcome; or

---

*In the following discussion extensive bibliographical citings will be omitted since the resulting list would be prohibitive. Fortunately, an exhaustive bibliography of the psychotherapy research literature has now appeared and is available (Strupp, 1964). From the topical index provided one can find an exhaustive bibliography of studies for each of the therapy variables discussed below. Also, several specific reviews provide some integration of the many studies and can be usefully consulted (Auld & Murray, 1955; Breger & McGaugh, 1965; Cartwright, 1957; Eysenck, 1961; Gardner, 1964; Goldstein, 1962; Grossberg, 1964; Herzog, 1959; Marsden, 1965; Stieper & Wiener, 1965; Zax & Klein, 1960). Finally, the chapters on "Psychotherapeutic Processes" and "Counseling" in the *Annual Review of Psychology* (1950–1965) as well as the American Psychological Association's two volumes on *Research in Psychotherapy* (Rubinstein & Parloff, 1959; Strupp & Luborsky, 1962) are both indispensable sources for critical reviews of research.

matching experimentals and controls on these relevant initial patient measures. Meaningful results will not occur if one continues to aggregate patients ignoring the meaningful variance of relevant patient characteristics.

Therapist Uniformity Assumption. Perhaps an even more devastating practice in psychotherapy research has been the selecting of various therapists for a research design on the assumptions that these therapists are more alike than different and that whatever they do with their patients may be called "psychotherapy." Theoretical formulations seem to have perpetuated this assumption since they have traditionally focused on describing "The Therapy" which is ideally appropriate for all kinds of patients. The myth has been perpetuated that psychotherapy in a research design represents a homogeneous treatment condition; that it is only necessary for a patient to receive psychotherapy, and that mixing psychotherapists (whether of the same or different orientations) makes no difference.

This kind of loose thinking seems to have grown out of what Raimy (1952) has called the "egg-shell era" of psychotherapy wherein it was rare for a therapist to tape record his sessions or in other ways to make public his therapeutic behavior.

> Almost without exception . . . psychotherapists adopted the attitude that patients and clients were frail, puny beings who would flee the field if anyone except their own private psychotherapist touched them. In view of the lack of evidence to the contrary, such an attitude was at one time entirely justified since, in simple ethics, the welfare of the patient does come first. The fact that the attitude also had other supports, particularly the fact that it provided defensive measures for the therapist's unsteady ego-structure, made no difference. (Raimy, 1952, p. 324).

In this aura of mystery it became easy for one to think of "the One" psychotherapy which would maximally benefit all patients. As Colby (1964) relates: "As long as what went on in therapeutic sessions remained secret, myths of consensus within paradigms were easily perpetuated. For example, among psychoanalysts there grew the myth of a single agreed-upon perfect technique" (p. 348). The advent of general tape-recording has made records of the therapist's behavior progressively more available to other clinicians and researchers, and it has become apparent that differences in technique and personality exist, even within schools, and that disagreement prevails.

Despite this token admission of therapist differences, the Uniformity Assumption still abounds in much psychotherapy research. Patients are still assigned to "psychotherapy" as if it were a uniform, homogeneous treatment, and to psychotherapy with different therapists as if therapist differences were irrelevant. As Rotter (1960) observes:

> Although the trend is generally away from the notion of psychotherapy as an entity, there is still too much concern with *the* process of therapy. For many there is an assumption that there is some special process which takes place in patients, ac-

counting for their improvement or cure. . . .In a similar way the role of the therapist is conceived of as one ideal set of behaviors which will maximally facilitate the mysterious process. The alternative conception that psychotherapy is basically a social interaction which follows the same laws and principles as other social interactions, and in which many different effects can be obtained by a variety of different conditions, is frequently neglected. (p. 408)

In addition, the Myth ignores the growing body of evidence that psychotherapists are quite heterogeneous along many dimensions (e.g., experience, attitudes, personality variables) and that these differences seem to influence patient outcome. Some therapy may be more effective than others; and it seems not too unlikely that some therapy may be more deleterious than no therapy at all (Rogers, Gendlin, Kiesler, & Truax, 1966). As Meehl (1955) states: "In our present ignorance it is practically certain that clients are treated by methods of varying appropriateness, largely as a function of which therapist they happen to get to. Also, it is practically certain that many hours of skilled therapists are being spent with unmodifiable cases" (374).

If psychotherapy research is to advance it must first begin to identify and measure these therapist variables so relevant to eventual outcome (personality characteristics, technique factors, relationship variables, role expectancies, and the like). One can then build therapist differences into his design by having several experimental groups, with therapists at respectively different levels of relevant dimensions. Or, one can match therapists on relevant factors. To continue the practice of assigning some patients to psychotherapy and others to a "control" group seems futile.

Unfortunately, this kind of naive conceptualization has dominated studies evaluating the effects of psychotherapy where therapy and control groups are compared. Typically, the results have been discouraging in that no significantly greater improvement has been demonstrated for the "therapy" patients (Eysenck, 1961). As Gendlin (1966) argues:

> Research in psychotherapy has suffered from the fact that psychotherapy was not definable. It has meant that, if an experimental therapy group was compared to a non-therapy control group, some of the supposed therapy subjects were not really receiving something therapeutic at all . . . .The effect of averaging the changes in the "experimental" group as compared with the "control" group often showed no significant differences. To bring this home, imagine trying to investigate the effects of a drug with an experimental group taking the drug and a control group receiving a placebo. Imagine that some (perhaps half) of your "experimental" group are actually taking a preparation without the effective ingredients of the drug . . . and you don't know which ones these are. Then, too, perhaps one or two "controls" are actually getting the drug on the side. Your "experimental treatment" group is not always getting the treatment. (p. 524)

An implication of this consideration is that if one could analyze the variability (rather than or in addition to the mean differences) of the experimental and control groups in these many studies, the therapy groups would be expected to show a much greater range of improvement behavior than the controls. This would follow if some of the "experimental" patients indeed were exposed to some quite "bad or indifferent psychotherapy."

Sanford (1953) states this still differently: "From the point of view of science, the question 'Does psychotherapy do any good?' has little interest because it is virtually meaningless. . . . The question is which people, in what circumstances, responding to what psychotherapeutic stimuli." And Gilbert (1952) urges:

> One of the extremely important problems in psychological counseling and therapy is that concerning the need for being able to describe and quantify different types of psychotherapeutic relationships. The possibility of accomplishing this is basic to further studies concerning the relative effectiveness of different types of counseling procedures. Studies of this nature will be necessary before it will ever be possible to make any scientific statements regarding such basic questions as the relative effectiveness of different counseling procedures with different types of counselee problems, or the relative effectiveness of a single over-all approach to all types of counseling problems as compared with diverse approaches based upon various diagnostic categories. (p. 360)

Finally, Kiesler (1966) states in summarizing the outcome results of a 5-year study of individual psychotherapy with schizophrenics (Rogers *et al.*, 1966):

> The picture emerging is that if we compare the therapy patients as a group to the control patients no differences emerge. Yet—and this seems to me to be the crucial question for outcome studies—if we divide the therapy cases by means of a theoretically relevant therapist variable (in this case level of "conditions" offered) the results are quite consistent with theoretical expectation. Hence, my final point would be that before we can validly assess the outcome or therapy evaluation problem, it is vitally necessary that we attempt to isolate therapist dimensions that will accurately reflect the heterogeneity of therapist performance. If we continue to evaluate therapy as a homogeneous phenomenon we will continue to obtain invalid results. (p. 85)

In summary, it would seem quite essential and useful to bury these Uniformity Myths once and for all. Until our designs can incorporate relevant patient variables and crucial therapist dimensions—so that one can assess which therapist behaviors are more effective with which type of patients—we will continue to perpetuate confusion. Psychotherapy research must come to grips with the need for factorial designs—as recommended a decade ago by Edwards and Cronbach (1952)—wherein different types of patients are assigned to different types of therapists and/or therapy, so that one can begin to discover the parameters needed to fill in a meaningful paradigm for psychotherapy.

As a postscript, it is often not remembered that different theoretical formulations and techniques have at least originally been derived from patients of different types. As Stein (1961) observes:

One source of difference between schools of psychotherapy that is often overlooked and which needs to be made explicit is the difference in types of patients on which the founders of the different schools based their initial observations. Maskin summarizes this point rather well when he says: "Freud used hysteria as the model for his therapeutic method, depression as the basis for his later theoretical conjectures. Adler's clinical demonstrations are rivalrous, immature character types. Jung's examples were constructed to a weary, worldly, successful, middle-aged group. Rank focussed upon the conflicted, frustrated, rebellious artist aspirant. Fromm's model is the man in a white collar searching for his individuality. And Sullivan's example of choice is the young catatonic schizophrenic." To this one might add that Roger's original formulations were based on college students. (p. 6–7)

Assuming these theoreticians were all perspicacious and accurate in their observations, the historical fact that their different formulations were derived from experience with different classes of patients would seem to reinforce strongly the necessity and appropriateness for abandoning the Uniformity Assumption in psychotherapy research.

REFERENCES

Colby, K. M. Psychotherapeutic processes. *Annual Review of Psychology,* 1964, **15**, 347–370.

Edwards, A. L. & Cronbach, L. J. Experimental design for research in psychotherapy. *Journal of Clinical Psychology,* 1952, **8**, 51–59.

Gendlin, E. T. The social significance of the research. In C. R. Rogers, E. T. Gendlin, D. J. Kiesler, & C. B. Truax, (Eds.), *The therapeutic relationship and its impact: A study of psychotherapy with schizophrenics.* Madison: University of Wisconsin, Press, 1966, 523–541.

Gilbert, W. Counseling: Therapy and diagnosis. *Annual Review of Psychology,* 1952, **3**, 351–380.

Herron, W. G. The process-reactive classification of schizophrenia. *Psychological Bulletin,* 1962, **59**, 329–343.

Kiesler, D. J. Some basic methodological issues in psychotherapy process research. *American Journal of Psychotherapy,* 1966, **2**, 135–155.

Meehl, P. E. Psychotherapy. *Annual Review of Psychology,* 1955, **6**, 357–378.

Raimy, V. C. Clinical methods: Psychotherapy. *Annual Review of Psychology,* 1952, **3**, 321–350.

Rogers, C. R., Gendlin, E. T., Kiesler, D. J., & Truax, C. B. *The therapeutic relationship and its impact: A study of psychotherapy with schizophrenics.* Madison: University of Wisconsin Press, 1966.

Rotter, J. B. Psychotherapy. *Annual Review of Psychology,* 1960, **11**, 381–414.

Sanford, N. Clinical methods: Psychotherapy. *Annual Review of Psychology,* 1953, **4**, 317–342.

Stein, M. I. (Ed.) *Contemporary psychotherapies.* New York: Free Press of Glencoe, 1961.

Strupp, H. H. The outcome problem in psychotherapy revisited. *Psychotherapy: Theory, Research and Practice,* 1964, **1**, 1–13.

Winder, C. L. Psychotherapy. *Annual Review of Psychology,* 1957, **8**, 309–330.

9

A Grid Model for the Psychotherapies*

DONALD J. KIESLER

It is easy to criticize existing systems without suggesting constructive alternatives. It is the purpose of this section to suggest strongly that alternative theories to those currently in vogue are at hand; the components of some have already been explicitly stated in various places; but unless these theoretical statements are systematically explicated, conforming to a paradigm similar to the one presented here, their impact and heuristic value will continue to be minimal.

Relatively few clinicians on the current psychotherapy scene adhere strictly to Freudian, existential, or behavior therapy regimes. Most describe themselves as eclectic, which implies that they extract "pieces" from each of the systems, modify them in accordance with their own experiences, and innovate as need arises. It is my contention that this eclectic lore, comprising the insights of clinicians who have been forced to modify traditional systems in dealing with different types of patients, offers the best promise for useful theoretical statements. Unfortunately, much of this lore is inexplicit and this is the way it is usually stated: "Clinician A has a real feeling for working with paranoid schizophrenics and knows for example that if he is warm toward paranoids he'll drive them away. Clinician B has specialized in obsessive-compulsives and knows that reflection plays right into their ruminative defenses. Therefore he systematically challenges their contradictory statements. Clinician C communicates well with sociopaths and feels it is very important initially to outmanipulate and outshout his patients."

Obviously, if these clinical hunches are correct, then some very different therapist behaviors are occurring as a result of the type of patient, and the personality of the therapist. The problem with the hunches are that they

*From D. J. Kiesler, A grid model for theory and research. In L. D. Eron & R. Callahan (Eds.), *The relation of theory to practice in psychotherapy.* Chicago: Aldine, 1969. Pp. 135–145. Copyright © 1969 by Leonard D. Eron and Robert Callahan. Reprinted by permission of the author and Aldine Publishing Company.

comprise loosely defined, inexplicit systems. Further, it is not very clear what one means by "obsessive-compulsive," "paranoid schizophrenic," or "sociopath"; interclinician reliability in assigning these labels to particular patients is rather low. Yet these are not insurmountable problems, particularly if some imaginative and articulate theoreticians arrive on the scene.

What is sorely needed, therefore, is not *a* theory of psychotherapy, but quite a few theories of psychotherapy—theories respectively for obsessive-compulsives, hysterics, anxiety reactions, phobics, process undifferentiated schizophrenics, depressive reactions, sociopaths and the like. Strupp applies the same emphasis in Chapter 2 when he talks of systematic studies which will serve to restrict specific therapeutic techniques to specific patients. The important point is that these new formulations need to be stated explicitly and specifically enough so that the objections summarized in the previous section do not apply.

Figure 1 presents schematically a model for the various psychotherapies that avoids the inadequacies of present theories—the patient, therapist, and outcome uniformity assumptions. The multidimensions of therapist activity are specified explicitly as are the in-therapy and concurrent or subsequent extra-therapy changes on patient behavior that should occur.

The examples of patient types chosen and the specific therapist and patient behaviors shown reflect to a degree the author's thinking about these types of patients. But the specific variables presented are unimportant for the present purpose. The crucial aspect of the model is that it demonstrates the kind of theoretical specificity that is necessary if we are to make progress with the psychotherapies.

Notice the three surfaces of the model described in the legend. *Surface A* reflects the different types of patients for which separate theoretical statements are needed. The illustrative types chosen here—obsessive-compulsives, hysterics, mixed depressive-manics, and process undifferentiated schizophrenics—are arbitrarily chosen. In this regard, Wolpe as well as Stampfl and Levis should be commended for their focus on a restricted type of patient, the phobic. This kind of restriction of patient type, which avoids the patient uniformity myth, is needed in all theorizing about behavior modification. You will notice further on Surface A descriptions of what is meant by the various patient types, descriptions referring to the patient's manner of defensive communication or talking about himself. This emphasis derives from the author's attempts to operationalize one dimension of patient's talking-about-themselves behavior in the interview (Kiesler, Mathieu, & Klein, 1964; Kiesler, Klein, & Mathieu, 1965; Kiesler, 1966; Kiesler, Mathieu, & Klein, 1967; Rogers, Gendlin, Kiesler, & Truax, 1967). Also it emphasizes the belief that researchers have ignored to a great extent the possibility that a patient's language behavior provides a good basis for eventual reliable and relevant psychiatric classification. As Kiesler (1966) states:

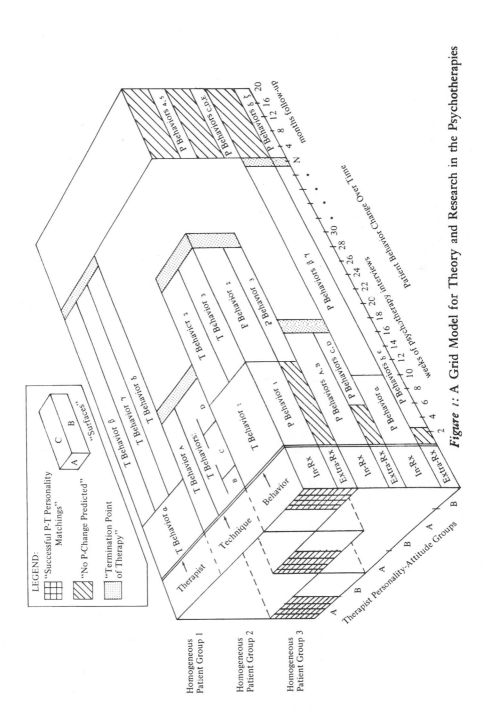

Figure 1: **A Grid Model for Theory and Research in the Psychotherapies**

A suggested answer to both of these nosological difficulties is that we may be looking in the wrong places for a reliable and valid diagnostic scheme. Perhaps the answer to the classification problem lies in differential patient behavior found in the therapy hour itself. If therapists in fact deal differently in therapy with different patients, then perhaps the patient cues to which the therapist differentially responds can be isolated and reliably measured from the interaction. If the manner in which the patient talks about himself in therapy indeed provides a reliable differentiation of patients, then the likelihood seems good that the process dimensions isolated would be directly relevant to differential therapeutic techniques. It seems that this possibility has been overlooked to date. (p. 127)

Strupp argues in Chapter 2: the investigator of psychotherapy must abstract and quantify relevent aspects of the verbal interchange. Ruesch (1961) makes a similar point:

. . .only when we learn to diagnose the difficulties of our patients in terms of the same scientific universe in which we explain our therapeutic methods will we be able to evaluate therapy in a meaningful way. As long as the diagnosis is made in terms of one system and therapy is explained in terms of another system we cannot match therapy to pathology. Therefore it seems feasible that patients be diagnosed in terms of their ability to communicate and the disturbances that interfere with it. The therapeutic diagnosis thus is principally based upon the evaluation of the communicative behavior of the patient, and therapeutic communication is designed to overcome the difficulties.(p. 74)

Turn now to *Surface B* in Figure 1. This represents a specification of the kind of changes that should occur in the respective types of patients. (1) Notice immediately that we are now not talking about "therapeutic outcome" but rather about obsessive-compulsive outcome, hysteroid outcome, depressive-manic outcome, etc. This depicts clearly that we need different dimensions of change for different types of patients. Hence, we are avoiding here the outcome uniformity myth. (2) A clear distinction is made between two areas of patient change—that evident in the interview behavior of the patient (in-therapy change), and that apparent in the patient's behavior outside of therapy (with his peers, family, on the job, etc.), which is extra-therapy change. (3) Although it is not explicitly depicted in Figure 1, one should offer a specific rationale as to how, or whether, the in-therapy patient changes relate to the postulated extra-therapy changes. (4) It should also be evident that patient change is a multidimensional construct for a particular type of patient. Several different in- and extra-therapy behaviors should show change. (5) Further, the time dimension is specified, as well as the interaction of time with the specific patient changes. Some patient changes occur early in the therapy sequence, others will manifest themselves later, and still others cannot be expected until some time after therapy terminates. This aspect of the model emphasizes the necessity for repeated measures of patient changes (rather than the naive pre-post measurement of most "outcome" studies) along the several dimensions, and the important requirement of extended follow-up measurement for some patient-change behaviors. (6) The important variables of dosage and duration of therapy contact are also included. This implies that for some patients the changes expected should be accomplished over a four-month period; while for others two or more years of contact will be necessary. Some patients may require brief contacts daily, others may get by with an hour a week, and still others may need an hour daily for several weeks, and then little contact until the next crisis. Therapy dosage and duration of contact need to be theoretically specified.

Patient change obviously represents a complex construct, and needs to be specified in this kind of detail theoretically before we can usefully begin to research the "outcome" of "psychotherapy." This kind of theoretical specificity will aid researchers in making the operational and sampling decisions necessary to assess the predicted patient changes over the therapy sequence and subsequent follow-up periods.

Turn now to *Surface C* of Figure 1. This represents the related factors of therapist intervention that theoretically produce the specific patient changes for the respective types of patients. The surface avoids the therapist uniformity myth by attempting to specify the different therapist behaviors necessary to produce differential change with different types of patients.

Three general aspects of therapist behavior have been emphasized by theory and research: (1) therapist "personality differences," exemplified by the research endeavors of Whitehorn and Betz (Betz, 1962); (2) therapist relationship-attitudes (e.g., positive regard, and congruence) emphasized by Rogers and the existentialists; and (3) therapist technique behavior—specific verbal and/or nonverbal manipulations by the therapist (e.g., "confrontation" or "interpretation").

It may be that therapist personality type needs to be matched in some way with patient type, as the figure suggests (*cf.* the "success" cells). It may further be the case that the attitudinal "conditions" emphasized by Rogers are important with every type of patient, however, although they may be necessary they are *in*sufficient conditions for effective patient changes. Finally, it seems very likely that if personality and attitudinal therapist factors are appropriate, it still remains that technique manipulations are extremely important and will vary with type of patient. Strupp in Chapter 2 also emphasizes the need for research in therapist skill as well as attitude and personality. Importantly, theoretical formulations must explicitly tie together these various aspects of the therapist's behavior, and specify the differences in behavior for the various types of patients.

As the model suggests, therapist behavior is very likely multidimensional and sequential. And inasmuch as changes desired in the patient are multidimensional, with different changes at different periods of time in the interactional sequence, the therapist model needs to specify individual therapist behaviors and their points of operation over time which correspond with respective changes in the patient. For example, after an initial period of communicated regard and empathy, "confrontation of contradictions" may be needed for a certain type of patient if his abstract talking is to be made more concrete.

SOME IMPLICATIONS OF THE MODEL

It seems this kind of model, if correct, has important implications for research, training, and clinical practice. It argues for much more restricted and specific designs in research. For example, a group of homogeneous obsessive-compulsives, operationally defined (and here theoretical formulation would be a boon), could be assigned to therapists varying both in personality type and technical behavior. The latter behavior could be operationally pre-scribed to therapists in line with theoretical speculation. The sequence of techniques to modify respective patient behaviors could also be indicated. This would permit conclusions regarding the interaction of therapist personality, technique, and patient type (e.g., Technique B with therapist Personality C works best with obsessive-compulsives and thereby becomes the therapist-treatment of choice.)

Similarly, in training therapists, we may first classify students regarding relevant personality dimensions. Assuming next that we have demonstrated the knowledge that would fill in the model in Figure 1, we say to a particular student, "It is very unlikely with your personality type that you'll ever work effectively with psychopathic patients. Instead, it seems likely you will do very well with obsessive-compulsives and with paranoid schizophrenics. Further, we know that a relatively rational approach of 'confrontation of contradictions' and focus on patient role-playing behavior outside the inter-view are the treatments of choice for these patient types. Hence, we will focus our supervisory efforts primarily with these types of patients. We're going to make you an effective specialist—an expert in interpersonal relationships for obsessive-compulsive patients and paranoid schizophrenic patients. You'll not be all things to all patients, but you will be one hell of a specialist as we have described."

Finally, in clinics and private practice more time will be spent in the selection of patients, and we'll have a variety of psychotherapy specialists on the staff. The diagnostic and placement staffing might sound something like the following: "Patient X is obviously a hysteroid personality. Dr. B, you're a specialist with hysteroids—we've already established that your personality and techniques are the best for this type of patient. Hence, we are assigning Patient X to you. We certainly don't want to assign him to Dr. E, since we know that pairing has to be incompatible and the patient would terminate after three interviews."

In summary, then, the basic skeleton of a paradigm for psychotherapy seems to be something like the following: The patient communicates something; the therapist communicates something in response; the patient communicates and/or experiences something different; and the therapist, patient, and others like the change (although they may like it to different degrees, or for divergent reasons). What the therapist communicates (the independent variables) is very likely multidimensional (and the patterning of this multidimensionality needs to be specified), and may be different at different phases of the interaction for different kinds of patients. Similarly, what the patient communicates and/or experiences differently (the dependent variables) is likely multidimensional (and the patterning of that multidimensionality needs to be clarified) and may be different at distinct phases of the interaction. The enormous task of psychotherapy theory and research is that of filling in the variables of this paradigm. (Kiesler, 1966, pp. 129–130)

It is hoped that the grid model presented here depicts this task more clearly and exemplifies some promising leads for the much needed theories of the psychotherapies.

REFERENCES

Betz, B. J. Experiences in research in psychotherapy with schizophrenic patients. In H. H. Strupp & L. Luborsky (Eds.), *Research in psychotherapy II*, Washington, D. C.: American Psychological Association, 1962, 41–60.

Breger, L., & McGaugh, J. L. Critique and reformulation of "learning-theory" approaches to psychotherapy and neurosis. *Psychological Bulletin*, 1965, **63**, 338–358.

Breger, L., & McGaugh, J. L. Learning theory and behavior therapy: A reply to Rachman and Eysenck. *Psychological Bulletin*, 1966, **65**, 170–173.

Colby, K. M. Discussion of papers on therapist's contribution. In H. H. Strupp & L. Luborsky (Eds.), *Research in psychotherapy II*. Washington, D. C.: American Psychological Association, 1962, 95–101.

Colby, K. M. Psychotherapeutic processes. In *Annual Review of Psychology*, 1964, **15**, 347–370.

Ford, D. H., & Urban, H. B. *Systems of psychotherapy*. New York: Wiley, 1963.

Ford, D. H., & Urban, H. B. Psychotherapy. *Annual Review of Psychology*, 1967, **18**, 333–372.

Kiesler, D. J. Some myths of psychotherapy research and the search for a paradigm. *Psychological Bulletin*, 1966, **65**, 110–136.

Kiesler, D. J., Klein, M. H., & Mathieu, P. L. Sampling from the recorded therapy interview: The problem of segment location. *Journal of Consulting Psychology*, 1965, **29**, 337–344.

Kiesler, D. J., Mathieu, P. L., & Klein, M. H. Sampling from the recorded therapy interview: A comparative study of different segment lengths. *Journal of Consulting Psychology*, 1964, **28**, 349–357.

Kiesler, D. J., Mathieu, P. L., & Klein, M. H. Patient experiencing level and Interaction-Chronograph variables in therapy interview segments. *Journal of Consulting Psychology*, 1967, **31**, 224.

Levis, D. J. Implosive therapy: The subhuman analogue, the strategy, and the technique. In S. G. Armitage (Ed.), *Behavior modification techniques in the treatment of emotional disorders*. Battle Creek, Michigan: V. A. Publication, 1967, 22-37.

Phillips, E. L. *Psychotherapy: A modern theory and practice*. Englewood Cliffs, N. J.: Prentice-Hall, 1956.

Raimy, V. (Ed.) *Training in clinical psychology.* New York: Prentice-Hall, 1950.

Rogers, C. R., Gendlin, E. T., Kiesler, D. J., & Truax, C. B. *The therapeutic relationship and its impact: A study of psychotherapy with schizophrenics.* Madison, Wisconsin: University of Wisconsin Press, 1967.

Ruesch, J. *Therapeutic communication.* New York: Norton, 1961.

Stampfl, T. G. Implosive therapy: The theory. In S. G. Armitage (Ed.), *Behavior modification techniques in the treatment of emotional disorders.* Battle Creek, Michigan: V. A. Publication, 1967, 12–21.

Strupp, H. H. Psychoanalytic psychotherapy and research. In L. D. Eron & R. Callahan (Eds.), *The relation of theory to practice in psychotherapy.* Chicago: Aldine, 1969, 21–62.

Wolpe, J. Conditioning: The basis of modern psychotherapy. In L. D. Eron & R. Callahan (Eds.), *The relation of theory to practice in psychotherapy.* Chicago: Aldine, 1969, 1–20.

10

Strategy of Outcome Research
in Psychotherapy*

GORDON L. PAUL

Shlien (1966) has summarized the overall impact of the past 25 years of psychotherapeutic research by pointing out, "Continued subscription [to psychotherapy] is based upon personal conviction, investment, and observation rather than upon general evidence" (p. 125). Eysenck's (1952) first review of the outcome literature concluded, "The figures fail to support the hypothesis that psychotherapy facilitates recovery from neurotic disorder" (p. 323). His more recent reviews (Eysenck, 1961, 1965) have led to essentially the same conclusions. In the face of such evidence, only two alternatives present themselves: (*a*) Psychotherapy does not "work"; that is, it is ineffective and should be abandoned, or (*b*) past studies have been inappropriate or inadequate evaluations of the efficacy of psychotherapy. The consensus of research workers who have considered the basic principles and methods for the evaluation of psychological treatment strongly favors the second alternative (e.g., Edwards & Cronbach, 1952; Hoch & Zubin, 1964; Rubinstein & Parloff, 1959; Strupp & Luborsky, 1962).

Parloff and Rubinstein (1959) have summarized the sociological obstacles to progress in outcome research which, combined with methodological difficulties in criterion definition, resulted in what Zubin (1964) calls a "flight into process" (p. 127). Large-scale researchers came to focus on the process of therapist-client interaction. Thus, sociological difficulties were circumvented by the importance of personality theory, and criterion problems were eased by a focus on intratherapy measures. The assumed relationship of such studies to treatment outcome rests on the common belief that more process studies are necessary to identify all important variables before evaluations can be meaningfully made (Hoch, 1964). Similarly, "The evaluation of the effects of therapy is not a task we can handle with existing tools" (Hyman & Berger, 1965, p. 322).

---

*From *Journal of Consulting Psychology,* 1967, **31**, 109–118. Copyright 1967 by the American Psychological Association. Reprinted by permission.

A major problem with the process approach is that the importance of a variable or theory for outcome cannot be established without concurrent assessment of outcome (Greenhouse, 1964). It is precisely through outcome studies with concurrent measurement or manipulation of variables whose influence is unknown that important variables are likely to be identified. If the influence of all variables were known, the question of evaluation would be spurious from the beginning. Additionally, many statements such as that of Hyman and Berger appear to result from a confusion of what Reichenbach (1938) has called the context of discovery and the context of justification. While it may be true that psychological science may never be in a position to measure the truth of the complex experiences which take place between two or more persons (context of discovery), verifying the degree to which the goals of such an interaction are reached or not reached (context of justification) is logically no different for psychotherapy than for any other change-agency (Sanford, 1962).

Apart from emotional and sociological obstacles, the principles and methods of outcome research are basically the same as any other experimental design problem, except for the greater number and complexity of variables. As with all research in psychology, the basic purpose is to discover phenomena—behavioral events or changes—the variables which affect them, and the lawfulness of the effects. Likewise, the greatest difficulty has come from research errors, that is, discrepancies between what is concluded and what can be concluded as a consequence of the experimental operations. Unfortunately, the majority of outcome research has suffered from what Underwood (1957) terms "lethal errors"—discrepancies in which there is no way that a scientifically meaningful conclusion can be reached from the procedures used. "These cases are best exemplified by blatant confounding of stimulus variables from different classes (environmental, task, subject) so that behavior changes measured cannot be said to be the result even of variables within a given class" (Underwood, 1957, p. 90).

VARIABLES IN PSYCHOTHERAPY RESEARCH

The major variables or domains involved in psychotherapy research, irrespective of theoretical preconceptions, are summarized in Table 1. Levinson (1962) and Kiesler (1966) have also considered these basic problems. Each of the variables listed in Table 1 may be treated as independent variables through selection or manipulation, exerting main effects and interactions within domains and between domains.

The essential ingredients are at least one client and one therapist who get together over some finite period of time. Clients come to treatment in order to obtain help in changing some aspect of their behavior which they, or someone else, find distressing. These distressing behaviors (1a) may vary in

Table 1. Major Variables (Domains) Involved in Psychotherapy Research

1. Clients
   a. Distressing behaviors (cognitive, phisiological, motoric)
   b. Relatively stable personal-social charactersitics
   c. Physical-social life environment

2. Therapists
   a. Therapeutic techniques
   b. Relatively stable personal-social characteristics
   c. Physical-social treatment environment

3. Time
   a. Initial contact
   b. Pretreatment
   c. Initial treatment stage
   d. Main treatment stage
   e. Termination (pretreatment stage)
   f. Posttreatment
   g. Follow-up

number and nature and may change over time. Clients may also vary on relatively stable personal-social characteristics (1b) such as age, intelligence, and expectancies. 1a and 1b thus comprise the usual experimental class of subject variables. Clients work with therapists who utilize therapeutic techniques (2a) through which they attempt to alleviate the distress of the client. Like the client's distressing behaviors, therapeutic techniques may vary in number and nature and may change over time. Therapists, just as clients, may vary on relatively stable personal-social characteristics (2b) and, in addition, on characteristics related to treatment, such as subscription to particular "schools" of therapeutic theory, experience, and type of "conditions" established. Thus, 2a and 2b comprise the usual experimental class of task variables. Although 1c and 2c comprise the usual class of environmental variables, they are listed with clients and therapists due to the greater likelihood of confounding adjacent classes. The client's physical-social life environment (1c) includes essentially all the intercurrent life experiences impinging upon him outside of the treatment situation, for example, family, drugs, and work situation. The physical-social treatment environment (2c) refers to the institutional setting in which treatment takes place. This domain may vary from private to public, fee or no fee; it may be a hospital, clinic, or private office.

   The third category of Table 1, that of time, is usually considered a task variable. Time is separated here for expository purposes because, in addition to task variation, the events in time also mark points of research focus. As a task variable, time may vary in terms of length of treatment contact and number of sessions, that is, the time between pretreatment (3b) and posttreatment (3f). Within treatment proper (3c,d,e) time may vary within and between different stages. Likewise, time may vary between initial contact (3a) and pretreatment (3b) and between posttreatment (3f) and follow-up (3g). The second aspect of the time dimension delineates points of research focus for study or measurement of the main effects and interactions of variables, either between time periods or within time periods.

QUESTION PROBLEM

From the above list of variables and the corresponding points in time for their occurrence and measurement, it is possible to determine the necessary operations for obtaining answers to specific questions and, conversely, to see where research errors have occurred. The most obvious problem with past outcome research has been in the stage of asking questions. The initial question posed, "Does psychotherapy work?" is virtually meaningless. Psychotherapy comprehends a most diversified set of procedures ranging from suggestion, hypnosis, reassurance, and verbal conditioning to systematic sets of actions and strategies based upon more or less tight theoretical formulations. Narrowing the question to specific schools of psychotherapy, such as "Does client-centered therapy work?" or "Does behavior therapy work?" is no more meaningful than the general question, since the range of procedures remains as diversified within schools as within psychotherapy in general. Furthermore, such questions fail to take into account the characteristics of therapists (2b) which may contribute to efficacy. Even if psychotherapy were a homogeneous entity, these questions fail to specify the "what" for "does it work?" Here again, the wrong questions were asked. "Does it work for neuroses?" "Does it work for schizophrenics?" As with schools of psychotherapy, the range of individual differences within standard diagnostic categories remains so diversified as to render meaningless any questions or statements about individuals who become so labeled. The labeling process itself is notoriously unreliable, and criteria for inclusion in a particular class are vague and overlapping. Questions asked in this manner are doomed to committing lethal errors from their time of conception, allowing confounding and confusion of Domains 1 and 2 from the beginning.

The third problem with questions that have been asked in outcome research is with the term "work" itself, that is, the criteria of success or improvement. While there may be general agreement that if psychotherapy works, the client will "feel better" and "function better" (Frank, 1959), the specific goals in accomplishing this end will be as varied as the problems which are brought to treatment. Without specifying the "what" in a question of the nature, "For what does it work?" the question of success remains as confused and hetero-geneous as the domains of psychotherapy and clients at large.

What is the appropriate question to be asked of outcome research? In all its complexity, the question towards which all outcome research should ultimately be directed is the following: *What* treatment, by *whom* is most effective for *this* individual with *that* specific problem, and under *which* set of circumstances? Relating the basic question to the domains listed in Table 1, we find: What treatment (2a, therapeutic techniques), by whom (2b, ther-apists with relatively stable personal-social characteristics), is most effective (change in 1a, the client's distressing behaviors, from 3b, pretreatment, to 3f and g, posttreatment and follow-up) for this individual (1b, clients with relatively stable personal-social characteristics), and under which set of circum-stances (1c, the client's physical-social life environment, and 2c, the physical-social treatment environment)? Posed in this manner, two points are obvious: (*a*) No single study of any degree of complexity will ever be capable of answering this question, and (*b*) in order for knowledge to meaningfully accumulate across separate studies and provide a solid empirical foundation for subsequent research, it will be necessary for every investigation to ade-quately describe, measure, or control each of the variables or domains listed in Table 1.

CRITERION PROBLEM

One of the most recurrent methodological difficulties in outcome research has been the criterion problem. Lack of agreement among criteria, not only between investigators, but between clients, therapists, and other sources in the same investigation was one factor which resulted in the flight into process. A major basis for the lack of relationship among criteria lies in the fact that different frames of reference may be used by persons in different roles for making overall judgments of success or improvement. Most investigators have selected criteria from some theoretical frame of reference, ignoring the hetero-geneity of client populations. Criteria so selected are likely to be, at best, partially related to criteria selected from some other frame of reference. Parloff and Rubinstein's (1959) statement that an "investigator's selection of specific criteria [is] a premature and presumptuous value judgment" (p. 278) appears valid when the criteria are based upon some preconceived theoretical judgment which bears no demonstrated relationship to the client's problems, or when the criteria are deemed to be the attainment of some "ideal" which is necessarily value laden with the mores of a particular class, culture, or investigator. The normal population is heterogeneous in the extreme, allowing for broad ranges of variability in ways of living. Irrespective of any theoretical position, the real question of outcome on logical and ethical grounds is whether or not the clients have received help with the distressing behaviors which brought them to treatment in the first place (Betz, 1962; Hoppock, 1953; Rickard, 1965). As recently stated by Jerome Frank and his colleagues (Battle, Imber, Hoehn-Saric, Stone, Nash, & Frank, 1966),

> In the absence of adequate knowledge of the causes of psychiatric complaints, we assume that psychotherapy has removed the causes if the complaints are permanently relieved, and no new ones are substituted for them. (p. 185)

While using such tailored criteria does bypass the homogeneity problem which arises from the use of varying frames of reference, it does not remove the necessity for adequately defining the dependent variables at some level of quantification with adequate reliability and validity. Although many techniques for measuring change have been used in the past, few of these methods have proved to be acceptable (Zax & Klein, 1960). Subjective reports of change by clients or therapists are notorious for their lack of reliability and validity, and specific problems negate the use of many psychological tests (Paul, 1966).

The most important and meaningful test of outcome is the change in clients' distressing behaviors outside of treatment (Luborsky & Strupp, 1962). Some guidelines for assessment may be obtained by considering the process which results in client-therapist contact; that is, the client does something, under a set of circumstances, which disturbs someone sufficiently that action results—entering treatment (Ullmann & Krasner, in press). The "something" he does has been identified as the distressing behaviors which lead him to treatment. However, since this something occurs under a set of circumstances it is unnecessary to attempt measurement of change under all circumstances. Rather, assessment should be more or less situation specific. As Zax and Klein (1960) point out, the least used but most promising criteria are, then, objective behavioral criteria external to the treatment situation. The advantages of such "work sample" assessments, which may include self-report measures, have been presented elsewhere (Paul, 1966). While multiple measures of outcome are necessary, the dependent variable in any outcome evaluation must be, to return to Table 1, change in the distressing behaviors which brought the client to treatment (1a), from pretreatment (3b) to posttreatment (3f), and follow-up (3g), assessed external to treatment proper by unbiased means.

APPROACHES TO OUTCOME RESEARCH

Given the basic question and criterion specifications, as with all research, the means of obtaining answers or partial answers becomes a problem of strategy. That is, what is the place of and need for different levels of outcome research? What can the varied approaches such as case studies, simplifications, and different levels of controlled experiment contribute? In view of the range and complexity of the variables involved, continuing series of well-controlled, factorially designed experiments appear to be not only the most efficient means to obtain knowledge relevant to the ultimate questions (Edwards & Cronbach, 1952), but probably the only way. Both before and after factorially designed experiments there is a real value for lower levels of investigation and for studies designed to answer different questions, especially in the determination of mechanisms of change. However, these investigations must be evaluated on the basis of their possible level of product.

Since outcome studies attempt to determine cause-effect relationships, the ultimate necessity of factorial investigations is apparent upon consideration of two principles of basic research: (*a*) There is really only one principle of experimental design, and that is to "design the experiment so that the effects of the independent variables can be evaluated unambiguously" (Underwood, 1957, p. 86), and (*b*) in order to do this, "to draw a conclusion about the influence of any given variable, that variable must have been systematically manipulated alone somewhere in the design" (Underwood, 1957, p. 35). These principles again highlight the need of describing, measuring, or controlling each of the variables or domains listed in Table 1 to prevent confounding.

The problem of necessary experimental controls for the prevention of confounding (Frank, 1959) is clear in factorial designs. Additionally, tactical decisions within a factorial study need to be made on the basis of the strength of knowledge in an area at any given time. Since the major points concerning needed controls and the practical and empirical problems of conducting factorial outcome studies have been presented elsewhere (Paul, 1966), these points will only be summarized here, with focus on strategies which appear desirable at our current level of knowledge.

An adequate definition of the client sample and the related practical problems of providing sufficient time for appraisal, adequate information prior to treatment assignment, and large enough groups constitute the first concern of the outcome study. Since change in clients' distressing behaviors (1a) is always a dependent variable, selection of the sample involves a decision on heterogeneity. In view of the likelihood that the severity of distressing behaviors will vary, even within the same class (e.g., obese women), and that resistance to change may vary across classes (e.g., obese women versus morphine addicts), the tactical choice favors selection of clients on the same class of target behaviors.

Even with selection on a homogeneous class of target behaviors, there is likely to be a wide variation in relatively stable personal-social characteristics (1b). Clients might be classified on the basis of 1b variables, and these classes might then be treated as independent variables (e.g., elderly, lower-class males of average intelligence versus adolescent, middle-class females of superior intelligence). However, practical considerations suggest that the best strategy for early studies would be the selection of homogeneous samples described in enough detail for meaningful comparisons to be made across studies. With quantification of major characteristics, correlational analyses of client characteristics with outcome can provide suggestive evidence of possible influencing parameters and thus sharpen independent variables for subsequent outcome studies.

While the distressing client behaviors in Domain 1a will always be involved as independent and dependent variables, and while the relatively stable person-social characteristics in Domain 1b may be independent variables, described or controlled, the variables in Domain 1c, the physical-social life environment of the clients, can seldom be described in detail or treated as independent variables. The task then becomes one of control, that is, to provide for the eventuality that behavioral modifications which may be observed are not due to extraexperimental life experiences. The only way of controlling for these factors appears to be to use a comparable no-treatment control group that is observed and assessed at the same time and for the same amount of time as the treatment groups. Such a group also controls for the effects of repeated testing and for so-called "spontaneous" changes over time.

Own-control designs (i.e., comparisons of 3a-3b change with 3b-3f change for the same clients) are desirable for obtaining base rates on the stability of distressing behaviors, but they do not adequately control for changes which may be related to the passage of time, season, or extraexperimental experiences. Therefore, the problem becomes one of dividing the sample into equivalent experimental and control groups. Experimentally, there are three ways of obtaining equivalent groups. The first method is to match groups, not only on target behaviors, but also on all other major variables believed to be significant from Domains 1b and 1c, randomizing on other aspects. A second possibility is to equate groups by stratified sampling of major categories without matching individuals. The third method is straight random assignment. For any method, randomization of variables not matched or measured is important. In factorial studies, the present strategical choice appears to favor, at least, stratification on target behaviors and motivation. The danger of experimental procedures destroying the equivalence of the no-treatment control group in relation to other groups may be partially circumvented by strategic use of an own-control waiting period for a later treatment as the no-treatment control for current treatment groups.

Constituting the next concern are an adequate definition of the therapists and techniques of treatment and the related practical problems of providing sufficient time for assessment or training prior to treatment contact, monitoring of intratherapy procedures, and obtaining enough cooperative individuals. The usual independent variable of most interest in the outcome study is the specific therapeutic technique (2a) proposed to be effective in alleviating behavioral distress. A decision on heterogeneity is even more important with regard to therapeutic technique, since the replication of independent variables is involved. In dealing with established treatment procedures, this problem becomes even more complicated, because most experienced psychotherapists have developed their techniques to a more or less individual art. One strategic approach to this problem would be to allow complete flexibility among therapists with their preferred techniques, determine those who are reliably effective, and then return to audio or video recordings of the effective therapists to determine what they did, or conduct more elaborate process studies with these therapists as subjects. The difficulty with this approach is that it provides no information on what is ineffective treatment, nor does it allow ready comparison to other therapeutic techniques.

On the other hand, if each set of treatment techniques is relatively homogeneous within treatment groups across therapists, immediate knowledge of what constitutes effective treatment would be available. Thus, whether dealing with old or new treatment procedures, the tactical choice favors homogeneity within groups, preferably provided with a single monitor-supervisor for all therapists within individual treatments.

By using homogeneous treatment procedures, the chief problem of control is to distinguish between the effects of Domains 2a and 2b, that is, the effects of the relatively stable personal-social characteristics of the therapist versus those of the specific set of therapeutic techniques. A related problem is that of distinguishing between the specific effects of particular therapeutic techniques and the nonspecific effects which are involved in any therapeutic contact—the "placebo-effect" (Rosenthal & Frank, 1958). An adequate control for placebo effects would then be another form of treatment in which clients have equal faith, but which would not be expected to lead to behavioral change on any other grounds. By having each therapist conduct both a treatment to be evaluated and an attention-placebo treatment with several clients, equating the length and number of sessions and all other time factors, not only may nonspecific placebo effects be distinguished, but a base rate is provided for the improvement resulting from the relatively stable person-social characteristics of the individual therapists. As with client characteristics (1b), therapist characteristics (2b) may be treated as additional independent variables (e.g., experienced versus inexperienced). However, in view of the present state of knowledge, the best strategy for early studies might limit evaluation of therapist characteristics to correlation with outcome to aid in sharpening of hypotheses for future evaluation.

In practice, the physical-social treatment environment (2c) will probably be constant for any given investigation. In this case, the major requirement is an adequate description of the facility and usual operating procedures to allow comparisons across studies. Should more than one facility be involved, however, it is important to control for possible confounding by conducting all treatments, including the attention-placebo, in all facilities. While the separate influence of the treatment setting itself appears, within normal limits, to be the least important domain, settings could be evaluated as an independent variable by having each therapist conduct each of the different treatments with several clients in two or more facilities.

With regard to the time dimension, each of the time periods listed in Table 1 should be specified and held constant, unless time is to be treated as an independent variable. Assessments should be taken at the same points in time and the number and duration of sessions held constant across groups. If time is to be treated as an independent variable, for example, in questioning whether spacing or duration of sessions were important, it would also be necessary to systematically vary these aspects across relevant control groups.

If the investment of time and money is made for all of the above therapists and controls, it would also appear to be good strategy to evaluate two or more treatments within the same design. This could be accomplished by extending therapists across more than one treatment, in addition to the attention-placebo treatment, or by introducing different therapists into the design to conduct both a different type of treatment and the attention-placebo treatment. In either case, main effects may be evaluated for treatments and for therapists, as well as interactions. It would also seem reasonable to choose the most promising competing treatments for any particular disorder for comparative evaluation. Further, if these treatments were derived from competing theoretical formulations, an additional contribution could be made to basic science, as well as to the ethical-technological aspects.

Since factorial studies of the above type do involve a tremendous investment of time, money, and personnel, it is important to consider the place and value for lower levels of investigation and for studies designed to answer different questions both before and after factorially designed experiments. A summary of the major approaches relating to outcome research, along with a designation of the confounding possible and resulting level of knowledge obtainable for each is presented in Table 2. As indicated above, the factorially designed experiment with no-treatment and attention-placebo controls is the only approach which offers the establishment of antecedent-consequent relationships for specific treatments without possible confounding. With this type of design, analytic conclusions may be reached for complex variables, such as a total treatment system.

Once the effectiveness of a complex treatment is established across specified problems, populations, and therapists, a number of these alternative approaches become valuable research strategies. One of the most valuable approaches is that of "simplification" (Bordin, 1965), that is, abstracting from the originally observed phenomena in the clinical setting and transferring them to the laboratory, where greater precision can be obtained in experimental isolation, manipulation, and control. The term experimental analogue is often given to this approach, since in the process of simplification, one or more of the variables or domains relevant to psychotherapy is deemed to be analogous

Table 2. Summary of Major Approaches to Outcome Research

Approach	Confounding possible	Level of product
Case study (without measurement)	Within & between all domains	Crude hypotheses.
Case study (with measurement)	Within & between all domains	Correlational conclusions. Strengthened hypotheses.
Nonfactorial group design (without no-treatment control)*	Within & between all domains	Same as above. Hypotheses strengthened as individual studies move across all domains.
Nonfactorial group design (with no-treatment control)	Within client (1a, b) Within treatment (2,a, b, c)	Antecedent-consequent relationship established between classes. Determinants strengthened as individual studies move across domains.
Factorial group design (with no-treatment control & attention-placebo control	None necessary	Antecedent-consequent relationship established for specifics within and between classes. analytic conclusions for complex variables.
Laboratory simplification	None necessary	Antecedent-consequent relationship established for specifics within & betweenclasses for analogues. Analytic conclusions for specific. variables.

*Lower possible confounding, higher level product for "A-B-A own-control approach (see text).

to those existent in the natural clinical setting (Maher, 1966). To the extent that the analogue shares the essential characteristics of clinical procedures and phenomena, this approach is a powerful and economical means for determining the mechanisms of operation and specific parameters of influence for complex variables identified in the factorial group design. However, any changes in procedure or hypotheses developed for other phenomena which grow from experimental analogues need to be confirmed in the clinical setting.

While both laboratory simplifications and factorial group designs in the clinical setting allow analytical conclusions to be reached, lower levels of investigation also have strategic value for the ultimate question of outcome. Nonfactorial group designs with no-treatment controls can establish antecedent-consequent relationships between treatment and outcome in the same manner as factorial designs. However, since the nonfactorial design cannot separate within-class confounding, its utility must be considered in relationship to the available knowledge concerning the effectiveness and applicability of treatment techniques. Following a factorial study, the nonfactorial design may be valuable in extending treatment evaluation across domains, that is, to different types of clients, problems, therapists, treatment settings, and variations in the time domain. The limiting factor with this usage is that, for the accumulation of knowledge to remain precise, new variation can be introduced into only one domain at a time. The second strategic use of the nonfactorial design with a no-treatment control is to provide, prior to the factorial experiment, global validation of promising treatment procedures and of new combinations of known methods. Since confounding is possible within classes of variables, from a scientific point of view, the latter usage serves only a mapping function. Practically, however, this mapping function has considerable value; only the promising therapists or treatment procedures need be included in later factorial outcome studies, and only effective treatment procedures need be continued in clinical practice. Additionally, therapists or techniques which cause clients to get worse can be immediately identified and redirected.

The three lower approaches in Table 2 (the nonfactorial design without no-treatment controls and case studies with or without measurement) cannot provide evidence of antecedent-consequent relationships because confounding is possible between domains and classes as well as within. The individual case study without external measurement is of use only in the earliest phase of the clinical development of techniques. The case study with measurement before, during, and after treatment constitutes the first step in validation by establishing correlational conclusions and communicating procedures to others. The hypotheses of a promising treatment procedure and its parameters can be strengthened as case studies accumulate across domains and through the uncontrolled nonfactorial design; however, these approaches can at best serve an early, crude mapping function and can never validate a specific technique. One particular approach involving a nonfactorial group design without no-treatment controls does not quite fit with these statements. This is the "A-B-A own-control" design in which the client's distressing behavior is reduced, increased, and again reduced contingent upon therapeutic techniques (Ullmann & Krasner, 1965). By demonstrating these temporal relationships reliably across groups, the likelihood of between-class confounding by spontaneous fluctuation in time or extraexperimental life experiences is quite low. The level of product for this design approaches that of the nonfactorial group design with no-treatment controls.

One other approach to outcome research which appears from time to time is the "retrospective study" in which clinical records are searched to obtain "measurement" or description on all variables, including the outcome measure itself. Although the rationale of such studies may be the same as prospective experiments, the crudeness of the data and methodological problems involved are so nearly insurmountable that these studies appear to contribute little more than confusion. With careful application of appropriate methodology and strategy, hope exists that 25 more years of research will no longer find psychotherapy characterized as "an undefined technique applied to unspecified problems with unpredictable outcome" (Raimy, 1950, p. 93).

REFERENCES

Battle, C. C., Imber, S. D., Hoehn-saric, R., Stone, A. R., Nash, E. R., & Frank, J. D. Target complaints as criteria of improvement. *American Journal of Psychotherapy,* 1966, **20,** 184−192.

Betz, B. Experience in research in psychotherapy with schizophrenic patients. In. H. H. Strupp & L. Luborsky (Eds.), *Research in psychotherapy.* Vol. 2. Washington, D. C.: American Psychological Association, 1962, 41−60.

Bordin, E. S. Simplification as a strategy for research in psychotherapy. *Journal of Consulting Psychology,* 1965, **29,** 493−503.

Edwards, A. L., & Cronbach, L. J. Experimental design for research in psychotherapy. *Journal of Clinical Psychology,* 1952, **8,** 51−59.

Eysenck, H. J. The effects of psychotherapy: An evaluation. *Journal of Consulting Psychology,* 1952, **16,** 319−324.

Eysenck, H. J. The effects of psychotherapy. In H. J. Eysenck (Ed.), *Handbook of abnormal psychology.* New York: Basic Books, 1961, 607−725.

Eysenck, H. J. The effects of psychotherapy. *International Journal of Psychiatry.* 1965, **1,** 99−144.

Frank. J. D. Problems of controls in psychotherapy. In E. A. Rubinstein & M. B. Parloff (Eds.), *Research in psychotherapy.* Vol. 1. Washington, D. C.: American Psychological Association, 1959, 10−26.

Greenhouse, S. W. Principles in the evaluation of therapies for mental disorders. In P. H. Hoch & J. Zubin (Eds.), *The evaluation of psychiatric treatment.* New York: Grune & Stratton, 1964, 94−105.

Hoch, P. H. Methods of evaluating various types of psychiatric treatments: Discussion In P. H. Hoch & J. Zubin (Eds.), *The evaluation of psychiatric treatment.* New York: Grune & Stratton, 1964.

Hoch, P. H., & Zubin, J. (Eds.) *The evaluation of psychiatric treatment.* New York: Grune & Stratton, 1964.

Hoppock, R. What is the "real" problem? *American Psychologist,* 1953, 8, 124.

Hyman, R., & Berger, L. Discussion of H. J. Eysenck's "The effects of psychotherapy." *International Journal of Psychiatry,* 1965, **1,** 317−322.

Kiesler, D. J. Some myths of psychotherapy research and the search for a paradigm. *Psychological Bulletin,* 1966, **65,** 110−136.

Levinson, D. J. The psychotherapist's contribution to the patient's treatment career. In H. H. Strupp & L. Luborsky (Eds.), *Research in psychotherapy.* Vol. 2. Washington, D. C.: American Psychological Association, 1962, 13−24.

Luborsky, L., & Strupp, H. H. Research problems in psychotherapy: A three year follow-up. In H. H. Strupp & L. Luborsky (Eds.), *Research in psychotherapy.* Vol. 2. Washington, D. C.: American Psychological Association, 1962, 308−329.

Maher, B. A. *Principles of psychopathology.* New York: McGraw-Hill, 1966.

Parloff, M. B., & Rubinstein, E. A. Research problems in psychotherapy. In E. A. Rubinstein & M. B. Parloff (Eds.), *Research in psychotherapy.* Vol. 1. Washington, D. C.: American Psychological Association, 1959, 276−293.

Paul, G. L. *Insight vs. desensitization in psychotherapy: An experiment in anxiety reduction.* Stanford: Stanford University Press, 1966.

Raimy, V. C. (Ed.) *Training in clinical psychology.* Englewood Cliffs, N. J.: Prentice-Hall, 1950.

Reichenbach, H. *Experience and prediction.* Chicago: University of Chicago Press, 1938.

Rickard, H. C. Tailored criteria of change in psychotherapy. *Journal of General Psychology,* 1965, **72,** 63–68.

Rosenthal, D., & Frank, J. D. Psychotherapy and the placebo effect. In C. F. Reed, I. E. Alexander, & S. S. Tomkins (Eds.), *Psychopathology: A source book.* Cambridge: Harvard University Press, 1958, 463–473.

Rubinstein, E. A., & Parloff, M. B. (Eds.), *Research in psychotherapy.* Vol. 1. Washington, D. C.: American Psychological Association, 1959.

Sanford, N. Discussion of papers on measuring personality change. In H. H. Strupp & L. Luborsky (Eds.), *Research in psychotherapy.* Vol. 2. Washington, D. C.: American Psychological Association, 1962, 155–163.

Shlien, J. M. Cross-theoretical criteria for the evaluation of psychotherapy. *American Journal of Psychotherapy,* 1966, **1,** 125–134.

Strupp, H. H., & Luborsky, L. (Eds.) *Research in psychotherapy.* Vol. 2. Washington, D. C.: American Psychological Association, 1962.

Ullmann, L. P., & Krasner, L. (Eds.) *Case studies in behavior modification.* New York: Holt, 1965.

Ullmann, L. P., & Krasner, L. *Abnormal behavior: A psychological approach.* Englewood Cliffs, N. J.: Prentice-Hall, in press.

Underwood, B. J. *Psychological research.* New York: Appleton-Century-Crofts, 1957.

Zax, M., & Klein, A. Measurement of personality and behavior changes following psychotherapy. *Psychological Bulletin,* 1960, **57,** 435–448.

Zubin, J. Technical issues: Discussion. In P. H. Hoch & J. Zubin (Eds.), *The evaluation of psychiatric treatment.* New York: Grune & Stratton, 1964, 122–128.

11

Comparisons of Psychiatric Treatments: Problems and Pitfalls*

ALEX D. POKORNY AND C. JAMES KLETT

In the present era of change and innovation in psychiatric treatment, one of the most urgent needs is that different treatment methods be compared in terms of relative effectiveness. Newer approaches certainly need to be compared with the older or 'standard" methods. Even some of the relatively older methods need to be compared more objectively and thoroughly.

Such comparisons of treatments, however, present numerous methodological problems in design, execution, and interpretation. A number of these will be identified and discussed in this paper. As an illustration, we will use Project 8 of the VA Cooperative Studies in Psychiatry (Gorham *et al.*, 1964). This was a multiple-hospital comparison of group psychotherapy alone, chemotherapy alone, and combined treatment, using as subjects 150 schizophrenic veteran patients. The principal finding was that, in most symptom areas, chemotherapy alone or in combination with psychotherapy was superior to psychotherapy alone.

In the following discussion of a series of technical problems in comparisons of treatments, we will describe the solutions, safeguards, or compromises which were adopted in the planning of this study. Some of the items, however, had not been anticipated, and only came to our attention in the course of the study or during the subsequent analysis. In those areas, potential remedies are suggested.

(1) *Patients selected for one treatment may not be appropriate for the other treatment.* If one conceives of an extreme or exaggerated example of this, the point is obvious or even ludicrous: e.g. patients selected for a herniorrhaphy would not improve on antimalarial therapy. This general principle becomes relevant and important only when the two treatments are for approximately the same class of patients. Ordinarily, the mere fact that two treatments are being compared in a research project will imply that both are

*From *Diseases of the Nervous System*, 1966, 27, 648–652. Reprinted by permission.

applicable to the same patients. The real difficulty arises when the difference between the cases for which a treatment is appropriate is more subtle. If the treating persons were to select cases individually for each treatment, there is a strong likelihood that the two groups would not be alike even though the differences might not be obvious.

The usual criteria for selection of patients for psychotherapy are somewhat different than those used in prescribing tranquilizing drugs. This implies that a suitable candidate for one form of therapy might not be expected to respond as well to another. There might be still other patients who are not considered good candidates for either treatment, or some that would be expected to respond to both. What strategy should be employed in drawing the sample of patients to compare the two treatments? It is obviously not a satisfactory solution to pick the best candidates for the respective treatment and then compare groups. Patients selected for psychotherapy are presumably systematically different from those not selected. All patients are not equally suitable candidates for chemotherapy. Unless patients are randomly assigned to the treatments, there can be no valid statistical evaluation of relative effectiveness. It is for this reason that retrospective evaluations of treatment are always suspect.

The nature of the patient sample also determines the generalizability of the results. Suppose that a sample of consecutively admitted schizophrenic patients is randomly assigned to psychotherapy or chemotherapy and the evaluation shows chemotherapy to be the treatment of choice. The proponents of psychotherapy might justifiably complain that psychotherapy is not appropriate for all newly admitted schizophrenic patients. However, if the design of the study is otherwise sound, this complaint does not in any way decrease the validity of the results. In terms of the sampling, the experimental question was "What is the relative effectiveness of chemotherapy and psychotherapy *in newly admitted schizophrenic patients?*" It may be, however, that a valid answer has been found for the wrong question and that careful thought would have led to the use of some other form of sampling.

Other strategies are possible that will answer different questions but will also affect generalization. Suppose that only patients who are judged to be good candidates for psychotherapy are admitted to the study. If this patient class is randomly assigned to the two treatments and chemotherapy is found to be superior, it would be difficult to construct a strong case for the use of psychotherapy. However, if chemotherapy is found to be inferior with this group, proponents of chemotherapy could legitimately complain that psychotherapy was given an edge by the sampling procedure. This would not affect the validity of the conclusion that psychotherapy is superior to chemotherapy *with patients who are good candidates for psychotherapy.* Obviously, the same kind of arguments could be made if sampling is conducted on the basis of suitability for chemotherapy.

In Project 8, one of the requirements was that the cases selected should be suitable for either one of the treatments. After a patient was entered into the study, he was given a code number which had been set up to randomize the treatments. This yielded a conclusion which can be generalized to that patient class. Multiple-therapy studies of this kind, however, magnify the usual problems of standardization of case-selection. Patients should be suited for either form of treatment. Furthermore, they should be *equally* suitable for both forms of treatment, which implies a quantitative knowledge of the effectiveness and applicability of the treatment, the very matter which is presumably under study. It is often helpful to consider the disease entity or diagnostic category (Greiner, 1962). It is much easier to compare two treatments, such as electroconvulsive therapy and antidepressant drugs, which are effective in the same type of patient, than it is to compare treatments whose principal effectiveness is with widely different types of patients, e.g. fever therapy and psychotherapy. However, the relative scarcity of specific treatments in the psychiatric field makes this less of a problem.

(2) *The goals and the criteria for success of the two treatments may differ.* In treatment with psychotropic drugs, the criterion is usually prompt subsidence of symptoms, even single "target symptoms." With psychotherapy, on the other hand, the criterion of success is much more diffuse and also much more far-reaching; we usually expect long-term or lasting changes, not only in symptoms, but in social adjustment and interpersonal relationships, self-sufficiency, etc. To evaluate two such treatments, a range of criteria is probably required to ensure a fair comparison. If one treatment is consistently superior on all criteria, as tended to be the case in Project 8, the conclusions drawn can be simply stated and decisions about which treatment to use can be easily made. However, if one treatment is superior in certain respects and the second treatment superior in others, the clinician may want to retain both treatments and use them selectively to achieve certain goals. Or he may have to make a value judgment about the relative importance of the various goals.

(3) *Available measures seem to be standardized mostly for the process or effects of one treatment modality.* The various behavior rating scales which have been found very useful in psychotropic drug research, especially with psychotics, are less sensitive to the kind of changes which follow psychotherapy. Furthermore, some measures are completely inapplicable to other forms of therapy. All of the measures of quality and degree of participation in psychotherapy, individual and group, are limited to that modality. Certain self-report measures, as well as some psychological tests which have come into favor because they successfully reflect changes with existing treatment techniques, may not work with new treatments; that is, these same measures or tests may not be sensitive or equally sensitive to the effects of the new treatments. To compare treatments and generalize the results it is essential that the measures are equally applicable to both. Otherwise the findings will

have to be qualified by phrases such as "as measured by the MMPI."

This problem was not completely solved in Project 8. The compromise adopted was to use a battery of measures, some of general usefulness and some especially tailored to one or the other of the treatments. Fortunately, the results were internally consistent on all measures. If it had been otherwise, there might have been serious problems of interpretation.

(4) *Rates of action of compared treatments may differ.* This applies to the lag between start of treatment and the first decrease in symptoms. For example, in the treatment of depression, electroconvulsive therapy acts more rapidly than antidepressant drugs. Most somatic and drug treatments act more rapidly than psychotherapy. The difference also applies to duration of treatment, how long a treatment method has to be applied to achieve its full effect. There is a marked difference in the time required for such treatments as brain surgery, tranquilizers or convulsive therapy, and such treatments as psychoanalysis or vocational retraining and rehabilitation.

In a comparison of two treatments whose rates of action differ, it is difficult to select a duration of the study which will give full opportunity to the slower treatment without unduly delaying the "fast" treatment group which can result in the loss of many cases by discharge following successful completion of treatment.

One approach is to do repeated measurements so that there can be evaluation at several points in time. There may still be a difference in the optimal interval between measurements. Another solution is to leave the treatment time variable within limits. This might offend the purists but still lead to a valid conclusion.

In Project 8, this general problem was handled by selecting a treatment period which provided a good *trial sample* of response to treatment. Even though the 12-week period did not allow the treatments to show their full effectiveness, it was long enough for both treatments to show definite effects. It should be noted that as soon as a fixed time interval is selected, it too becomes part of the experimental question and answer; i.e., treatment A is superior to B over an X week period.

(5) *The two treatments may not be equally simple to start.* Drug therapy may be started almost immediately after admission. Somatic therapies usually require permission, laboratory examinations, perhaps consultations, etc. Psychotherapy may be delayed until time is cleared in the schedule of the staff. Group therapy may be delayed until a group is assembled.

In this situation, is it better to start rating on the day of admission or the day of beginning of therapy? If it is the latter, and there is a characteristic difference in how long patients of the two groups have waited, a systematic bias may be introduced.

One partial solution is to delay start of treatment until either one of the treatments is ready to go; the protocol thus requires a certain standard delay.

Though this means that treatment is being "withheld" from some patients for a few days, this is usually not a serious problem.

(6) *One treatment may be easier to specify than the other.* In general, the somatic therapies and drug therapies are fairly likely to be given in a standard way and in such a manner that the procedure could be repeated by someone else. With such procedures as activity therapy, psychotherapy, and social psychiatry techniques, however, it is very hard to standardize and specify exactly what is to be done or what has been done.

We tried to handle this in Project 8 by being considerably more elaborate and detailed in the description of the group psychotherapy and by being exact wherever possible in regards to duration, time schedules, the maximum permissible skips, etc. The training and experience requirements of the therapist were also spelled out. There was a full description of the nature of the group therapy, the focus, the typical contents or topics, etc.

(7) *Where there is a combined-therapy group, it is even more necessary that treatments be standardized.* Otherwise, good or bad effects of one treatment may be masked by compensatory variations in the other. In Project 8, if the group psychotherapy stirred up one patient, this might be hidden from observation if the treatment doctor were free to increase drug dosage. Another patient might show decrease in symptoms as a result of the psychotherapy, only to have this partly counteracted by the treating doctor who might then lower drug dosage. A high dose of drugs might actually make a patient unsuitable for psychotherapy.

To prevent this type of counteracting effect, it is necessary to standardize the treatments. This means, then, that the treatments are not given optimally or with individual flexibility. In Project 8, restrictions were placed upon the degree to which dosage could be adjusted for the individual patient.

(8) *There may be a differential drop-out rate;* e.g., unlike psychotherapy, a drug might lead to side-effects causing patients to be terminated. On the other hand, drugs might control psychotic symptoms more rapidly, enabling more patients to continue. Using an essentially fixed dosage can lead to trouble if it is set too high or too low. Some treatments like lobotomy, might have no drop-out rate at all, but might have some mortality. The problems in relation to dropouts have been discussed by Lasky (Lasky, 1962). This problem can be handled reasonably well if one is aware of it.

(9) *Uncooperativeness is more of an obstacle in some treatments than in others.* The patient does not have to be completely cooperative to participate in electroconvulsive therapy, drug therapy, or lobotomy. On the other hand, a degree of cooperativeness is required for individual or group psychotherapy. This may lead to a differential rate of dropouts and in turn may result in spuriously high mean scores for those patients who *complete* psychotherapy.

Two remedies for this problem are to evaluate all of the *original* group of patients and to base analyses on them and not simply the group that completes the full treatment course; or, only such patients should be selected in the first place who are expected to be cooperative with both treatments. This sampling requirement also affects generalization.

(10) *In comparison of radically different treatments, blindness often has to be compromised or even abandoned.* It is easy enough to substitute a placebo for an active drug, but there is no good "placebo" for psychotherapy, a total push program, etc. One way of handling this is to have several treatment and control groups, e.g. with each of the treatments alone, with combined treatment, with placebo wherever possible, with neither treatment, etc. Since each such treatment and control group requires a substantial number of cases, this complex kind of design leads to greatly increased requirements in numbers of patients, with some "wasting" of cases.

The treatments also tend to be administered by different professional groups, leading to possible biases in their ratings. In Project 8 we examined the attitudes of the various professional groups involved towards chemotherapy of psychiatric illness. It appeared that nurses and psychiatrists had more positive attitudes toward chemotherapy than did psychologists. This seems to fit in with the fact that psychiatrists prescribe psychotropic drugs and nurses dispense them, whereas psychologists do not participate directly. One might predict that psychologists and psychiatrists would have a more positive attitude towards psychotherapy than would nurses.

A partial remedy was to have some of the evaluations performed by a "visiting" team of raters who were not connected with the treatment of these patients and who had no awareness of which treatment a particular patient was receiving. This has the disadvantage, however, that the more complete and detailed knowledge possessed by the treatment staff is lost.

DISCUSSION

One general theme in the preceding discussion is that the various technical problems are magnified if the goals and criterion measures are oriented to the treatments, but are lessened if the focus is on the patients, the symptoms, and on long-term changes. If we had the knowledge, the skills, and the tools to identify, describe, and classify patients precisely and to rate their symptoms quanititatively, most of th' problems mentioned would become insignificant. For each experiment, a certain class of patients could be selected, and then the various available treatments could be evaluated and compared, one after another, using as criteria only the degree and permanence of symptom change.

Since such precise categorizations and quantitative evaluations are not yet possible, we must work with the tools at hand. This means that we must use the available rating instruments, tests, examination procedures, and other indicators of change, even though many of these are oriented to a specific treatment process. We also have to make use of short-term changes, on the assumption that they will be valid indicators of long-term changes. This assumption can and should be verified, but it is not practical to wait for the ultimate results of one experiment before beginning another.

Use of presently available tools raises a number of technical problems, which have been discussed in the body of this paper. Our intent has been to identify these, so that investigators may take steps to neutralize or minimize them. Another point we have tried to emphasize is that whatever experimental features are adopted to deal with the problem of adequately evaluating different treatments, they become part of the experimental questions, i.e., is one treatment better than another *under these circumstances.* Therefore careful consideration has to be given to whether the original research question is being modified by the use of particular research strategies.

SUMMARY

1. Comparisons of the effectiveness of different psychiatric treatment methods are extremely important. Yet such comparisons present many complexities and technical problems.

2. Ten such problems in a two-treatment comparison are identified and discussed. A multi-hospital drug vs. group psychotherapy study is used as an illustration.

3. Possible solutions and safeguards related to some of these problems are suggested.

REFERENCES

Gorham, D. R., Pokorny, A. D., & Moseley, E. C. Effects of a phenothiazine and/or group psychotherapy with schizophrenics. *Dis. Nerv. Syst.,* 1964, **25,** 77–86.

Greiner, T. Selecting patient-participants for drug investigations. *J. of New Drugs,* 1962, **2,** 199–205.

Lasky, J. J. The Problem of sample attrition in controller treatment trials. *J. Nerv. and Ment. Dis.,* 1962, **135,** 332–337.

PART III
Clinical Prescriptions

Commentary

In this Part we will review psychotherapy research literature for the purpose of deriving clinically useful prescriptions in major psychodiagnostic categories. The bases for each prescription are empirical investigations in which the experimental findings could be related directly to at least one antecedent therapeutic variable. This approach distinguishes itself from a tradition that has long characterized the psychotherapy literature — that of basing prescriptive-like recommendations on subjective, impressionistic, and often biased case studies. While individual case studies may be useful for suggesting hypotheses to be tested subsequently, the serious sources of confounding of uncontrolled therapist, patient, and treatment variables inherent in case study reports precludes statements about cause-effect relationships (Paul, 1969). Thus, we have omitted such individual case studies in deriving our therapeutic prescriptions. We have, however, reviewed and organized the results from "single-group design" studies in which the pre-post treatment effects of a single psychotherapy variable (e.g., a therapy technique) on a homogeneous sample of subjects are determined. For example, the percentage of schizophrenic patients rated as improved following milieu therapy (e.g., Foreyt & Felton, 1970), or the decrease in anxiety after systematic desensitization with agoraphobics (e.g., Agras, 1967), or the effectiveness of biofeedback with hypertensive patients in decreasing blood pressure (e.g., Bensen et al., 1971) are illustrative of such studies.

In each instance the efficacy of the treatment is assessed by comparing the patient's level of functioning following therapy to his or her level preceding therapy. To this extent, the single-group design is nothing more than a compilation of case studies and thus suffers from the same sources of experimental error as the single case study report. In both designs, a no-treatment control group, to establish a base-rate of improvement in the absence of a specific form of intervention, is conspicuously absent. However, unlike individual case studies, the single-group design permits possible correlational statements about patient characteristics and therapeutic outcomes. In our statement below about prescriptive treatments for phobic disorders, we have organized these correlations to serve as the basis for a low level nondifferential prescription. As noted in this Part, we have used the term "nondifferential" since prescriptive recommendations are derived from the cumulation of correlational data rather than from direct comparisons of one therapeutic variable with another or with a control condition.

As our earlier prescriptive schema indicated, more advanced levels of prescription are "differential" in nature. *Differential prescriptions* are derived from investigations designed to assess the relative effects of at least two experimentally controlled conditions. In its most basic form this involves one group of patients receiving a form of psychotherapy, compared to a matched control group of patients either not receiving treatment (e.g., wait list, no contact control) or receiving an inert treatment in the form of nonspecific attention (placebo control). In a slightly more complex variety, two psychotherapeutic variables (e.g., techniques) are directly compared in addition to the inclusion of no-treatment and/or attention control groups.

More complex differential prescriptions emerge from studies that have employed factorial experimental designs. The essential feature of this design is that two or more levels of either a patient, therapist, or treatment variable (factor) is investigated within the same experiment. A unique and crucial property of factorial designs is that they permit a direct evaluation of the interactions between the factors under investigation, thereby providing a comprehensive description of the interrelationships between the variables at the various levels represented in the experiment. As Paul (1969) notes:

> ... the interactions and differential effects of treatment variables may be separated for different types or levels of distressing target behavior and for different types or levels of relatively stable personal-social characteristics of clients by selecting independent variables and forming experimental and control groups to represent classes of variables factorially (p. 51).

In this fashion, answers to the prescriptive question — what treatment, by whom, is most effective for which individuals with what problem? — are more closely approximated. Unfortunately, factorially designed outcome studies in psychotherapy are so few in number as to currently preclude the formulation of reliable prescriptions of the hierarchically more advanced form generated from such types of investigations.

Table 1 summarizes the relationship between the diagnostic categories to be reviewed and the presence or absence of research investigations at each level of analysis. As shown, the current state of the literature in psychotherapy research that is *clinically* relevant for prescribing differential treatments appears to be at a median point, somewhere between single-group designs and factorially designed studies.

The bulk of the contemporaneous research evidence speaks to the establishment of cause-effect relationships between antecedent treatment techniques and consequent patient changes. This state of the literature is reflected directly in the orientation and content of the clinical prescriptions found in

Table 1. Diagnostic Categories and Presence or Absence of Research at Each Level of Analysis

Diagnosis	1. Nondifferential		2. Unidifferential			3. Bidifferential		4. Tridifferential
Level: Type:	1A	1B	2A	2B	2C	3A	3B	4A
Psychoneuroses:								
Phobic reactions	X		X	X	X	X		
Obsessive-compulsive	X		X					
Hysteria	X		X					
Depression	X							
Psychophysiological Disorders:								
Bronchial asthma	X		X		X			
Ulcerative colitis	X		X					
Hypertension and hypertensive headaches	X							
Migraine	X		X					
Sexual Deviations:								
Sexual orientation disturbance	X		X					
Orgasmic dysfunctioning	X				X			
Fetishism and transvestism	X				X			
Exhibitionism	X				X			
Anti-social behavior	X		X					
Smoking	X		X	X		X		
Obesity	X		X					
Insomnia	X		X					
Schizophrenia	X		X			X	X	

this Part. By far, the majority of prescriptions specify optimal matches between psychotherapy techniques, patient diagnosis, and treatment outcomes. Most conspicuously absent are studies which examine the role of the therapist and how the characteristics of the therapist interact with properties of the treatment technique and with characteristics of the patient to produce differential outcomes. Aside from its relative absence as an independent variable in studies of the therapeutic process related to outcome, information about the therapist's contribution to patient change is even sorely lacking on a correlational level. Typically, descriptions of the therapist's characteristics are left vague or unspecified. Ironically, in studies in which the influence of the therapist is examined directly, descriptions of the therapeutic technique and the characteristics of the patients remain too global for prescriptive purposes. For example, an abundance of research evidence exists demonstrating that differentiation of therapists by the Strong Vocational Interest Blank into Type A and Type B is predictive of differential success with schizophrenics (Whitehorn & Betz, 1954, 1960) and neurotics (Carson, 1967; McNair, Callahan, & Lorr, 1962), respectively. Despite these long-standing empirical relationships, the findings have largely remained "functionally autonomous" from the conduct and conceptualization of psychotherapy principally because these findings have not been systematically related to different therapy techniques. An exception is a recent study by James and Foreman (1973) which does point to the importance of relating therapist A-B types to specific forms of treatment. In this study it was found that B-status "therapists" (mothers) were more successful than A-status "therapists" in the treatment of their eneuretic children by Mowrerian conditioning procedures. Despite such exceptions, "the route by which therapist personality factors enter and influence technical operations needs to be mapped out much more thoroughly. At present, it is not at all clear how therapist personality and technical operations are to be differentiated..." (Strupp & Bergin, 1969, p. 37). The limited amount of research data on the interrelationships between therapist variables with treatment and patient factors suggests that prescriptions based exclusively on the interaction between these latter two variables must be accepted with this limitation in mind. Since many psychotherapy prescriptions do not include qualifications on the manner in which therapist factors — his personality, his background, his social adjustment, his cognitive style, his values — enter into the prescriptive formulation, the validity of the prescription in the hands of any particular therapist remains unknown.

Our formulation of psychotherapeutic prescriptions is predicated on the assumption that research in psychotherapy can be utilized in a manner that is much more relevant to the practice of psychotherapy than has been true in the past. In an attempt to provide the clinician with research information underlying the development of useful therapeutic prescriptions, we have summarized a very considerable number of psychotherapy investigations in the tables that follow. Each table is organized around a single psychodiagnostic group and contains, for each study summarized, the following information:

1. *Patient characteristics.* Formal diagnosis (utilizing primarily DSM II nomenclature), sex, age, and, where reported, other prescription-relevant characteristics — e.g., duration of symptoms, social class, education, and so forth.

2. *Therapist characteristics.* Profession, orientation, number, sex, experience level, etc. Inspection of the tabularized research information, however, will reveal to the reader that it is generally the case that qualities of the participating therapists remain unspecified in most contemporary psychotherapy research.

3. *Treatment characteristics.* Therapy techniques employed, number of sessions, and duration of treatment.

4. *Outcomes.* Measures employed, differential treatment effects at termination and, where available, upon follow-up.

Following each summary table of investigative findings, and based upon these findings, one or more psychotherapeutic prescriptions are offered for the diagnostic group represented. Initially we sought with these data to provide the clinician with answers to the question, "Given a patient who is labeled a (diagnosis), what is currently the most effective form or forms of treatment, offered by whom, that will produce what specific changes?" However, because of the relative paucity of research on the therapist's contribution to the outcome of therapy, in the majority of instances we revised the general form of the prescriptions so as to answer instead the question, *"Given a patient who is labeled a (diagnosis), what is currently the most effective form or forms of treatment that will produce what specific changes?"*

Our answers to this prescriptive question are restricted in several ways. First, our selection of relevant research was limited to include only investigations of individual psychotherapy with adult patients. While this excludes research on child and adolescent therapy, group therapy, sensitivity training, and psychopharmacological treatment, the scope of problems included and the range of treatment techniques analyzed is quite extensive. Second, we have generally excluded studies which used heterogeneous groups of patients as subjects, such as "psychoneurotics," "psychotics," or "hospitalized patients." These categories are too broad for prescriptive purposes and are remnants of the "patient uniformity myth" identified by Kiesler (1966). Third, the empirical foundation and thus the consequent level of confidence in the prescriptions vary across different diagnostic categories and are directly related to the number and quality of differential studies conducted within a diagnostic group. Thus, while there has been a wealth of comparative research with the interpersonally anxious college student and the hospitalized schizophrenic, there exists a paucity of differential studies with hysterics and obsessive-compulsives. Clearly, the prescriptions derived for the former groups deserve less hesitant and restricted implementation than those derived for the latter diagnostic groupings.

This completes our depiction of the manner in which our clinical prescriptions were derived and the considerations entering into both their potential utility and limitations. For both the patients who may be their recipients and the researcher-clinicians who hopefully will improve upon our initial effort here, our prescriptions and the tabular summarizations of their empirical bases now follow. The order of presentation is:

Psychoneuroses

PHOBIC REACTIONS

Social Phobias

Social Anxiety and Nonassertiveness

Social anxiety refers to instances in which individuals report anxiety about social situations and these feelings motivate an avoidance of the precipitator (e.g., members of the opposite sex, dating, socializing). Nonassertiveness refers to individuals who report intense difficulty saying "no" to unreasonable requests. Both problems are characterized by an essential deficit in the initiation and conduct of socially appropriate interpersonal behaviors.

To date, research has been directed toward attempts to teach precisely those social performance skills lacking in the response repertoire. These attempts have involved the exclusive application of behavioral rehearsal or some closely related variant (e.g., role playing, psychodrama, self-reinforcement, structured guidance training). Reliably, *behavioral rehearsal* has been shown to be more effective than no treatment in relieving the emotional distress produced by social situations (Dua, 1970; Martinson & Zerface, 1970; McFall & Lillesand, 1971; McFall & Marston, 1970; Rehm & Marston, 1968).

Research on the effects of psychotherapy with problems of social anxiety and nonassertiveness have compared insight-oriented psychotherapy (e.g., client-centered therapy) with behavioral rehearsal (e.g., Dua, 1970; Lazarus, 1966; Martinson & Zerface, 1970; Rehm & Marston, 1968). In each instance and across a variety of cognitive, emotional, and behavioral measures of improvement, *behavioral rehearsal* was demonstrated to be reliably more effective.

Speech Anxiety

All forms of psychotherapy that have been investigated are more effective than no treatment in reducing interpersonal anxiety. These treatments consist of *systematic desensitization* (Johnson *et al.,* 1971; Mylar & Clement, 1972; Paul, 1967), *insight-oriented psychotherapy* (Paul, 1966, 1967), *behavioral rehearsal* (Johnson *et al.,* 1971), *implosive therapy* (Mylar & Clement, 1972), *rational-emotive therapy* (Karst & Trexler, 1970; Trexler & Karst, 1972); and *fixed role therapy* (Karst & Trexler, 1970).

Several treatments have been shown to effectively reduce anxiety associated with public speaking. A review of this literature suggests that treatments (e.g., *systematic desensitization, behavioral rehearsal, implosive therapy, fixed role therapy*) specifically designed to directly alter concrete aspects of speech anxiety are reliably more successful than approaches (e.g., psychoanalytic therapy, client-centered therapy, rational-emotive therapy) which focus primarily or exclusively on inferred processes which are abstractly related to the immediate behavioral expressions of interpersonal anxiety.

Agoraphobia

The agoraphobia syndrome signifies individuals who exhibit generalized fears of going outside, particularly alone. According to Marks (1970), the majority of agoraphobics are women who, in addition to fears of going out, also experience collateral symptoms ranging from diffuse panic attacks, feelings of depression and depersonalization, to persistent obsessive ruminations. In contrast to other phobic states involving circumscribed and relatively specific evoking conditions, agoraphobics tend to be more generally anxious and, at times, may appear undifferentiable from such clinical syndromes as anxiety states, affective disorders, or obsessive neuroses. It appears as one of the commonest (approximately 60%) and also the most distressing phobic reaction seen by practicing clinicians (Marks, 1970). Nevertheless, despite its prevalence and the oppressiveness of the symptomatology, *no one form of therapy has been demonstrated to be reliably effective in relieving agoraphobia.* To date, three approaches have been investigated experimentally: (a) systematic desensitization, (b) aversion relief therapy, and (c) implosive therapy. Unlike the other phobias, in which questions about the comparative effectiveness of different treatments are germane, even the absolute effectiveness of one particular treatment (i.e., pre to post treatment improvement) for agoraphobia has yet to be generally established.

As previously mentioned, research on agoraphobia potentially yielding nondifferential prescriptions is highly equivocal. Two investigations that used within-subject change or difference scores, in which measures were taken prior to and immediately following therapy, reported significant patient improvement. Thus, Agras (1967) found that 30 systematic desensitization sessions effectively enabled four out of five agoraphobic patients to walk one mile alone. Orwin (1973), using a form of aversion relief training called "the running treatment," exposed patients to moderately fear-arousing situations while the patients were recovering their breath from having just participated in vigorous running exercises. In this fashion, "respiratory relief" occurred in the presence of previously avoided situations. Results indicated that all eight subjects became symptom-free following 12 to 90 sessions. However, when the effects of aversion relief training were compared to a matched untreated control group (Solyom *et al.,* 1972), no statistically significant differences emerged, although more subjects in the aversion relief group benefited on more variables and to a greater degree than the control subjects.

Marks (1970) presented evidence showing that agoraphobics, relative to the responsiveness of other phobics to systematic desensitization, displayed significantly less improvement after desensitization therapy. This poorer showing by agoraphobics to desensitization was attributed to their tendency to relapse repeatedly. Prognosis was also poorer for patients with a history of either panic attacks or obsessions. Similarly, Glick (1970) reported that only 30% of agoraphobic patients treated by systematic desensitization were noted as improved compared to a 60% improvement rate of other phobic problems (e.g., elevators, crowds, animals, school, being alone) also treated by desensitization.

Research findings on the comparative effectiveness of different treatments are too few and the findings are too tentative to allow even meaningful speculations about optimal patient-treatment outcomes. In the only systematic investigation on agoraphobia, Gelder and Marks (1966) compared systematic desensitization with an "insight-oriented" approach designed to relate past experiences with current interpersonal problems. Neither the measures of symptom improvement, nor social adjustment, nor anxiety reduction were significantly different between these groups. More improvement in work adjustment was found following desensitization than after insight-oriented psychotherapy.

In a series of related studies Marks, Gelder, and their associates investigated the comparative effectiveness of systematic desensitization in heterogeneously comprised groups of phobic patients. Although the groups contained a variety of different phobic types (e.g., specific, social), approximately 45% of the subjects were diagnosed as agoraphobic and the results may thus have a bearing on our understanding of the differential treatment of this problem. It was found that systematic desensitization was more effective than either hypnosis (Marks, Gelder, & Edwards, 1968) or an "insight-oriented" group psychotherapy (Gelder & Marks, 1968). However, flooding (implosive therapy) proved more effective than systematic desensitization with the agoraphobic patients but desensitization was differentially more effective in alleviating the specific phobias (Boulougouris *et al.,* 1971).

Significantly, the therapeutic gains, in the form of therapists' ratings of improvement, self-report of anxiety, and heart-rate and galvanic skin responsivity during imagery, were maintained at a 12-month follow-up. In addition, the finding of a differential effectiveness of two forms of treatment correlated with two different patient characteristics is an extremely important and promising finding, in need of replication and further examination.

Specific Phobias

Test Anxiety

The analysis of therapy outcomes with test anxiety has focused primarily on: (a) self-report measures of anxiety (e.g., Fear Survey Schedule, Alpert-Haber Achievement Anxiety Scale, Sarason's Test Anxiety Scale, Taylor Manifest Anxiety Scale) and (b) improvement in test grades. Since prescriptive statements optimally are directly related to specific outcomes, the first section below discusses prescriptions based on changes in felt anxiety, followed by prescriptions based on classroom grades as the measure of improvement.

The bulk of the evidence (approximately 90% success) in studies of a single treatment compared to a no-treatment group points to the efficacy of *systematic desensitization* for alleviating the anxiety associated with test-taking situations (Cohen, 1969; Crighton & Jehu, 1969; Donner, 1970; Donner & Guerney, 1969; Emery & Krumboltz, 1967; Freeling & Shemberg, 1970; Garlington & Cotler, 1968; Katahn, Strenger & Cherry, 1966; Kondas, 1967; Meichenbaum, 1972; Mitchell & Ng, 1972; Smith & Nye, 1973; Suinn, 1968).

Definitive conclusions about the effectiveness of systematic desensitization in comparison to other treatments remain somewhat equivocal and tentative. While Prochaska (1971) demonstrated that implosive therapy based on either symptomatic or psychodynamic cues of test anxiety is equally successful, it appears that systematic desensitization can be more effective than implosive therapy (Smith & Nye, 1973). Studies directed toward identifying the specific active ingredients in systematic desensitization, however, have yielded inconsistent findings. From the four studies comparing systematic desensitization with muscular relaxation training alone, two found both treatments equally effective in reducing anxiety (Johnson & Sechrest, 1968; Laxer & Walker, 1970), one study reported a superiority for systematic desensitization (Freeling & Shemberg, 1970), and one investigation obtained results supporting the efficacy of relaxation training alone (Laxer *et al.,* 1969).

Recently, the combined use of *systematic desensitization with "cognitive-problem solving"* approaches have obtained impressive results in affecting a reduction in test-taking anxiety (Allen, 1971; Meichenbaum, 1972; Mitchell & Ng, 1972). In each instance, the combination of systematic desensitization with group counseling about more effective study habits (Allen, 1971; Mitchell & Ng, 1972) or with an insight-oriented therapy emphasizing coping imagery and self-instructional training to remain task relevant (Meichenbaum, 1972) have been shown to be more effective than systematic desensitization alone in reducing the emotional component of test anxiety.

In contrast to the reliable effectiveness of systematic desensitization in reducing test-taking anxiety, no consistent findings have emerged favoring a particular therapy when improvement in test grades is the measure of success and the treatment is compared to an untreated group of subjects. The majority of studies indicate that neither systematic desensitization (Allen,

1971; Emery & Krumboltz, 1967; Garlington & Cotler, 1968; Kondas, 1967; Laxer *et al.,* 1969; Laxer & Walker, 1970; Mitchell & Ng, 1972) nor relaxation training alone (Johnson & Sechrest, 1968; Laxer, *et al.,* 1969; Laxer & Walker, 1970) produce effects different from untreated groups of test anxious subjects.

Improvements in test grades have reliably occurred when *systematic desensitization is combined with cognitive-problem solving approaches.* Thus, Meichenbaum (1972) found a cognitive modification procedure superior to systematic desensitization and Allen (1972), Katahn, Strenger, and Cherry (1966), and Mitchell & Ng, (1972) all used both group systematic desensitization and a more traditional counseling method together and found the combination to yield significantly better results than either treatment alone.

The superiority of systematic desensitization plus cognitive-problem solving orientations may relate to the specific responsiveness of this marriage to the nature of test anxiety. According to Liebert and Morris (1967) and Wine (1971), the major components of test anxiety are "worry" (i.e., a concern about performance) and "emotionality or arousal." The combined application of cognitive-problem solving and systematic desensitization, respectively, may match these mechanisms and thereby produce changes in *both* the anxiety and the test performance response modes.

Aviation

The only controlled experiment with individuals professing a fear of airplane flying was conducted by Goorney (1970). The subjects were six British pilots and navigators referred for treatment. Therapy consisted of *systematic desensitization,* first with the feared situations presented in imagery followed by *in vivo* training sessions. Results indicated reductions in self-reports of anxiety and in MMPI scales to levels comparable to those of nonphobic aircrews. Five of the patients returned to full flying duties, which was maintained at a three-year follow-up.

Aquaphobia

Sherman (1972) compared systematic desensitization to the effects of gradually exposing aquaphobics to a hierarchically arranged series of *in vivo* water activities. Significant behavioral and subjective improvement was associated primarily with the repeated *in vivo* exposures, while the reduction of anxiety that accompanied systematic desensitization showed little evidence of transfer to real-life aquatic situations. In conclusion, the results of this well-controlled study suggest that *repeated in vivo gradual exposure to water activities* is, currently, the treatment of choice for aquaphobia.

Acrophobia

In two studies, Ritter (1969a, 1969b) found *"contact desensitization,"* in which the therapist first demonstrated or modeled the desired behavior and then physically guided the patient in successfully performing the behavior (e.g., held the patient's legs while he stood atop a ladder), significantly more effective than when the therapist demonstrated and verbally prompted or supported the patient or when the therapist merely modeled the desired behavior.

Phobias of Internal Stimuli

Fears of Heart Attacks, Cancer, Strange Illnesses, Deaths

Kumar and Wilkinson (1971) reported the effective use of a *thought stopping* procedure in reducing considerably the frequency, the pathological quality, and the intensity of phobic ideations. Briefly, this procedure involved the therapist repeatedly interrupting the patient by yelling the word "stop" following each occurrence of the undesirable thought. The patients also rehearsed by employing subvocal self-instructions to "stop" during each undesirable thought, followed by more pleasant thoughts. The improvement judged to be evident in each patient was also judged to have been maintained at a 12-month follow-up. However, since the findings reflect only pre- to post-therapy changes, in the absence of at least a no-treatment control group, these findings and their prescriptive relevance must be viewed cautiously and tentatively.

Table 2. PHOBIC REACTIONS

	Patient					Therapist	
Name	Diagnosis	No.	Sex	Age	Other	Description	No.

Level 1. Nondifferential prescriptions
Type 1A: Psychotherapy A for patients X

Agras, 1967	agoraphobia	5	3F 2M	x̄=31.6	duration of phobia = 2–10 yr.	unspecified	–
Garlington & Cotler, 1968	test anxiety	3	all F	25	–	graduate students	4
Glick, 1970	multiple phobias	23	16F 7M	14–52 x̄=30.8	outpatients, mdn. duration = 5 yr.	physician	1
Goorney, 1970	aviation phobia	6	all M	x̄=30.5	pilots or navigators	experi- menter	1
Kumar & Wilkinson, 1971	"internal stimuli"	4	3F 1M	22–44	fears of heart attacks, cancer, death	unspecified	1
Orwin, 1971	multiple phobias	–	–	–	–	unspecified	–
Orwin, 1973	agoraphobia	8	6F 2M	23–45	duration of problem = 1.5–32 yr.	nurses, para- professionals	–
Snider & Oetting, 1966	test anxiety	12	all M	–	college students	experi- menter	1
Solyom & Miller, 1968	multiple phobias	8	7F 1M	x̄=32	–	unspecified	–
Suinn, 1968	test anxiety	28	–	–	college students	graduate students	3

Treatment			Outcomes		
Type	No. Sessions	Total Duration	Assessment Procedure	Results	Follow-up
systematic desensitization	x̄=30 (15–70)	–	physical; behavioral test	4 Ss judged improved; 1 S unchanged	none
systematic desensitization vs. no-treatment control	10–11	6–7 wk.	self-rating of fear; grades	systematic desensitization >no-treatment control	1 mo.; no no grade dif- ferences
systematic desensitization	x̄=7.1 (1–18)	–	t rating	52% improved	5–20 mo.; 39% improved
systematic desensitization	–	1–6 mo.	self-report of anxiety; psychometric tests	reduction to average level	2–3 yr.; results main- tained
thought stop- ping & relaxation training	8–10	4 wk.	self-report of anxiety	reduction in frequency of phobic thoughts & anxiety in each S	1 yr.; changes maintained
aversion relief (respiratory)	1–2	–	t rating	6 Ss lost pho- bic symptoms	none
aversion relief (respiratory); running	12–90	–	behavioral test	all Ss symptom- free	none
autogenic training	–	3 wk.	self-report of anxiety; grades	Ss rated treat- ment effective; increase in grades	none
aversion relief	x̄=19.5	–	self-report of anxiety & behavior	6 out of 7 Ss free of pho- bic symptoms	10 mo.– 3 yr.
systematic desensitization vs. no-treatment control	7.8	4 wks.	self-report of anxiety; behavioral test	systematic desensitization >no-treatment control	none

Table 2 cont.

Name	Patient					Therapist	
	Diagnosis	No.	Sex	Age	Other	Description	No.
Watson & Marks, 1971	specific phobias	10	8F 2M	19–41	chronic symptoms	psychiatrists	–

Level 2. Unidifferential prescriptions
  Type 2A: Psychotherapy A vs. psychotherapy B for patients X

Name	Diagnosis	No.	Sex	Age	Other	Description	No.
McFall & Lillesand, 1971	social anxiety	33	18M 15F	–	nonassertive; college students	–	1M 1F
McFall & Marston, 1970	social anxiety	42	24F 18M	–	nonassertive; college students	graduate students	3M
Martinson & Zerface, 1970	social anxiety	24	all M	–	nondaters; college students	–	5M
Rehm & Marston, 1968	social anxiety	36	all M	–	college students; discomfort with females	graduate students	4
Johnson et al., 1971	speech anxiety	30	–	–	8th graders	unspecified	–

Treatment			Outcomes		
Type	No. Sessions	Total Duration	Assessment Procedure	Results	Follow-up
flooding	2–3	4–5 hr	t rating; self-rating of anxiety; behavioral test, interview; physical	sign. reduction in fear on all measures	3–6 mo.; results maintained
behavioral rehearsal (overt) vs. behavioral rehearsal (covert) vs. attention control	4	2–3	self-report of anxiety; behavioral test	behavioral rehearsal (covert) > behavioral rehearsal (overt) > attention control	none
behavioral rehearsal + feedback vs. behavioral rehearsal vs. attention control vs. no-treatment control	4	3 wks.	self-report of anxiety; behavioral test; physio.	behavioral rehearsal + feedback= behavioral rehearsal > attention control= no-treatment control	none
individual counseling vs. arranged coed interactions vs. no-treatment control	5	5 wks.	self-report of anxiety; behavioral test	arranged coed interactions > individual counseling=no treatment control	8 wks.; results maintained
self-reinforcement vs. relationship therapy vs. no-treatment control	–	5 wks.	self-report of anxiety; behavioral test; psychometric tests	self-reinforcement > relationship therapy & no-treatment control	7–9 mo.
systematic desensitization vs. behavioral rehearsal vs. no-treatment control	9	5 wks.	self-report of anxiety	systematic desensitization =behavioral rehearsal > no-treatment control	none

Table 2 cont.

| Name | Patient | | | | | Therapist | |
	Diagnosis	No.	Sex	Age	Other	Description	No.
Karst & Trexler, 1970	speech anxiety	22	15F 7M	–	college students	psychologist; graduate student	2
Mylar & Clement, 1972	speech anxiety	39	all M	–	graduate students	audio tapes	–
Paul, 1967	speech anxiety	89	62M 27F	17–24 mdn.= 19	college undergraduates; self-referrals	experienced in Rogerian & neo-Freudian approaches	5
Trexler & Karst, 1972	speech anxiety	33	17F 16M	–	college students	graduate student	1
Gelder & Marks, 1966	agoraphobia	20	15F 5M	$\bar{x}$=34.5	$\bar{x}$ duration of problem =7 yrs.	psychiatrists	–

Treatment			Outcomes		
Type	No. Sessions	Total Duration	Assessment Procedure	Results	Follow-up
fixed role vs. rational emotive vs. no-treatment control	3	—	self-report of anxiety	fixed role > rational emotive > no-treatment control	6 mos.
systematic desensitization vs. implosion vs. no-treatment control	5	3 wks.	self-report of anxiety; behavioral tests	systematic desensitization =implosion > no-treatment control	1 mo.; changes maintained or increased
systematic desensitization vs. relationship therapy vs. attention control vs. no-treatment control	5	6 wks.	self-ratings, behavioral test	at time of follow up: systematic desensitization → 85% improved; relationship therapy & attention control → 50% improved; no-treatment control → 22% improved	2 yrs.
rational emotive vs. attention control (relaxation) vs. no-treatment control	4	—	self-report of anxiety; behavioral test; physiological measure	rational emotive > attention control & no-treatment control	6–7 mo.; changes maintained or increased
systematic desensitization vs. relationship therapy	63	21 wks.	psychometric tests of symptoms; self-report of anxiety; behavioral ratings	systematic desensitization =relationship therapy (no changes in either condition); systematic desensitization > relationship therapy for improved work adjustment	12 mos.

Table 2 cont.

Name	Patient Diagnosis	No.	Sex	Age	Other	Therapist Description	No.
Ritter, 1969 (a)	acro- phobia	15	13F 2M	20–55	female	unspecified	1
Solyom et al., 1972	agora- phobia	27	23F 4M	$\bar{x}=35$	$\bar{x}$ duration of illness =12.7	psychia- trists	3
Gelder & Marks, 1968	multiple phobias	7	2M 5F	$\bar{x}=38$	5 agora- phobics; 1 social phobia; 1 thunder	psychia- trists inexperi- enced t	4 1
Hussain, 1971	agora- phobia, social phobias	40	13M 27F	$\bar{x}=28.4$	severely handicapped by symptoms	unspecified	–
Marks, et al, 1968	agora- phobia, social phobias	·28	10M 18F	33	12 agora- phobics; 8 social phobics; 8 specific phobics	unspecified	–
Watson & Marks, 1971	specific phobias; agora- phobia	16	–	$\bar{x}=30$	$\bar{x}$ duration of illness= 12.3 yrs.	psychia- trists	7
Allen, 1971	test anxiety	75	36M 39F	$\bar{x}=19.4$	college students	graduate students	2

Treatment			Outcomes		
Type	No. Sessions	Total Duration	Assessment Procedure	Results	Follow-up
contact desen-sensitization vs. noncontact desen-sitization vs. no-treatment control	1	24 min.	self-report of anxiety; behavioral test	contact desen-sitization > noncontact desensitization =no-treatment control	none
aversion relief vs. pseudoconditioning control vs. habituation control	24	3 mos.	psycho-metric tests; self-rating of anxiety	no difference between groups	none
group therapy vs. systematic desensi-tization (crossover design)	–	4 mos.	self-ratings of anxiety, t ratings, judge's ratings	systematic desensitization > group therapy	none
systematic desensi-tization (thiopental or saline) vs. flood-ing (thiopental or saline) (crossover design)	12	45 min. twice/ wk.	self-rating of anxiety; t rating of improvement	systematic desensitization (thiopental)= systematic desensitization (saline); flooding (thiopental) > flooding (saline)	none
systematic desensi-tization vs. hypnosis	12–24	12–24 wks.	psycho-metric tests; self-report of anxiety; t ratings	systematic desensitization > hypnosis (non sign.)	6 wks. & 4½ mos.
flooding vs. flooding (irrele-vant fears)	16	6 wks.	self-report of anxiety; physiological; t ratings	both treat-ments equally effective	6 mos.
systematic desensi-tization vs. counseling vs. systematic desen-sitization + counseling vs. attention control vs. testing control vs. minimal contact control	7	7 weeks.	self-report of anxiety; physiologi-cal; grades	systematic desensitization + counseling > systematic desensitization =counseling= controls	none

Table 2 cont.

| Name | Patient | | | | | Therapist | |
	Diagnosis	No.	Sex	Age	Other	Description	No.
Allen, 1973	test anxiety	84	63F 21M	–	college students	graduate students	2
Cohen, 1969	test anxiety	19	–	–	college students	graduate students	1
Crighton & Jehu, 1969	test anxiety	28	–	–	college students	unspecified	2
Emery & Krumboltz, 1967	test anxiety	54	36M 18F	–	college students	graduate students	9
Freeling & Shemberg, 1970	test anxiety	28	24F 4M	–	college students	unspecified	–
Johnson & Sechrest, 1968	test anxiety	41	–	–	college students	experi- menter	1

Treatment			Outcomes		
Type	No. Sessions	Total Duration	Assessment Procedure	Results	Follow-up
counseling + relaxation vs. counseling vs. attention control vs. no-treatment control	21	7 wks.	self-report of anxiety; grades	counseling= counseling + relaxation > attention control=no-treatment control	none
group systematic desensitization with or without group interaction & progressive hierarchy vs. no-treatment control	12	6 wks.	self-report of anxiety; grades	all systematic desensitization groups > no-treatment control; no difference between experimental groups	none
systematic desensitization vs. nondirective therapy vs. no-treatment control	20+	about 10 wks.	psychometric tests of affect; sleep disturbance; grades; self-report of anxiety	systematic desensitization =nondirective therapy (both effective)	none
systematic desensitization (individual vs. standard hierarchy) vs. no-treatment control	16	8 wks.	self-ratings of anxiety; grades	systematic desensitization (individual)= systematic desensitization (standard) > no-treatment control; no difference in grades	none
systematic desensitization vs. imagery vs. relaxation	6	6 wks.	anagram task	systematic desensitization =relaxation= imagery	none
systematic desensitization vs. relaxation vs. no-treatment control	5	45 min./ session	self-report of anxiety; grades	systematic desensitization > relaxation= no-treatment control	1–6 mo.

Table 2 cont.

| Name | Patient | | | | | Therapist | |
	Diagnosis	No.	Sex	Age	Other	Description	No.
Katahn et al., 1966	test anxiety	14	8F 6M	–	college students	psychologist & graduate students	3
Kondas, 1967	test anxiety	13	–	21.9	college students	psychologists	2
Laxer et al., 1969	test anxiety	116	–	–	secondary school students	college graduates with teaching experience	4
Laxer & Walker, 1970	test anxiety	110	–	–	secondary school students	counselors	3
Mann, 1972	text anxiety	80	40M 40F	–	7th & 8th graders	unspecified	–
Meichenbaum, 1972	test anxiety	21	15M 6F	17–25	college students, 1 high school senior	graduate student	1

Treatment			Outcomes		
Type	No. Sessions	Total Duration	Assessment Procedure	Results	Follow-up
group therapy + systematic desensitization vs. no-treatment control	8	8 hrs.	self-report of anxiety; grades	group therapy +systematic desensitization > no-treatment control	1 academic semester
systematic desensitization vs. relaxation vs. no-treatment control	10	3½–10 wks.	self-report of anxiety; physiological measure	systematic desensitization > relaxation= no-treatment control	5 mos.
systematic desensitization vs. relaxation vs. no-treatment control	30	6 wks.	self-rating of anxiety; grades	relaxation=systematic desensitization=no-treatment control; relaxation > no-treatment control	none
systematic desensitization vs. relaxation vs. behavioral rehearsal vs. relaxation + behavior rehearsal vs. attention control vs. no-treatment control	20	8 wks.	self-rport of anxiety; grades	systematic desensitization =relaxation > controls=behavioral rehearsal =behavioral rehearsal + relaxation	none
modeling + rehearsal vs. observe only vs. no-treatment control	6	3 wks.	self-report of anxiety; behavioral test	experimental groups > no-treatment control	4 wks.; results maintained
systematic desensitization vs. cognitive modification vs. no-treatment control	8	8 wks.	behavioral test; self-report of anxiety; grades	cognitive modification =systematic desensitization > no-treatment control	1 mo.

Table 2 cont.

Name	Diagnosis	No.	Sex	Age	Other	Description	No.
			Patient			Therapist	
Mitchell & Ng, 1972	test anxiety	30	–	–	college students	unspecified	–
Osterhouse, 1972	test anxiety	54	–	–	college students	psychologists	2
Prochaska, 1971	test anxiety	61	all M	–	college students	audio tape	–
Smith & Nye, 1973	test anxiety	34	18F 16M	–	college students	graduate students	4
Sherman, 1972	aquaphobia	54	all F	17–19	college students	graduate students	11

Treatment			Outcomes		
Type	No. Sessions	Total Duration	Assessment Procedure	Results	Follow-up
systematic desensitization vs. group counseling vs. systematic desensitization & counseling vs. no-treatment control	9	9 wks.	self-report of anxiety; grades; study habits	systematic desensitization + counseling > systematic desensitization > counseling= no-treatment control	23 wks.
systematic desensitization vs. study skills training vs. no-treatment control	6	6 wks.	self-report of anxiety; behavioral test	systematic desensitization > no-treatment control=skill training (for anxiety reduction only)	none
implosion (symptoms) vs. implosion (dynamics) vs. implosion (general axiety) vs. attention control vs. no-treatment control	3	3 wks.	grades; self-report of anxiety	implosion (symptoms)= implosion (dynamics) > other groups	12 wks.
systematic desensitization vs. implosion vs. no-treatment control	7	3½ wks.	self-report of anxiety; behavioral test; grades	systematic desensitization =implosion > no-treatment control; systematic desensitization > implosion (for grades only)	1 academic quarter for grades only
systematic desensitization vs. predesensitization vs. no-treatment controls (with or without repeated exposures)	3–10	—	self-report of anxiety; behavioral test	repeated exposures > no repeated exposures	4 wks.

Table 2 cont.

Name	Patient					Therapist	
	Diagnosis	No.	Sex	Age	Other	Description	No.
Ritter, 1969 (b)	acro-phobia	22	13F 9M	$\bar{x}$=36.9 14–49	self-referrals	female	1
McReynolds & Tori, 1972	wounds, blood, surgery	28	all F	–	college students	unspecified	–
Richardson & Suinn, 1973	math anxiety	52	37F 15M	–	college students	–	–
Suinn & Richardson, 1971	math anxiety	143	–	–	college students	–	–

Treatment			Outcomes		
Type	No. Sessions	Total Duration	Assessment Procedure	Results	Follow-up
contact systematic desensitization vs. modeling + behavior rehearsal vs. modeling	1	35 min.	self-report of anxiety; behavioral test	contact systematic desensitization > modeling + behavioral rehearsal > modeling. Only in contact systematic desensitization, fear reduced significantly from pre to post	none
systematic desensitization vs. relaxation vs. no-treatment control	1	50 min.	self-report of anxiety; behavioral test	systematic desensitization > relaxation & no-treatment control	none
systematic desensitization vs. massed systematic desensitization vs. no-treatment control	2–9	2–3 wks.	self-rating of anxiety; behavioral test	systematic desensitization =massed desensitization > no-treatment control; no difference between groups on behavioral test	none
systematic desensitization vs. anxiety management training vs. no-treatment control	3	—	self-report; math aptitude test	both treatment groups only showed reductions in anxiety; systematic desensitization led to aptitude improvement	none

Table 2 cont.

Name	Patient					Therapist	
	Diagnosis	No.	Sex	Age	Other	Description	No.
Graff *et al.*, 1971	school-related anxiety	84	31F 53M	–	college students	graduate students	4

Type 2B: Psychotherapist 1 vs. psychotherapist 2 for patients X

Name	Diagnosis	No.	Sex	Age	Other	Description	No.
Donner & Guerney, 1969; Donner, 1970	test anxiety	28	all F	–	college students	psychologist	1
Kahn & Baker, 1968	social anxiety, acrophobia, test anxiety	16	–	–	college students	graduate student	7

Type 2C: Psychotherapy A for patients X vs. patients Y

Name	Diagnosis	No.	Sex	Age	Other	Description	No.
McMillan & Osterhouse, 1972	test anxiety	20	–	–	10 Ss high on general anxiety; 10 Ss low on general anxiety	unspecified	–

Treatment			Outcomes		
Type	No. Sessions	Total Duration	Assessment Procedure	Results	Follow-up
systematic desensitiza- tion vs. ex- tinction vs. no-treatment control vs. attention control	11	4 wks.	test anx- iety scales	systematic de- sensitization = extinction > no-treatment control = attention control	2 mos.; results main- tained
systematic desensitization (therapist present) vs. systematic desensitization (therapist ab- sent) vs. no- treatment control	8	7 + wks.	grades; self-report scale of anxiety	systematic de- sensitization (therapist pre- sent) = system- atic desensiti- zation (thera- pist absent) > no-treatment control	5 mos; system- atic de- sensiti- zation (ther- apist present) → great- er im- proved grades
systematic desensitization (therapist present) vs. systematic desensitization (therapist ab- sent)	12	6 hrs.	self-report of anxiety	systematic de- sensitization present = systematic de- sensitization absent (both improved)	none
systematic desensitization	3	6 hrs. (3 wks.)	self-report of anxiety; grades	low general anxiety > high general anxiety for grades only	none

Table 2 cont.

	Patient				Therapist	
Name	Diagnosis	No. Sex	Age	Other	Description	No.

Level 3. Bidifferential prescriptions
  Type 3A: Psychotherapy A vs. psychotherapy B for patients X vs. patients Y

Boulougouris *et al.*, 1971	agora-phobia, specific phobias	16	7M 9F	–	"severe phobias" 11 out-patients, 5 inpatients	psychiatrists, residents, medical students	10
Solyom *et al.*, 1971	agora-phobia, specific phobias	20	13F 7M	$\bar{x}=35$	18 out-patients, 2 inpatients	psychiatrists	3
DiLoreto, 1971	inter-personal anxiety	100	58F 42M	18.8 19.3	college students	experience 1½ – 4 years	6

Treatment			Outcomes		
Type	No. Sessions	Total Duration	Assessment Procedure	Results	Follow-up
systematic de-sensitization vs. flooding (cross-over design)	12	5 wks.	t ratings; self-report of anxiety; physiol. measures	flooding > systematic de-sensitization in reducing anxiety; systematic desen-sitization best for specific phobias than agoraphobias. Flooding better for agoraphobias & = to sys-tematic de-sensitization with specific phobias	1 yr.; changes main-tained
aversion relief vs. systematic desensitization	$\bar{x}=34$	22 wks.	t ratings; psycho-metric tests; self-report of anxiety	aversion relief best with Ss high on obsessive, hysterical, hypo-chondriacal symptoms. Sys-tematic desen-sitization best with high anxious Ss	none
systematic de-sensitization vs. rational emotive vs. relationship therapy vs. atten-tion control vs. no-treatment control	—	11 hrs.	self-report of anxiety; t ratings	all treatments > controls; re-lationship better with introverts; rational emotive better with ex-troverts; sys-tematic desen-sitization equal-ly effective with introverts or extroverts	3 mos.; changes main-tained

OBSESSIVE-COMPULSIVE NEUROSIS

This neurotic syndrome refers to individuals who experience either intrusive and persistent thoughts that seriously impair daily decision making or to individuals who are plagued with irresistible urges that impel repetitive and ritualistic behaviors. While obsessional ruminations may occur in conjunction with compulsive acts, one clinical feature may predominate with an absence of the other. With obsessions, the mode of symptom expression is ideational in nature and may take the manifest form of either "obsessive thoughts" or "obsessive doubts." Obsessive thoughts are repetitive ideas that persistently intrude into consciousness. They usually consist of either forbidden and personally unacceptable sexual and aggressive wishes or involve affectless and seemingly meaningless thoughts which nevertheless command the individual's exclusive attention. Obsessive doubting is characterized by states of perpetual indecision, feelings of uncertainty, and prolonged periods of brooding about the inappropriateness of past decisions. The counterpart to obsessive doubting is compulsive ritualistic behavior (Buss, 1966). These stereotyped behavioral sequences appear to be maintained by the anxiety reduction which accompanies their occurrence and the heightened discomfort experienced when the individual resists the temptation to perform the ritual.

In a less symptomatic and diagnostic sense, the term "obsessive-compulsive" has also been used to describe a particular style of thinking, perceiving, and feeling (Shapiro, 1965). Such individuals are characterized by a rigidity of thinking, narrowly focus their attention to technical details, tend to be obstinate and lack spontaneity, and appear to live under self-imposed directives about what should and should not be done, wanted, felt, and thought. Although specific recurrent obsessions or compulsions may be absent, psychotherapy patients with an obsessive-compulsive character structure exhibit the same essential paralyzing indecisiveness of the obsessive-compulsive (symptom) neurotics.

Currently, there is a limited amount of research which speaks to the effective use of psychological treatments of either the symptomatic or the characterologic forms of the obsessive-compulsive syndrome. Kringlen (1965) found that most obsessional neurotics received a somatic form of therapy, particularly electroconvulsive treatment (ECT), and attributed this to the prevalent view that psychotherapy is of limited use with this type of patient. However, research data bearing on the relative effectiveness of ECT does not support its prescriptive use with obsessive neurotics. Table 3 summarizes the treatment outcomes of various forms of therapy in 100 cases of obsessional neurosis (Grimshaw, 1965). As shown, approximately 50% of the cases which received ECT reported improvement, while the other 50% remained either unchanged or became worse. This contrasts with an improvement rate of 66% following one to four years of insight-oriented (nonpsychoanalytic) psycho-

Table 3. Outcomes of 100 cases of obsessional neurotics following different forms of treatment, as reported by Grimshaw (1965).

Treatment	Number of Cases	Outcome
ECT	31	9 much improved 7 improved 15 unchanged or worse
Systematic psychotherapy	14	5 much improved 4 improved 5 unchanged
Supportive psychotherapy	36	15 much improved 9 improved 12 unchanged or worse
Leucotomy	3	1 much improved 2 unchanged
No treatment	16	11 much improved 5 unchanged or worse

therapy and 64% following supportive psychotherapy (e.g., reassurance, discussions of current problems, etc). It should be noted that both forms of psychotherapy were conducted in conjunction with the use of tranquilizing drugs and sedatives. Despite the higher rates of improvement following psychotherapy, the percentage of patients reporting either improvement or "deterioration" is highly similar to the baserates in these categories of obsessional patients who did not receive any specific form of treatment. Thus, while improvement cannot be attributed to either form of psychological treatment, these data clearly speak against the widespread use of ECT in the management of obsessional neurosis.

Two psychodynamic approaches that have received some empirical documentation are Frankl's Logotherapy technique of "paradoxical intention" and short-term psychoanalytic psychotherapy. Conclusions about the effectiveness of either type of psychodynamic therapy must be viewed as highly tentative since the analyses upon which the results are based are derived from an accumulation of case studies, conducted in the absence of comparison controls or differentially treated groups. For example, Sifneos (1966) described a psychoanalytically oriented short-term psychotherapy for the treatment of mild obsessional neurotics. The therapy was designed to be "anxiety-provoking" and emphasized specific areas of emotional conflict related to the patient's presenting symptoms, with the goal of providing insight into the patient's defenses as well as fostering alternative ways of coping with anxiety. Some of the specific ingredients of the therapy involved: (a) keeping the transference relationship positive by confronting the patient's expressions of resistance, in an attempt to teach how feelings for the therapist are duplications of past feelings for other people, (b) concentrating on areas of unresolved conflicts so as to foster an understanding of the defenses used to avoid anxiety, (c) avoiding both longstanding characterological problems and the development of negative transference issues, and (d) emphasizing how the patient's difficulties in interpersonal relations derive from the ambivalent attitudes acquired during the Oedipal situation. Unfortunately, the results of the treatment were presented in vague, subjective, and impressionistic terms, with references to "positive changes in the patients' attitude toward their symptoms, improved self-esteem, but with minimal alterations in their symptomatology." These findings are consistent with the generally limited and unimpressive changes following "supportive" or "insight-oriented" psychotherapy with obsessional patients as reported by Grimshaw (1965) and support the position that the effectiveness of such approaches in altering specific obsessional behaviors with these patients has yet to be demonstrated empirically.

Gerz (1966) reported that "paradoxical intention," when used in the context of psychodynamic psychotherapy and tranquilizing drugs (e.g., imipramine, chlordiazepoxide, diazepam), was correlated with the successful outcome of four out of six obsessive-compulsive neurotics. In this approach the therapist attempts to gain control of the therapeutic relationship by ordering the patient to engage in his symptoms. This maneuver is designed to place the patient in a "therapeutic double-bind" (Haley, 1963). If the symptom occurs, the patient is viewed as following the therapist's instructions but the secondary gains derived from the symptoms remain unsatisfied; on the other hand, if the patient does not engage in the symptom, despite defying the therapist's instructions, the reduced occurrence of the problematic behavior is seen as a positive therapeutic gain. Victor and Krug (1967) reported a single case study involving the exclusive use of paradoxical intention in the treatment of compulsive gambling. Although the patient was able to stop his compulsive gambling for the first time in 20 years, he also reported feelings of agitation, a desire for alternate forms of sensual arousal, and he began to masturbate frequently.

Behavior therapy approaches have attempted to habituate the patient to the discomforting situations associated with the compulsive behaviors. Rachman, Hodgson, and Marks (1971) and Hodgson, Rachman, and Marks (1972) found that *"in vivo"* desensitization and flooding, either applied alone or in combination, produced significantly more improvement than muscular relaxation with obsessive-compulsive neurotics. In the flooding condition, patients entered highly disturbing situations for progressively longer periods of time but were encouraged to refrain from carrying out the compulsive rituals. Patients provided with *"in vivo"* desensitization were encouraged to gradually enter each of a hierarchically arranged series of disturbing situations during which the patient imitated the therapist's nonavoidance and nonritualistic behaviors. With hospitalized obsessive-compulsive patients, an important adjunct to the successful transfer of treatment to nonclinical settings involved the participation of the patient's relatives in providing support and encouragement for alternative noncompulsive behaviors and nonreinforcement of behaviors associated with compulsiveness.

In summary, treatments such as *paradoxical intention, "in vivo" desensitization, flooding* that specifically focus on eliminating the sources of motivation that maintain an individual's compulsive rituals (e.g., guilt, anxiety) and also provide reinforced opportunities to engage in alternative, noncompulsive behaviors have been shown to be of therapeutic value with obsessive-compulsive neurotics. This conclusion pertains exclusively to the management of compulsive acts, since there is an absence of controlled therapy outcome studies which evaluate the modification of obsessive ruminations. However, several case studies employing behavioral approaches such as thought-stopping (Stern, 1970) and altering the patient's expectations (Meyer, 1966) suggest possible useful techniques for the treatment of obsessions.

Table 4. OBSESSIVE-COMPULSIVE NEUROSIS

| Name | Patient | | | | | Therapist | |
	Diagnosis	No. Sex	Age	Other		Description	No.

Level 1. Nondifferential prescriptions
  Type 1A: Psychotherapy A for patients X

Gerz, 1966	obsessive-compulsive	6	–	–	–	unspecified	–
Kringlen, 1965	obsessive-compulsive	122	55M 67F	x̄=34	x̄ duration of hospital-ization = 2.1 mos.	unspecified	–
Sifneos, 1966	obsessive-compulsive	un-spec-fied	–	–	acute, high motivation to change, above average IQ	psychiatrist	–

Level 2. Unidifferential prescriptions
  Type 2A: Psychotherapy A vs. psychotherapy B for patients X

Grimshaw, 1965	obsessive-compulsive	100	–	–	nonpsychotic	unspecified	–
Hodgson, et. al., 1972	obsessive-compulsive	5	4F 1M	x̄=32	x̄ duration of symptoms = 8 yrs.	unspecified	–
Ingram, 1961	obsessive-compulsive	64	–	–	hospitalized inpatients	unspecified	

Treatment			Outcomes		
Type	No. Sessions	Total Duration	Assessment Procedure	Results	Follow-up
paradoxical intention + drugs + psychodynamic therapy	–	6 yrs.	t ratings	4 recovered, 2 improved significantly	unspecified
electroconvulsive shock	–	–	t ratings	50% unchanged, 35% slightly improved, 9% improved, 5% worse	30 yrs.; ₁6 became psychotic
short-term psychoanalysis	–	–	t ratings	little behavior change in symptoms; no longer bothered by symptoms	unspecified
insight psychotherapy vs. supportive psychotherapy vs. leucotomy vs. electroconvulsive shock vs. no-treatment control	–	–	t ratings	no difference in social adaptation between groups; 64% improved across treatments	6 mos.– ₁14 yrs. ($\bar{x}$=5.08 yrs)
in vivo desensitization + flooding vs. *in vivo* desensitization vs. flooding	30	6 wks.	t ratings; patient self-report of anxiety	*in vivo* desensitization + flooding> either alone	6 mos.
leucotomy vs. hospitalization alone	–	–	t ratings	leucotomy > hospitalization alone	5.9 yrs.

HYSTERIA

The psychotherapy outcome literature with hysterical patients beyond single case-study reports (e.g.; Beyme, 1964; Malmo, 1970; Meichenbaum, 1966) consists exculsively of groups of patients provided with a relatively uniform set of therapeutic conditions. These "compiled case-studies," summarized in Table 5, were conducted in the absence of any type of comparison control condition and are therefore structurally comparable to individual case documentations. Thus, because of the complete confounding of patient, therapist, and treatment ingredients inherent in these studies (i.e., psychotherapy A for patients X), prescriptive statements in this area are currently precluded.

DEPRESSION

In contrast to the extensive body of literature describing the causes and expressions of depression (e.g., Beck, 1967), there currently exists only a limited amount of empirically based research on psychotherapeutic treatments with this problem. The bulk of the therapy outcome literature in this area converges on the potentially effective use of *contingency management* procedures which serve to increase the rate of positive reinforcement contingent upon the occurrence of socially constructive and skilled behaviors. In this regard, the pioneering work by Lewinsohn and his associates (e.g., Lewinsohn & Atwood, 1969; Lewinsohn & Shaffer, 1971) is most promising. Briefly, this approach involves a dynamic and functional relationship between a behavioral assessment of the typical interaction patterns that produce low rates of positive reinforcement in the patient's home environment and the occurrence of behavioral indices of depression. On the basis of this analysis, treatment goals are defined and mutually agreed-upon procedures are instigated. These procedures are designed to reinstate denser schedules of positive reinforcement for successive approximations to socially skilled behaviors.

The efficacy of directive and active forms of intervention with neurotic depressives is further supported by the recent findings of Weissman and his associates (1974). These investigators reported on the beneficial effects of a *supportive psychotherapy* which were evidenced in the social adjustment of depressed female outpatients. Supportive therapy involved the identification of current practical and interpersonal problems, with the therapist recommending alternative and more adaptive (i.e., reinforcing) patterns of coping with the problematical situations. In its essential respects, this form of supportive treatment is comparable to the problem-solving orientation which characterizes the contingency management approaches. In addition, the effects of drugs (100-150 mg/day, amitriptyline hydrochloride) did not interact with the effects of psychotherapy, and "drugs did not have a negative effect on psychotherapy and psychotherapy did not have an adverse effect on the symptom reduction achieved by drugs" (Weissman *et al.*, 1974, p. 777). While supportive psychotherapy specifically improved the patient's work performance and reduced the interpersonal frictions, the anxious ruminations, and the inhibited communications previously experienced by the patients, these improvements in social adjustment were absent in patients maintained exclusively on drugs. Significantly, these positive gains did not emerge until six to eight months of treatment, suggesting that this form of supportive psychotherapy to improve depressed patients' interpersonal relations should not be viewed as "short-term" in nature.

Table 5. HYSTERIA

Name	Patient					Therapist	
	Diagnosis	No.	Sex	Age	Other	Description	No.
Bhattacharyya & Singh, 1971	hysterical fits	8	3M 5F	teen-age (married women)	Indian; fits leading to unconscious-ness once/day, only in presence of relatives	unspecified	1
Powers, 1972	hysterical personality	13	all F	17–34	married and unmarried	psychiatric social worker	1
Woolson & Swanson, 1972	hysterical personality	4	all F	23,23, 26,47	tense, suicidal ideation; 3 married	female	1

Treatment			Outcomes		
Type	No. Sessions	Total Duration	Assessment Procedure	Results	Follow-up
electric shock during and after each fit and withdrawal of social reinforcement (attention)	49–62	–	behavior	all Ss had no fits for 7 consecutive days & therapist unable to produce a fit by electric shock	6 mos.; 2 Ss had one fit upon returning home; 6 Ss had no fits
short-term psychoanalytic psychotherapy	1–2 sessions/wk.	8–10 mos.	t ratings	"minimal behavior change to successful personality change toward emotional maturity"	none
substituting specific alternative behaviors in place of problematical and ineffectual behaviors; training in operant conditioning procedures	–	about 4 mos.	t ratings	increase in "the use of more acceptable behavior, more capacity for affection, less frigidity, and ... more self assurance ..."	none

Table 6. DEPRESSION

Name	Patient					Therapist	
	Diagnosis	No.	Sex	Age	Other	Description	No.

Level 1. Nondifferential prescriptions
  Type 1A: Psychotherapy A for patients X

Burgess, 1969	neurotic depression	6	all M	18,18, 19,21, 26,40	all anxious about in- ability to perform; outpatients at coun- seling setting	author	1
Hersen *et at.*, 1973	neurotic depression	3	all M	32,53, 54	VA in- patients	–	–
Lazarus, 1968	neurotic (reactive) depression	11	–	–	–	author	1
Lewinsohn & Shaffer, 1971	neurotic depression	3	2M 1F	20,28, 28	out- patients	–	5
Shipley & Fazio, 1973 (Exp.I)	depression	22	–	–	college student volunteers; diagnosed by standardized rating scales of depression	graduate student	1

Treatment			Outcomes		
Type	No. Sessions	Total Duration	Assessment Procedure	Results	Follow-up
operant conditioning (fading task complexity, contingency management)	−	3 wks.	t ratings of improvement	all Ss able to perform in their life situations	6−9 mos.; 4 Ss symptom-free, 2 Ss remained in therapy
token economy (reinforcement for work behaviors)	−	16 days	behavioral ratings (talking, smiling, motor activity)	increase in nondepressive behaviors and decrease in depressive behaviors	none
time projection	1	−	t ratings	"6 responded excellently, 2 improved moderately, 3 unimproved"	none
operant conditioning (increasing the rate of positive reinforcement in interpersonal relations in the S's home)	−	3 mos. maximum	behavioral ratings of interpersonal interactions; self-report (mood) questionnaire	all Ss shown to be on a low schedule of positive reinforcement; increases in positive interpersonal reinforcement led to decreases in depression in 2 cases reported	none
problem solving (recommending alternative actions) vs. no-treatment control	1 hr. (No. unspecified	3 wks.	MMPI; self-ratings	problem solving > no-treatment control	none

Table 6 cont.

Name	Diagnosis	No.	Sex	Age	Other	Description	No.
		Patient				Therapist	

Level 2. Unidifferential prescriptions
  Type 2A: Psychotherapy A vs. psychotherapy B for patients X

Name	Diagnosis	No.	Sex	Age	Other	Description	No.
Shipley & Fazio, 1973 (Exp.II)	depression	27	–	–	same as Exp.I	graduate student	1
Weissman et al., 1974	neurotic depression (moderate)	106	all F	25–60 ($\bar{x}$=39)	depression at least 2 wks. in duration; nonschizo-phrenic, alcoholic, drug addict, subnormal IQ; working + lower-middle SES	psychiatric social workers; experienced	5

Treatment			Outcomes		
Type	No. Sessions	Total Duration	Assessment Procedure	Results	Follow-up
problem solving + high expectancy for success vs. problem solving alone vs. interest-support controls (high vs. no expectancy for success)	3	3 wks.	MMPI; self-ratings	no effect for expectancy; problem solving > interest-support control	none
supportive psychotherapy (hi contact) vs. brief interviews (lo contact); both combined with either amitriptyline drug, placebo, or no medication	1-2/wk.	8 mos.	social adjustment scale (work performance, interpersonal, communication, dependency, family anxiety)	no effect of drug treatment at 4 or 8 mos.; supportive therapy > brief interviews after 8 mos. of treatment	none

Psychophysiological Disorders

BRONCHIAL ASTHMA

Experimental analyses pertaining to the relative effectiveness of the psychotherapeutic treatment of the asthmatic patient have centered on procedures designed to attenuate the patient's emotional responsiveness. Training in muscular relaxation has been shown to correlate with improved respiration (Alexander, 1972; Alexander *et al.*, 1972; British Tuberculosis Association, 1968), particularly with patients that are nonreactive to subdermal injections of allergins and whose asthma appears primarily under the control of identifiable situational, affective, or cognitive factors (Philip *et al.*, 1972). The cumulative evidence suggests, however, that *systematic desensitization* is differentially most effective for the treatment of asthma (Moore, 1965; Moorefield, 1971). The most impressive findings, in terms of both experimental design and therapy outcome, have been provided by Moore (1965). She found that systematic desensitization, emphasizing hierarchies related to an asthmatic attack, an allergic attack, and a stressful situation, was more successful than relaxation training or suggestions about being relaxed in improving the "maximum peak flow," especially after five weeks of treatment.

ULCERATIVE COLITUS

Although the amount of outcome research with this disorder is quite meager, there are some intriguing, yet highly tentative results which speak to the potential role of psychotherapy in the treatment of ulcerative colitus. The most comprehensive, systematic, and prescriptively relevant research in this area has been conducted by Karush and his associates (1969) and O'Connor and his associates (1964). These investigators have analyzed the interrelationships of selected patient and therapist factors in the psychoanalytic treatment of ulcerative colitus. From their extensive and complex series of research reports at the Psychoanalytic Clinic for Training and Research at Columbia University's College of Physicians and Surgeons, we may begin to identify possible specific active ingredients that contribute to the successful outcomes of psychoanalytic treatments with colitus patients. A summary, derived and abstracted from this research, of these potential ingredients is outlined in

Table 7. The first column indicates the classification of colitus patients according to their predominant affective styles of feelings displayed toward significant others. A detailed description of these various types is found in the study by Karush and his associates (1969). Briefly, the Symbiotic patients appear ". . .as more or less helpless victims of others, . . .they are likely to brood and to blame others for their own shortcomings and frustrations, . . .the general appearance they give when disturbed is that of chronic depression embedded in a passive attitude of resignation and even apathy, and . . .paranoid thinking about others is often present" (Karush *et al.*, 1969, p. 212). In contrast, Individuated patients ". . .act as though they have a natural right to influence and control their environment according to their own wishes . . .and feel powerful and omnipotent and justified in trying to manipulate persons important to them, and . . .the failure to achieve their aims tends to produce varying degrees of depression and anxiety" (Karush *et al.*, 1969, p. 210). Finally, the Transitional patients present mixtures of both individuated and symbiotic attitudes without a distinct predominance of either. All three groups may be further subdivided in terms of characteristic styles of emotional reactivity as primarily labile, constricted, or a combination of both. The therapists were approximately evenly divided as active or passive, and this dimension was shown to be related to patient factors and to therapeutic effectiveness. In this regard, it was found that nonpsychotic patients showed more somatic improvement with active therapists while passive therapists produced greater improvement in psychotic patients. In addition, the therapist's interest, empathy, and hopefulness or optimism together emerged as a nonspecific active ingredient, correlating .90 with somatic improvement across the different patient types. In general, the patients who improved the most and exhibited enduring somatic changes were those who were most hopeful about being helped and entered into a relationship in which the therapist communicated high levels of interest, empathy, and optimism. Another therapist characteristic which significantly related to positive therapeutic gains was the ability to remain patient, accepting, and noncritical despite fluctuations in the patient's moods and temperaments. Together these relationship-enhancing factors bear a striking resemblance to the ingredients identified by Rogers (1957) as the necessary and sufficient conditions for therapeutic change.

The emergence of differential relationships between patient characteristics and various forms of intervention suggest the operation of specific active ingredients in addition to the nonspecific relationship factors discussed above. Interpretations focused on the analysis of unconscious aggressive and libidinal motivations, on resistances and the patient's characterological defenses, and on

---

*All Karush quotes on this and following page from A. Karush, G. E. Danials, J. F. O'Connor, and L. O. Stern. The response to psychotherapy in chronic ulcerative colitis. *Psychosomatic Medicine*, 1969, **31**, 201–226.

Table 7. Suggested Specific and Nonspecific Active Ingredients in the Psychoanalytic Treatment of Ulcerative Colitis.

Patient Factors	Therapist Factors	Treatment	Outcomes
Object Relations:	*Activity Level:*	*Interventions:*	*Somatic Improvement*
Symbiotic	Active - talkative,	Interpretations	
labile	directive		*Psychological Improvement:*
constricted		Support, catharsis,	
mixed	Passive - nondirective,	suggestions	ego strength
	quiet		moods (depression)
Individual		Environmental	anger, helplessness
labile	*Attitudes:*	manipulation	adaptability to environment
constricted	Interest		(family, work, marriage)
mixed		*Duration*	object attitudes and
	Empathy		relationships
Transitional		*Intensity*	
labile	Hopefulness		
constricted			
mixed	Noncritical		
	Tolerance		

the transference relationship. This form of intervention was most effective with individuated and transitional patients but totally ineffectual with symbiotic patients. The most productive form of psychoanalytically oriented therapy of symbiotic patients involved support and suggestions about possible alternative constructions of reality. "The symbiotic patient is helped most by the therapist who permits a strongly dependent transference to develop and who accepts an attitude of complaining helplessness without criticism, who empathizes with and tacitly encourages whatever feelings the patient can express" (Karush *et al.*, 1969, p. 216). Only until such a relationship existed was catharsis found to be beneficial with symbiotic patients. In general, "the more the patients were capable of individuated and self-reliant behavior, the more likely was abreaction of strong feelings to be followed by a remission of the colitis" (Karush *et al.*, 1969, p. 217). In contrast to the differential effects of interpretations and support, direct environmental manipulations in the form of intervention in the patient's family, school, or work life were unrelated to enduring somatic or psychological improvement. Rather, improvements in these various sectors of the patient's life were found to correlate significantly with the degree and duration of somatic improvement which, in turn, related positively to the duration and frequency of therapy.

In conclusion, these results, as well as those of Weinstock (1962), support the position that *psychoanalytically oriented psychotherapies* are prescribed for the treatment of ulcerative colitis patients who are relatively well differentiated (individuated and transitional) in their object relations and are attempting to remain independent in their interpersonal relations. For colitis patients who are overly dependent and symbiotic in their interpersonal relations, a supportive or *nondirective psychotherapy* appears most appropriate. Of particular interest is the possibility that direct manipulation of environmental contingencies, which characterizes the operant conditioning approaches to behavior modification, in particular, may be proscribed for the treatment of ulcerative colitis.

HYPERTENSION AND HYPERTENSIVE HEADACHES

Despite vast differences between hypertension and hypertensive headaches (e.g., Alexander & Flagg, 1965), recent advances in the domain of *biofeedback* have consistently provided the most positive results in the treatment of these disorders (e.g., Bensen *et al.*, 1971; Budzynski *et al.*, 1969; Shapiro *et al.*, 1970). In general, the biofeedback techniques involve the application of two fundamental principles of operant conditioning: (a) immediate knowledge of results, and (b) response shaping. For example, Budzynski, Stoyva, and Adler (1969) provided tension headache patients with audio feedback indicating the state of the muscle action potentials in their forehead area. Low frequency tones were presented whenever the frontalis muscle was relaxed and higher frequency tones signaled whenever the frontalis was tense. Gradually the task requirements were made progressively more difficult so that greater degrees of muscle relaxation were required to maintain low tonal frequencies. In addition, a gradually increasing number of no-feedback trials were interspersed among the feedback trials to enhance transfer of the training effects to situations not including the feedback tones. The same essential procedure and principles have been successfully applied to the reduction of blood pressure (Shapiro *et al.*, 1970), although the clinical research literature has not, as yet, established the reliability, generality, and endurance of the effects of biofeedback training.

MIGRAINE

The migraine syndrome is characterized by periodically reoccurring severe headaches which originate unilaterally but become more diffuse as the attack persists. The initial pain may be accompanied by feelings of irritability, nausea, photophobia, and by prodromal disturbances of scotomata, paresthesia, and speech difficulty (Wolff, 1948). The physiological mechanisms that appear to mediate migraine attacks relate to an initial vasoconstriction of cerebral and cranial arteries followed by a vasodilation of these vessels. Thus, Ergot and other vasoconstrictive drugs usually produce relief of pain following the initial prodromal phase of migraine attacks.

Successful psychotherapeutic interventions of migraines have employed "self-control" procedures designed to teach the patient means of regulating autonomic nervous system functioning, which may possibly mediate the vascular or emotional components of the attacks. This has been accomplished principally through the use of either *autogenic training* (e.g., Sargent *et al.*, 1973; Shultz & Luthe, 1969) or *systematic desensitization* (e.g., Mitchell, 1971a). Autogenic training has been effective in preventing attacks and in interrupting their onset by having patients perform autogenic exercises when the prodromal symptoms begin to appear. For example, the autogenetic handwarming exercise, which serves to increase blood flow in the hands, has been shown to be 80% effective in ameliorating migraine reactions (Sargent *et al.*, 1973). Systematic desensitization combined with assertion training shows initial promise in reducing migraine headaches as well as problems related to interpersonal relations in general (Mitchell, 1971a, 1971b).

Table 8. PSYCHOPHYSIOLOGICAL DISORDERS

	Patient					Therapist	
Name	Diagnosis	No.	Sex	Age	Other	Description	No.

Level 1. Nondifferential prescriptions
 Type 1A: Psychotherapy A for patients X

Alexander, 1972	asthma	25	14M 11F	10–15	residents of treatment centers	experienced	3
Alexander *et al.*, 1972	asthma	36	18M 18F	10–15	residents of treatment center	experienced	3
Collison, 1968	asthma	20	13M 7F	$\bar{x}$=26	nonhospitalized	unspecified	–
Moorefield, 1971	asthma	9	6M 3F	13–47; $\bar{x}$=27	$\bar{x}$ duration = 5.3 yrs.	unspecified	–
Weiss *et al.*, 1970	asthma	16	10M 6F	12–14	children, residential treatment center ($\bar{x}$=7 mos.)	unspecified	–
Karush *et al.*, 1969	ulcerative colitis	30	–	–	chronic; moderate-severe; 1 prior hospitalization	psychoanalytically trained psychiatrists	47
O'Connor *et al.*, 1964	ulcerative colitis	57	32F 25M	–	$\bar{x}$ duration = 15 yrs.	psychiatrist	1

Treatment			Outcomes		
Type	No. Sessions	Total Duration	Assessment Procedure	Results	Follow-up
relaxation vs. no-treatment control (own control design)	10	2 wks.	peak expiratory flow rates (PEFR)	increase in peak expiratory flow rates (PEFR) across sessions during relaxation	none
relaxation vs. no treatment control	6	8 days	peak expiratory flow rates (PEFR)	relaxation > no-treatment control	
relaxation (hypnotic induction) + coping suggestions	1—21	14 wks.	behavior rating	11 Ss — no attacks; 5 Ss — less severe attacks; 4 Ss — unimproved	none
systematic desensitization + hypnosis	4—23 $\bar{x}=13.4$	—	behavior rating	all Ss returned to normal functioning	8 mos.— 2 yrs.; no relapses
suggestion	1	—	respiration rate	no change	none
psychoanalytically oriented psychotherapy	1—4/wk.	3 mos. minimum	t ratings	symptoms — 20 improved, 10 unimproved; adjustment — 23 improved, 7 unimproved	1—11 yrs. ($\bar{x}=5.8$ yrs.)
psychoanalytically oriented psychotherapy	variable	—	interview, t ratings (career, sexual, family, self-esteem functioning)	time in psychotherapy unrelated to physical improvement; duration & intensity of psychotherapy related to improvement	—

Table 8 cont.

Name	Patient					Therapist	
	Diagnosis	No.	Sex	Age	Other	Description	No.
Weinstock, 1962	ulcerative colitis	28	–	–	previously hospitalized	experienced psychoana- lysts	20
Sargent et al., 1973	migraine, tension headache	28	22F 6M	21–63	–	–	–
Budzynski et al., 1969	tension headaches	5	4F 1M	–	–	· unspecified	–
Bensen et al., 1971	hyper- **tensi**on	7	5M 2F	$\bar{x}=47.9$	paid $5/ session	unspecified	–
Glen, 1968	duodenal ulcers	45	37M 8F	$\bar{x}=28$	$\bar{x}$ duration 5 yrs.	psychi- atrists, physicians	–

Treatment			Outcomes		
Type	No. Sessions	Total Duration	Assessment Procedure	Results	Follow-up
psycho-analytically oriented psycho-therapy and classical psycho-analysis	1–4/wk.	1½–5 yrs.	behavioral symptoms, t ratings	classical psycho-analysis-10/14 Ss symptom free; psycho-analytically oriented psychotherapy – 12/14 symptom free; number & intensity of pretreatment symptoms negatively correlated with im-provement	3–18 yrs.; 79% symptom free
relaxation (autogenic)	–	1–22 $\bar{x}=7.7$	t ratings; self-reports	12/15 migraines improved, 3 un-improved; 2/4 tension headaches improved, 2 un-improved	none
biofeedback	2–3/wk.	4 wks.–2 mos.	self-report of head-ache fre-quency & intensity; EMG of frontalis	significant re-duction or elimination of headaches	2–3 mos.; results maintained
biofeedback (operant conditioning, shaping)	$\bar{x}=21.7$	–	blood pressure	5 Ss significant-ly decreased blood pressure	none
psycho-analysis vs. attention control	24 (therapy group only)	3 wks.–6 mos. (control group only)	acid output	psychoanalysis = attention control	12 mos.

Table 8 cont.

	Patient					Therapist	
Name	Diagnosis	No.	Sex	Age	Other	Description	No.

Level 2. Unidifferential prescriptions
  Type 2A: Psychotherapy A vs. psychotherapy B for patients X

British TB Association, 1968	asthma	176	–	10–60	minimum of 2 attacks in past year	physicians	–
Moore, 1965	asthma	12	–	–	6 adults; 6 children	experimenter	1
Grace *et al.*, 1954	ulcerative colitis	177	107F 70M	15–54	duration of disorder = 1 mo.– 10 yrs.	physicians	–
Mitchell, 1971 (b)	migraine	17	–	17–44	$\bar{x}$ frequency of attacks= 11.1/wk.	unspecified	–

Treatment			Outcomes		
Type	No. Sessions	Total Duration	Assessment Procedure	Results	Follow-up
hypnosis (auto) vs. relaxation	12	1 yr.	behavior (wheezing, broncho- dilator use)	males: hypnosis = relaxation (both improved); females: hypnosis > relaxation; experienced hypnotists > inexperienced hypnotists	none
systematic desensiti- zation vs. relaxation vs. relaxation and suggestions (crossover design)	1½ hr./ wk.	2 mos.	behavior (no attacks, ease of breathing, increased peak expir- atory flow rates)	systematic desensitiza- tion > relax- ation + suggestion = relaxation alone	none
direct psycho- therapy vs. diet + drugs	–	2 yrs.	mortality rate, oper- ation rate, rate of serious complica- tions	direct psycho- therapy > diet + drugs	none
systematic desensitiza- tion + assertive training vs. relaxation vs. no-treatment control	15	7–8	psychometric tests of anxiety & social adjust- ment; fre- quency of attacks	systematic desensitiza- tion + asser- tive training > relaxation = no-treatment control	16 wks.

Table 8 cont.

Name	Diagnosis	No.	Sex	Age	Other	Description	No.
		Patient				Therapist	

Type 2C: Psychotherapy A for patients X vs. patients Y

Name	Diagnosis	No.	Sex	Age	Other	Description	No.
Brown & Bettley, 1971	eczema	72	–	18–65	duration = 6 wks.– 3 yrs.	psychiatrist; dermatolo- gist	2
Phillip et al., 1972	asthma	20	–	14–49	outpatients; intrinsic (I) asthmatics vs. extrin- sic (E) asthmatics	unspecified	–

Treatment			Outcomes		
Type	No. Sessions	Total Duration	Assessment Procedure	Results	Follow-up
psychoanalysis + salve vs. relaxation + salve vs. salve alone	–	4–18	t ratings; self-reports	no difference between groups; psychological + dermatological treatment best with highly motivated Ss and those who had recent onset of other psychological symptoms	18 mos.
relaxation vs. no-treatment control	5	–	respiratory efficiency in response to irritant or neutral substances	I asthmatics benefited more from relaxation training than E asthmatics	–

Sexual Deviations

SEXUAL ORIENTATION DISTURBANCE

(Homosexuality) *

Research evidence concerning the outcomes of psychotherapy with homosexuals has clustered on the efficacy of either psychoanalysis or behavior therapies which employ a variety of aversive conditioning techniques. Ironically, both approaches are prescribed largely on the premise that homosexuality is motivated predominantly by anxiety associated with females (Barlow, 1973). Treatment, thus, becomes oriented toward eliminating these fears by reducing the attractiveness of males and by enhancing heterosexual arousal. The application of different aversive conditioning techniques by behavior therapists has attempted to modify specific motivational or arousal states that presumably mediate overt homosexual behaviors. For example, fear conditioning (e.g., McGuire & Vallance, 1964) attempts to specifically increase negative arousal (conditioned response – CR) to homosexual stimuli (conditioned stimuli – CSs) by pairing the CSs with unavoidable and inescapable electric shock (unconditional stimulus – UCS). The fear conditioning paradigm has also been used in combination with aversion relief training (e.g., Freund, 1960; Solyom & Miller, 1965; Thorpe *et al.,*1964). In this technique the termination of the aversive UCS is assumed to produce a state of "relief" which is paired with a heterosexual CS. In this fashion, the fear conditioning phase is designed to decrease the attraction to males (CSs) by supporting aversive CRs, while the aversion relief phase attempts to increase the attrac-

---

*The American Psychiatric Association recently voted to eliminate the "illness" designation of homosexuality by omitting the term from the *Diagnostic and Statistical Manual of Mental Disorders (DSM-II)*. In its place is substituted a new diagnostic category, "sexual orientation disturbance," which includes homosexuals who are in conflict about their sexual orientation and who want either to change it or learn how to more effectively accomodate to it. The present review, analysis, and presriptions are based on research which adopted the earlier conventional diagnostic category of "Homosexuality," and which did not differentiate between homosexuals who were or were not in conflict about their sexual identity. While the newer classification appears to be limited to homosexuals who are motivated to change, the extent to which the present conclusions are generalizable to this population must remain an empirical question.

tiveness to female CSs by associating them with the emotion of relief. Finally, a third form of aversive conditioning with homosexuals has adopted an escape-avoidance learning paradigm (Feldman & MacCulloch, 1965; MacCulloch & Feldman, 1967; Tanner, 1974). Briefly, in this procedure slides of males (CSs) that remain presented for more than eight seconds are followed by an escapable electric shock (UCS). However, if the patient makes the appropriate response which terminates the slide before eight seconds have elapsed, then the UCS is avoided. Periodically, female slides are presented concurrent with the anxiety relief which theoretically follows successful avoidance responses. The escape component is designed to decrease positive arousal to homosexual CSs and the active avoidance component is designed to increase positive arousal to heterosexual stimuli.

In contrast, psychoanalytic approaches have attempted to induce changes in homosexual behavior by providing the patient with insight into the unconscious processes by which females signal anxiety and the development of motives that maintain a generalized avoidance of adopting the masculine role (Bieber *et al.*, 1963; Curran & Parr, 1957; Ellis, 1956; Ovesey *et al.*, 1963; Woodward, 1958). According to Ellis (1956), the goal

> is not that of inducing the patient to forego all homosexual activity or desire... it is the exclusive or...obsessive...compulsiveness...the aim of psychotherapy is to free the confirmed homosexual from the fear or antagonism towards heterosexual relations and to enable him to have a satisfying love sex involvement with members of the other sex (p. 191).

Despite vast differences in treatment approaches, whether it be *a form of aversive conditioning or a psychoanalytically oriented psychotherapy*, each produces similar outcome effects. More specifically, the consequences of therapy usually are restricted to changes toward increased heterosexual arousal and thoughts, in the absence of a corresponding increase in heterosexual behavior. Fear conditioning, aversion relief, and avoidance learning procedures report "improved" arousal and cognitions to heterosexual stimuli in approximately 69% of the cases without apparent systematic differences between the different aversive conditioning techniques. Similarly, the nondifferential studies which assessed the effects of psychoanalysis indicated an average improvement rate of 64% in the arousal component of heterosexual responsiveness. Neither the aversive conditioning techniques nor psychoanalysis has marshaled evidence that a particular approach reliably produces changes in the overt social-behavioral component of heterosexual responsiveness.

The general finding that both aversive conditioning and psychoanalysis tend to produce an increase in heterosexual arousal in the absence of an increase in heterosexual behavior is actually consistent with the goals of treatment. In both orientations, efforts were directed toward altering mediating sources of arousal (e.g., fear of males) and cognition, assuming that reduced heterosexual fears will somehow result in increased heterosexual behavior. In light of the outcome results, the validity of this assumption is highly questionable. Rather, the results suggest that in addition to affecting motivational and cognitive changes, treatments should be responsive to the need to teach appropriate interpersonal heterosexual social skills. This is consistent with Barlow's (1972) recommendation that

> . . . heterosexual responsiveness is not a unitary concept, but actually consists of several distinct behavioral components. If this is the case, some combination of the above techniques . . . to instigate heterosexual arousal and social training to build heterosexual skills may constitute the most effective approach to the problem (p. 667).

Studies that directly compared the relative effectiveness of different treatments support the conclusion that fear conditioning, aversion relief training, and avoidance learning produce equivalent outcomes (Feldman & McCulloch, 1971; McConaghy, 1971; McConaghy & Barr, 1973). Each treatment is nondifferentially effective in increasing arousal to heterosexual cues but did not produce an increase in heterosexual social behaviors. The only direct comparison between aversive conditioning and a dynamic, insight-oriented psychotherapy has been reported by Feldman and McCulloch (1971). It was found that while fear conditioning and avoidance learning did not differ from each other in effectiveness, both were more effective in altering attitudes and arousal than 12 hours of a "psychotherapy" which principally explored and discussed with patients their attitudes toward females and associated personality difficulties. The limited duration of the "psychotherapy" and the numerous sources of confounding between the treatment and the one therapist that administered the treatment precludes even tentative conclusions about differential effectiveness based on this one investigation.

We may also examine characteristics of homosexual patients that have been associated with successful outcomes following different forms of therapy. The relationships between patient variables and the successful application of avoidance conditioning and psychoanalytic psychotherapies are summarized in Table 9. For both orientations, a patient's previous history, which contained pleasurable heterosexual interests and experiences, positively related with the successful outcome of treatment. Feldman and MacCulloch (1971) proposed that such an individual is more likely to experience cognitive dissonance about his sexual identity and thus is highly committed to the change process and the therapy enterprise. Consistent with this formulation is the finding by Bieber *et al.*, (1963) and Ellis (1956) that patients rated as most highly motivated to change improved the most following psychoanalytic psychotherapy.

Feldman and MacCulloch (1971) also found that the extent of "self-insecure personality" positively related to increases in heterosexual orientation following a psychoanalytically-based psychotherapy but was unrelated to out-

Table 9. Patient Characteristics Associated with Positive Treatment Outcomes of Homosexuality

Avoidance Conditioning	*Psychoanalytic Psychotherapy*
History of pleasurable heterosexual interests and experiences (Feldman & MacCulloch, 1971)	History of pleasurable heterosexual interests and experiences (Feldman & MacCulloch, 1971; Bieber *et al.*, 1963; Ellis, 1956) Self-insecure type – insecure, compulsive, self-blame (Feldman & MacCulloch, 1971) High motivation to change (Bieber *et al.*, 1963; Ellis, 1956)
Low anxiety or neuroticism (Feldman & MacCulloch, 1971)	
Low degree of conscientiousness (Feldman & MacCulloch, 1971)	

come when treatment involved either fear conditioning or avoidance learning. The self-insecure personality is described as displaying an

> increased impressionability, reduced power for active expression, pent-up working over of experience, chronic self-uncertainty, and self-blame ... obsessive or compulsive personalities are outwardly pedantic; correct, scrupulous, and yet inwardly exceedingly insecure. The self-insecure group as a whole is characterized by high standards with inner feelings of anxiety, guilt, inadequacy, and inferiority (p. 136).

Which ingredients in psychoanalytic psychotherapy interact with this patient variable is currently unknown but, should this relationship prove reliable, it certainly has important prescriptive implications.

ORGASMIC DYSFUNCTION

Frigidity

There is currently much ambiguity surrounding the meaning of the term "frigidity." Some writers have emphasized exclusively the relative infrequency of an orgasmic response as the crucial dimension defining frigidity. The infrequency, however, remains vague and may range from a complete absence of orgasms to an unspecified intermittent occurrence of orgasms. Others have taken into account the antecedent sources of stimulation under which orgasms may or may not occur with a particular woman. For example, Masters and Johnson (1970) have distinguished three forms of "situational orgasmic dysfunction" — masturbatory, coital, and random orgasmic inadequacy. A woman who is orgasmic during intercourse but not with other forms of sexual stimulation is "masturbatory orgasmic dysfunctional." "Coital orgasmic inadequacy" is reserved for women who may have orgasms with masturbation but not during intercourse. There are also women who irregularly and unpredictably experience orgasms during either masturbation or intercourse, or when on a vacation but never at home. This is called "random orgasmic inadequacy."

The more effective approaches to the treatment of each expression of orgasmic dysfunctioning have focused on the extinction of feelings, cognitions, and attitudes that serve to inhibit the woman's responsiveness to sexual stimulation. In this regard, *systematic desensitization* has been shown to be an effective and an efficient procedure for the removal of anxieties associated with sexual intimacy (Brady, 1966). It is particularly successful with introverted patients who, as Lazarus (1963) has shown, tend to express fears about sexual intercourse, whereas extroverted women tend to complain of vaginismus (an involuntary spastic contraction in the outer third of the vagina that usually prevents the woman from having sexual intercourse).

The most comprehensive, penetrating, and impressive findings, from both a clinical and scientific perspective, have emerged from *the treatment program developed by Masters and Johnson (1970)*. This program is based on their extensive analytical research in the "Human Sexual Response," and has been described thoroughly in their book, *Human Sexual Inadequacy*. It stands as the most ambitious attempt to treat the physiological, intrapsychical, and interpersonal dynamics that comprise the complex structure of sexual dysfunctioning. The treatment program involves a short-term (two weeks) educational and supportive psychotherapy effort that focuses on the marital relationship as the unit in need of change. The goal of eliminating specific manifestations of sexual dysfunctioning is accomplished by "dual-sex therapy teams" which provide each couple with information about the nature of sexual responsivity, made interpretations about the couple's communication problems and their fears of sexual performance, and guide the patients through a series of sensate exercises designed to convey an appreciation for the physical and psychological pleasures derivable through a mutual giving and getting of sensory stimulation.

> The marital partners learn that sexual function is not just a physical expression. It is touch, smell, sound, and sight, reflecting how men or women as sexual beings show what they feel and think, that bring responsive meaning to the sexual act (Masters & Johnson, 1970, p. 71).

The treatment of orgasmic dysfunctioning is oriented toward teaching each marital partner how to accommodate sexual behaviors so as to maximize responsiveness to erotic stimulation. For the woman, this may involve a graded series of sexual contacts with her husband which build upon her current positive erotic experiences evoked during their sexual activities. In turn, the husband learns to adjust his sexual expressions to conform within the latitudes of acceptance of his wife's sexual value system. In this fashion, each partner learns to be sensitive to and competent in providing the psychological and physiological requirements for giving and receiving the sexual stimulation which precedes orgasmic release. The specific techniques to accomplish these goals are discussed in detail by Masters and Johnson (1970).

The immediate results of treatment and the success obtained at a five-year follow-up are summarized in Table 10. The success rate in the treatment of primary and situational orgasmic dysfunctionings is similar, both immediately after treatment and during follow-up. The one exception is the category of random orgasmic inadequacy in which failure occurred in 37.5% of the cases.

Table 10. Successful Treatment of Orgasmic Dysfunctioning by Masters and Johnson (1970).

Diagnosis	No. Patients	Post-treatment	5-year Follow-up
Primary Orgasmic dysfunction	193	83.4%	82.4%
Situational Orgasmic dysfunction	149	77.2%	75.2%
Masturbatory orgasmic inadequacy	11	90.9%	
Coital orgasmic inadequacy	106	80.2%	
Random orgasmic inadequacy	32	62.5%	

Impotence

Masters and Johnson (1970) distinguish between two expressions of impotence in males. In primary impotence, the male has never been able to have intercourse because he could not obtain or maintain an erection sufficiently long enough to ejaculate in the vagina. Secondary impotence refers to men who experience erective failure during at least 25% of their sexual experiences.

The effective forms of treatment have attempted to alleviate anxieties associated with sexual intercourse. Different treatments, however, have emphasized different sources of anxiety. Friedman (1968) reported that the *systematic desensitization* of fears surrounding lovemaking activities resulted in an ability to have satisfying sexual intercourse in 80% of the cases in which erective problems had characterized the impotence. However, for patients whose impotence involved primarily an inability to ejaculate, satisfactory intercourse occurred in only 50% of the cases.

Masters and Johnson (1970) describe an "analog" to the systematic desensitization of impotence which basically involves (a) a reeducation component directed toward sexual matters interfering with spontaneous sexual expressiveness, (b) sensate exercises designed to teach the man to gradually overcome his performance fears about losing an erection during intercourse, and (c) progressively longer and more involved attempts at sexual intercourse in the absence of performance demands. Masters and Johnson (1970) report moderate success (approximately 74%) in the treatment of secondary impotence but only a 59% success rate with primary impotence.

FETISHISM AND TRANSVESTISM

The therapy research literature with fetishists and transvestites is limited to nondifferentially designed behavior therapy investigations, all employing an aversion conditioning technique. The two expressions of sexual deviation are being considered concurrently since all but one study has combined them empirically and the treatment procedures and outcomes have been shown to be similar. Yates (1970), after reviewing case studies with these problems, proposed that "differentiation between the two is often difficult and perhaps unnecessary with respect to treatment " (p. 236).

The specific aversion therapy procedures that are associated with improvement are punishment, fear conditioning, and aversion relief. Documenting the effects of a punishment procedure, Marks and Gelder (1967) and Marks, Gelder, and Bancroft (1970) presented electric shock contingent upon the occurrence of behaviors and fantacized images expressive of fetishism or transvestism. They found a decrease in deviant acts from an average of 4.5 before treatment to 0.2 approximately two weeks after the termination of treatment. Similarly, the frequency of deviant fantasies decreased from an average of 6.9 to 2.3 during a comparable period of time. These changes in deviant behavior and fantasies were maintained throughout the next two years.

Fear conditioning, using either electric shock (McGuire & Vallance, 1964) or apomorphine (Morgenstern et al., 1965) as the aversive stimulus paired with stimuli associated with fetishism or transvestism, has also received some support although the total number of cases treated by this method is relatively small. In one study (Morgenstern et al., 1965) it was reported that seven out of 13 transvestites completely stopped cross-dressing and the remaining six patients were rated by the therapists as "much improved." Thorpe and his associates (1964), expanding upon the fear conditioning model so as to include a relief conditioning component, paired words denotative of sexual deviance with the onset of electric shock and paired words denotative of sexual nondeviance with the cessation of the shock. They reported that following treatment thoughts about deviant behavior came to evoke feelings of disgust.

In conclusion, the sparse and methodologically weak research evidence points to the tentative prescription that *aversion conditioning techniques (punishment, fear conditioning, aversion relief)* are effective procedures for eliminating the overt behaviors and sexual attitudes involved in fetishism and transvestism.

EXHIBITIONISM

While there are several single case studies in the literature reporting on the successful treatment of exhibitionism by systematic desensitization (Bond & Hutchinson, 1960), punishment (Kushner & Sandler, 1966), fear conditioning (Evans, 1968, 1970), and psychodynamically oriented psychotherapy (Zechnich, 1971), none of these reports employed the controls necessary to assess a causal relationship between the treatment package and the therapeutic outcomes. The most systematic, comprehensive, and impressive correlational study was recently conducted by Maletzky (1974), in which a modified version of *covert sensitization* was shown to effectively eliminate overt exposing, fantasies, urges, and dreams in nine out of ten exhibitionists. The treatment involved the hierarchical presentation of imaginal scenes depicting exhibitionist activity which, in turn, evoked feelings of sexual arousal in the patient. These events were followed immediately by verbal descriptions of noxious images (e.g., vomiting, contact with feces and urine, feelings of embarrassment) as well as actual exposures to a naturally odiferous chemical called valeric acid. A "relief" component was also included in which removal of the noxious odor was accompanied by scenes depicting escape from the exposing situation. Finally, *"in vivo"* training was included where each patient sniffed a vial of the acid in actual situations that were previously associated with exposing behaviors. There was a complete elimination of covert and overt exhibitionist behavior in all patients at a 12-month follow-up period. These impressive findings, however, need to be replicated in a controlled investigation which includes, at minimum, an untreated comparison group and, at best, attention and differentially treated groups to identify the specific active ingredients in this most promising form of treatment for exhibitionism.

Table 11. SEXUAL DEVIATIONS

Name	Patient					Therapist	
	Diagnosis	No.	Sex	Age	Other	Description	No.

Level 1. Nondifferential prescriptions
  Type 1A: Psychotherapy A for patients X

Name	Diagnosis	No.	Sex	Age	Other	Description	No.
Bieber et al., 1963	homo-sexuality	206	all M	—	106 = homo-sexuals; 72 exclusively homosexual; 100 = heter-osexuals; self-referrals, 70% college educated	psychiatrists	77
Birk et al., 1971	homo-sexuality	18	all M	—	nonpsy-chotic; highly moti-vated to change	authors	4
Ellis, 1956	homo-sexuality	40	28M 12F	under 25 – 36+	36 Ss overt homo-sexual relations; 4 Ss ob-sessive homo-sexual thoughts; 31 Ss un-married, 5 married, 4 divorced	author	1

Treatment			Outcomes		
Type	No. Sessions	Total Duration	Assessment Procedure	Results	Follow-up
psychoanalytic psychotherapy	max. = 150	–	t ratings based on self-reports	42/106 remained homosexual; 30/106 remained bisexual; 27% exclusively heterosexual; success related to higher motivation, young age, previous heterosexual genital experience	unspecified times
avoidance conditioning + psychotherapy vs. attention control	20–25	6 wks.	self-report of sexual behavior; MMPI; projective tests; Kinsey ratings; judges' ratings	avoidance conditioning > attention control for Kinsey ratings & self-report of sex behavior; no difference on MMPI & judges' ratings	3½ yrs.
psychoanalytically oriented psychotherapy; goal = free patient from fear of heterosexual relation	5–220	–	self-report & t ratings of improvement	females improved significantly more; were more often married or divorced, more often severely disturbed; outcome significantly related to S's desire to achieve heterosexual adjustment; 64% males improved, 100% females improved	none

Table 11 cont.

Name	Patient					Therapist	
	Diagnosis	No.	Sex	Age	Other	Description	No.
Feldman & MacCulloch, 1965	homo-sexuality	16	all M	19–47	Kinsey rating = 3–6; 12 un-married, 4 married	psychol-ogist, psy-chiatrist	2
Freund, 1960	homo-sexuality	47	all M	–	unre-quited homo-sexual love (9), referred by rela-tives (7), no obvious external pressures (31)	unspecified	–
Ovesey et al., 1963	homo-sexuality	3	M	under 30	–	psychi-atrist	–
Solyom & Miller, 1965	homo-sexuality	6	all M	20–42	2 married	unspecified	–

Treatment			Outcomes		
Type	No. Sessions	Total Duration	Assessment Procedure	Results	Follow-up
avoidance conditioning + anxiety relief (anticipatory avoidance)	x̄=15	–	behavior; fantasy	11/16 improved; better prognosis with Ss younger than 40 yrs. of age	1–14 mos.
fear conditioning (chemical + anxiety relief conditioning)	max.= 24	–	self-report of heterosexual behavior	51% – no improvement; 15% – short-term heterosexual adaptation; 26% – adaptation for several yrs.; 5% – unknown	3 yrs.
psychoanalytic psychotherapy – focus on anxiety motivated heterosexual avoidance	–	317 hrs.	t ratings	all 3 Ss successful, good heterosexual adjustment	5 yrs. +
fear conditioning + anxiety relief	x̄=23.5	30 min. session	psychological; behavior	plethysmograph Rs increased to female pictures; discontinuation of homosexual behavior in all Ss; no improvement in heterosexual behavior	none

Table 11 cont.

Name	Diagnosis	No.	Sex	Age	Other	Description	No.
			Patient			**Therapist**	
Tanner, 1974	homo-sexuality	16	all M	–	–	unspecified	–
Brady, 1966	frigid-ity	5	all F	$\bar{x}$=24.6	**all married**; no orgasms during coitus	unspecified	–
Cooper, 1969	impo-tence	44	all M	–	outpatients	unspecified	–
Masters & Johnson, 1970	ejacu-lation problems, impotence, "frigid-ity," va-ginismus	510	approx. 50% M, F	23–76	referral, well motivated, well educated	team – 1 male, 1 female	2
Marks & Gelder, 1967	fetishism, transvestism	5	all M	30.2	hospitalized; cooperative	unspecified	–

Treatment			Outcomes		
Type	No. Sessions	Total Duration	Assessment Procedure	Results	Follow-up
avoidance conditioning vs. no-treatment control	20	8 wks.	penile tumescence to slides; self-report of arousal & sexual behavior; MMPI	avoidance conditioning > no-treatment control for less arousal to male slides, frequent sex with females, frequent socializing with females, lower MMPI scale 5	none
systematic desensitization; intravenous methohexital sodium (brevital) for relaxation	$\bar{x}=11$; 10–14	20 min. session	occurrence of orgasm during coitus	1 S prematurely terminated; all **4** achieved orgasms, $\bar{x}$ frequency = 50%	3–8 mos.
relaxation + sex education + psychotherapy	20	1 yr.	self-report by partners	19 improved, 25 unchanged or worse	none
supportive psychotherapy + sex education & sexual training	1/day	2 wks.	sexual performance; self-report of attitudes, interests, feelings	premature ejaculation = 98% successful; primary impotent males = 59% successful; secondary impotent males = 74% successful; "frigidity" = 81% successful; vaginismus = 100% successful	5 yrs
aversion (electric); (punishment of behavior & fantasy)	about 28	2 wks. + booster sessions	t ratings; behavior, self-report of attitudes	erections & fantasy during deviant behavior ceased; positive attitude change	at least 6 mos.

Table 11 cont.

Name	Diagnosis	No.	Sex	Age	Other	Description	No.
		Patient				Therapist	
McGuire & Vallance, 1964	homo-sexuals, compul-sive mas-turbators, trans-vestites, sadist, fetishist	6 3 2 1 1	all M	–	–	unspecified	–
Thorpe *et al.,* 1964	homo-sexuals, trans-vestite, fetishist	3 1 1	all M	27,31 40 21 32	–	unspecified	–
Maletzky, 1974	exhibi-tionists	10	all M	21–52	8 married, 9th grade-college education; duration= 1–31 yrs; frequency of exhibiting= 1–10/month	author	1
Semans, 1956	prema-ture ejacu-lation	8	all M	25–47	–	physician	1

Treatment			Outcomes		
Type	No. Sessions	Total Duration	Assessment Procedure	Results	Follow-up
classical fear conditioning (CS = fantasy, US = electric shock)	–	–	t ratings	3 homosexuals prematurely terminated; all other Ss showed mild to complete improvement	1 mo.
aversion relief (shock offset + word denoting normal sexual behavior)	16–30	–	self-report of behavior; psychometric tests	thoughts about deviant behavior, feelings of disgust in all Ss increased	1–3 mos.; results maintained
covert sensitization (valeric acid = noxious UCS)	11–19	15 wks.	self-report of covert exhibitionist behavior (urges, fantasies, dreams), overt behavior	x̄ covert exhibitionist responses declined from 16.5/month before psychotherapy to .6/month just after psychotherapy; x̄ overt exhibitionist responses decreased from 5/month to .1/month	1 yr., results maintained
operant shaping of progressively longer nonejaculation intervals	variable	variable	self-report of behavior change	successful in all cases	5 wks.–1 yr.

Table 11 cont.

Name	Patient					Therapist	
	Diagnosis	No.	Sex	Age	Other	Description	No.

Level 2. Unidifferential prescriptions
  Type 2A: Psychotherapy A vs. psychotherapy B for patients X

Name	Diagnosis	No.	Sex	Age	Other	Description	No.
Feldman & MacCulloch, 1967,1971	homo-sexuality	30	28M 2F	15–40+	Kinsey rating = 3–6; primary vs. secondary homo-sexuals; nonpsy-chotic; IQ >80	one male, one female; psychiatrists	2
McConaghy, 1971	homo-sexuality	40	all M	–	18 Ss previously arrested, 10 mar-ried	unspecified	–
McConaghy & Barr, 1973	homo-sexuality	46	all M	15–59	7 Ss married; all distressed by homo-sexuality	unspecified	–
Meyer, 1966	homo-sexuality	173	all M	–	–	experienced psycho-analysts, experi-enced behav-ior therapist	77 / 1

Type 2C: Psychotherapy A for patients X vs. patients Y

Name	Diagnosis	No.	Sex	Age	Other	Description	No.
MacCulloch & Feldman, 1967	homo-sexuality	29	all M	$\bar{x}$=29.2	self-insecure disorder vs. attention seeker vs. weak willed	unspecified	–

Treatment			Outcomes		
Type	No. Sessions	Total Duration	Assessment Procedure	Results	Follow-up
avoidance conditioning vs. classical conditioning (fear) vs. psychotherapy (attitudes toward females)	24 (avoidance conditioning), 12 psychotherapy)	25 min./ session	self-report questionnaire (validity/reliability data available) on sexual orientation	secondary homosexuals more responsive than primary homosexuals, regardless of treatment type; both learning approaches led to better maintenance of + outcome than psychotherapy; Ss < 30 yrs. of age improved more	$\bar{x}=46.2$ wks.
apomorphine aversion vs. aversion relief	28 & 15, respectively	5 days	penile tumescence to male slides; self-report	no differences between groups. Both showed improvement	1 yr.
avoidance conditioning vs. fear conditioning vs. backward conditioning	19	5 days + 1/mo. for 5 mos.	penile tumescence; self-report; behavior	no significant difference between treatments	none
psychoanalytic psychotherapy vs. avoidance conditioning (compared results of 2 studies)	70–450	–	self-report; heterosexual behavior	psychoanalytic psychotherapy > avoidance conditioning	none
anticipatory avoidance	$\bar{x}=20$ (5–30 +)	20 min./ session	self-report of sexual attitudes & interests; Kinsey rating	self-insecure Ss > attention seekers & weak willed	13.4 mos.

Table 11 cont.

Name	Diagnosis	No.	Sex	Age	Other	Description	No.
			Patient			Therapist	
Cooper, 1969 1970	frigid-ity	58	all F	–	$\bar{x}$ duration problem = 5–7 yrs.; 3 groups, varied in rated pleasure of coitus & occurrence of orgasms	unspecified	–
Faulk, 1971	frigid-ity	40	all F	–	–	unspecified	–
Friedman, 1968	impo-tence	19	all M	21–55	16 married; duration of problem = 3 mos.; erective, ejacula-tory, concep-tive prob-lems	unspecified	–

Treatment			Outcomes		
Type	No. Sessions	Total Duration	Assessment Procedure	Results	Follow-up
relaxation + counseling + sexual activity at home	20	1 yr.	orgasms; self-report of pleasure during intercourse	significant negative relationship between improvement & degree of pleasure & frequency of orgasms prior to therapy and positively related to marital status, prior pleasurable experiences with intercourse and acute onset of symptoms; 48% improved	none
"insight" psychotherapy	1–50	–	behavior; self-report of pleasure; attitudes	1/10 successful with Ss anxious & disgusted by intercourse; 15/27 successful with Ss nonanxious about intercourse	none
systematic desensitization	4–31	–	self-report of satisfactory sexual intercourse	80% erective problems successful; 50% ejaculatory problems successful; 0% conceptive problems successful	6 mos.– 1 yr.

Table 11 cont.

| Name | Patient | | | | | Therapist | |
	Diagnosis	No.	Sex	Age	Other	Description	No.
Evans, 1970	exhibi-tionists	20	all M	–	referred by psy-chiatrists	unspecified	–
Marks *et al.*, 1970	trans-vestites, fetishists, trans-sexuals, sadomaso-chists	24	all M	$\bar{x}=33$	–	unspecified	–
Morgenstern *et al.*, 1965	trans-vestism	13	all M	–	–	unspecified	–

Treatment			Outcomes		
Type	No. Sessions	Total Duration	Assessment Procedure	Results	Follow-up
fear conditioning + escape (CS=phrases of deviant activity US=electric shock)	16	26 wks.	self-report of behavior	success related to low frequency of deviant mas-turbatory fantasy & briefer history of exhibiting	6 mos.
aversion (electric); punishment of behavior & imagery	19	2–3 wks.	t ratings of sexual attitudes, self-report of sexual behavior & fantasies; heterosexual adjustment score	transsexual un-improved; other groups improved equally across all measures	2 yrs.; results maintained
fear conditioning (nausea)	39	–	behavior, self-report	7 Ss stopped cross-dressing; 6 others relapsed under later stress but none returned to pretreatment frequency of cross-dressing; Ss high on MF scale of MMPI and low on neuroticism on Mandsley Per-sonality Inven-tory responded more favorably	none

Anti-Social Behavior

Reality therapy appears to be the appropriate prescriptive choice for the reduction of anti-social behavior. Glasser (1965) describes this approach as follows:

> Reality therapy is made up of three separate but intimately interwoven procedures. First, there is the involvement; the therapist must become so involved with the patient that the patient can begin to face reality and see how his behavior is unrealistic. Second, the therapist must reject the behavior which is unrealistic but still accept the patient and maintain his involvement with him. Last...the therapist must teach the patient better ways to fulfill his needs within the confines of reality. (p. 21)

Thus, (1) therapist involvement, (2) therapist acceptance of pro-social behavior and rejection of anti-social behavior, and (3) explicit teaching of pro-social behaviors are the central ingredients of reality therapy. Evidence for the prescriptive value of this therapeutic approach with anti-social patients extends well beyond the relatively few (though positive) evaluations of reality therapy per se. The same triad of active ingredients described above largely characterizes three other types of therapeutic efforts with anti-social patients. Each of these approaches has received empirical support for its efficacy. We refer here to Massimo and Shore's (1967) comprehensive, vocationally oriented therapy, Sarason's (1968) use of modeling for behavioral training, and Persons' (1966) reliance upon a combination of support and the active teaching of acceptable behaviors. Note in each of these approaches, as in reality therapy, the focus on the development of pro-social behaviors, augmenting patient responsibility by increasing his ability to discriminate pro-social and anti-social behaviors, and use of active therapist involvement and commitment to provide added therapeutic potency for these teaching efforts. The significance of this concordance of findings is, however, possibly attenuated by the near-complete absence of relevant follow-up studies.

Table 12. ANTI-SOCIAL BEHAVIOR

Name	Patient					Therapist	
	Diagnosis	No.	Sex	Age	Other	Description	No.

Level 1. Nondifferential prescriptions
  Type 1A: Psychotherapy A for patients X

Name	Diagnosis	No.	Sex	Age	Other	Description	No.
Burchard, 1967	anti-social	12	–	10–20	mildly retarded	attendants, teachers, social workers	9
Burchard & Barrera, 1972	anti-social	11	11M	15–19	mildly retarded	staff members	–
Glasser, 1965	anti-social	–	–	14–18	reform school inmates	psychiatrists, psychologists, social workers	–
Massimo & Shore, 1967	anti-social	20	20M	15–17	suspended or withdrew from school	–	–
Meichenbaum et al., 1968	anti-social	10	10F	$\bar{x}=15$	training school	psychology interns	5
Moore et al., 1962	anti-social	70	70M	–	prison inmates	psychologist (1) & psychology graduate students (2)	3

Treatment			Outcomes		
Type	No. Sessions	Total Duration	Assessment Procedure	Results	Follow-up
contingency management (reinforcement or loss of reinforcements)	15	15 days	behavioral ratings of classroom & work behavior	frequency of positive behaviors varied directly with contingent reinforcement	—
time-out & response costs (tokens) for anti-social behavior	48	48 days	change in anti-social behaviors	higher levels of response cost & time-out yielded lower levels of anti-social behaviors for 5/6 Ss analyzed	—
reality therapy vs no-treatment control	—	—	reduction in parole violations	reality therapy > no-treatment control	—
comprehensive vocationally oriented vs. no-treatment control	—	10 mos.	vocational-academic behavioral ratings	comprehensive, vocationally oriented > no-treatment control on most criteria	—
contingency management (reinforcement program)	—	about 4 wks.	behavioral ratings of classroom behaviors	apparent benefit across criteria	—
reality therapy	—	—	guard ratings, number days in disciplinary unit	apparent benefit on both criteria	—

Table 12 cont.

Name	Diagnosis	No.	Sex	Age	Other	Description	No.
		Patient				**Therapist**	
Persons, 1965	anti-social	52	52M	$\bar{x}=22$	prison inmates	psychologist	1
Persons, 1966	anti-social	82	82M	15–19; $\bar{x}=16.5$	reform school inmates; $\bar{x}$ length of incarcerations = 11 mos.	psychologists (2) & social workers (3)	5
Schwitzgebel, 1967	anti-social	35	35M	$\bar{x}=16$	police record	psychologists, undergraduates	—
Szymanski & Fleming, 1971	anti-social	8	8M	14–16	probationers	prisoners	3

Level 2. Unidifferential prescriptions
  Type 2A: Psychotherapy A vs. psychotherapy B for patients X

Name	Diagnosis	No.	Sex	Age	Other	Description	No.
Arbuckle & Boy, 1961	anti-social	36	36M	—	jr. high school students	school counselors	2

Treatment			Outcomes		
Type	No. Sessions	Total Duration	Assessment Procedure	Results	Follow-up
eclectic vs. no-treatment control	20	10	anxiety & delinquency scales, disciplinary actions	eclectic > no-treatment control across criteria	–
individual (support + teaching acceptable behaviors) + group vs. regular institutional program	40	20 wks.	anxiety & delinquency scales, MMPI	individual + group > regular institutional program on decrements on anxiety & delinquency scales &most MMPI subscales	–
interview + contingency management vs. no treatment control	20	2–3 mos.	behavioral ratings (social & verbal)	interview plus contingency management > no-treatment control	–
relationship therapy	–	–	recidivism	minimal apparent apparent benefit	3 mos.
client-centered vs. detention after school vs. no-treatment control	12	12 wks.	self-ideal discrepancy; teacher ratings, peer group acceptance	significant pre-post improvement within client-centered group only on self-ideal discrepancy, teacher ratings, & peer group acceptance	6 wks; trend for client-centered group to be referred less often for disciplinary action

Table 12 cont.

Name	Patient					Therapist	
	Diagnosis	No.	Sex	Age	Other	Description	No.
Croft *et al.*, 1964	anti-social	50	50M	13–25	proba-tioners	staff members	–
Parlett & Ayers, 1971	anti-social	65	65M	–	prison inmates	–	–
Sarason, 1968	anti-social	–	–	15–18	juvenile center residents	psychol-ogy grad-uate students	2
Tyler & Brown, 1967	anti-social	15	15M	13–15	court committed	cottage staff	6

Treatment			Outcomes		
Type	No. Sessions	Total Duration	Assessment Procedure	Results	Follow-up
authoritarian-disciplinary vs. self-governing group	–	–	MMPI, IQ, arrests, work record	significant IQ gain in authoritarian-disciplinary condition	14 mos.; authoritarian-disciplinary committed fewer offenses
academic-programed instruction vs. academic traditional instruction vs. trade training	–	95 days	personality & perceptual scales	programed instruction > traditional instruction = trade training on superego strength & self-concept	–
modeling vs. role playing vs. no-treatment control	15	–	behavioral ratings, self-ratings	modeling > role playing > no-treatment control	–
time-out vs. reprimand for mis-behavior	–	40 wks.	behavioral ratings	time-out > reprimand	–

Smoking

Of the alternative treatments which have been empirically examined, *emotional role playing* appears to be the appropriate current prescription for the reduction of smoking. The role playing or behavioral rehearsal component augmented by the arousal-enhancing or fear-enhancing aspect of this approach has been demonstrated across a sufficiently large number of studies to be an effective smoking reduction approach. A wide array of other behavioral approaches have been associated with significant decreases in smoking (within-condition comparisons), but none have consistently done so relative to other treatments (between-condition comparisons). It may well be, therefore, that the nonspecific procedures that these approaches share are the active ingredients in their success in enhancing smoking reduction — i.e., structure, positive helper expectancy, good quality relationship, etc. Perhaps most crucial, however, is the issue of follow-up. None of the approaches examined yielded consistently positive follow-up outcomes. Emotional role playing, which seems most efficacious of the procedures studied, also yielded mixed outcomes regarding *sustained* smoking reduction over time. Recent reviews of the smoking literature (Bernstein, 1969; Keutzer *et al.*, 1968; Lichtenstein & Keutzer, 1971) have also noted that the basic problem in the modification of smoking behavior is not the initial production of short-term change, but the long-term maintenance of nonsmoking behavior.

Table 13. SMOKING

Name	Patient					Therapist	
	Diagnosis	No.	Sex	Age	Other	Description	No.

Level 1. Nondifferential prescriptions
  Type 1A: Psychotherapy A for patients X

Name	Diagnosis	No.	Sex	Age	Other	Description	No.
Azrin & Powell, 1968	smoking	5	3F 2M	over 21	30−50 cigarettes/ day	psychologist	1
Chapman et al., 1971	smoking	23	8M 15F	$\bar{x}$=40.3	15−60 cigarettes/ day	authors	2
Elliot & Tighe, 1968	smoking	25	2F 23M	18−40	minimum 20 cigarettes/ day	psychologists	2
Franks et al.,1966	smoking	9	4F 5M	−	20−40 cigarettes/ day	−	−
Harris & Rothberg, 1972	smoking	5	−	−	−	−	−
Platt et al., 1969	smoking	61	61M	20−59; $\bar{x}$=42	minimum 10 cigarettes/ day	−	−
Powell & Azrin, 1968	smoking	3	3M	over 21	30−50 cigarettes/ day	−	−

Treatment			Outcomes		
Type	No. Sessions	Total Duration	Assessment Procedure	Results	Follow-up
behavioral engineering (locked cigarette case, openable at increasingly longer intervals)	–	7–13 wks.	amount of smoking	gradual reduction to ½ pack per day	smoking returned to original level when treatment terminated
aversive conditioning + self-management	5–10	3–12 wks.	amount of smoking	21/23 stopped completely at end of treatment	8/23 abstinent after 1 yr.; frequency & duration of treatment related to amount of smoking reduction
contingency contracting + anti-smoking literature		16 wks.	amount of smoking	21 Ss abstained during 4 month program	1 year; 38% abstained
aversive conditioning	12	4 wks.	amount of smoking	most reduced amount of smoking	6 mos.; gains maintained
self-control training	8	4 wks.	amount of smoking	all Ss reduced smoking rate	2 mos.; "partial relapses"
emotional role playing vs. no-treatment control	1	–	amount of smoking	emotional role playing > no-treatment control ˙	4 mos.; gains not maintained by 65%
behavioral engineering (portable shock apparatus on cigarette case, intensity graduated)	– ˙	–	amount of smoking	smoking decreased as shock increased	smoking returned to original level

Table 13 cont.

Name	Diagnosis	No.	Sex	Age	Other	Description	No.
		Patient				Therapist	
Resnick, 1968	smoking	9	3F 6M	$\bar{x}=19.2$	$\bar{x}=22.3$ cigarettes/ day	author	1
Schmahl et al., 1972	smoking	28	17F 11M	$\bar{x}=27$	$\bar{x}=30$ cigarettes/ day	psychology graduate students	2

Level 2. Unidifferential prescriptions
  Type 2A: Psychotherapy A vs. psychotherapy B for patients X

Name	Diagnosis	No.	Sex	Age	Other	Description	No.
Engeln, 1969	smoking	82	82M	–	minimum 10 cigarettes/	–	–
Gerson & Lanyon, 1972	smoking	21	14F 7M	$\bar{x}=28$	$\bar{x}$ years smoking = 10	psychologist	1
Grimaldi & Lichtenstein, 1969	smoking	29	–	$\bar{x}=42.6$	$\bar{x}=26.1$ cigarettes/ day	females	2
Hark, 1970	smoking	51	–	–	–	–	–
Janis & Mann, 1965	smoking	26	26F	18–23	minimum 15 cig- arettes/ day	–	1

Treatment			Outcomes		
Type	No. Sessions	Total Duration	Assessment Procedure	Results	Follow-up
satiation	–	1 wk.	amount of smoking	66% stopped smoking completely	4 mos; gains maintained
aversive conditioning vs. placebo control	$\bar{x}=8$	varied	amount of smoking	no significant between-conditions differences; significant pre-post reductions within both conditions	6 mos; gains maintained
systematic desensitization vs. aversive conditioning vs. self-monitoring vs. no-treatment control	8	2 wks.	amount of smoking	all treatment groups > no-treatment control	1 mo.; significant gains maintained
covert sensitization + systematic desensitization vs. covert sensitization + group discussion	10	5 wks.	amount of smoking	significant pre-post reductions within conditions	13 wks.; gains maintained for first group only
contingent punishment vs. noncontingent punishment vs. attention control	7	3 wks.	amount of smoking	no significant between-condition differences; significant pre-post reduction within conditions	1 mo.; gains not maintained
coverant conditioning + monitoring vs. monitoring + attention monitoring	–	8 wks.	amount of smoking	coverant conditioning plus monitoring > monitoring	–
emotional role playing vs. exposure	1	–	amount of smoking; attitude scale	role playing > exposure	–

Table 13 cont.

Name	Patient					Therapist	
	Diagnosis	No.	Sex	Age	Other	Description	No.
Keutzer, 1968	smoking	213	118F 95M	20—69	–	–	2
Keutzer *et al.*, 1969	smoking	54	54F	19—27	–	–	–
Koenig & Masters, 1965	smoking	42	16F 26M	19—25	minimum = 20 cig- arettes/ day	psycholo- gists (2) and psy- chology graduate students (5)	7
Lawson & May, 1970	smoking	12	12M	$\bar{x}$=25	$\bar{x}$=28 cigarettes/ day	psycholo- gist	1
Lichtenstein & Keutzer, 1968	smoking	170	–	–	–	–	–
Mann, 1967	smoking	64	32F 32M	–	minimum = 10 cig- arettes/ day	–	–

Treatment			Outcomes		
Type	No. Sessions	Total Duration	Assessment Procedure	Results	Follow-up
coverant conditioning vs. aversive conditioning vs. negative practice vs. placebo control vs. no-treatment control	3	3 wks.	amount of smoking	all treatment groups > no-treatment control; no other between-group differences	–
emotional role playing vs. exposure	1	–	amount of smoking	emotional role playing = exposure	–
systematic desensitization vs. aversive conditioning vs. supportive nondirective	9	6 wks.	amount of smoking	no significant between-condition differences; significant pre-post reductions within conditions	6 mos.; gains maintained
covert sensization vs. contingency management vs. contracting vs. monitoring – discussions	14	5 wks.	amount of smoking	no significant between-condition differences	–
negative practice vs. breath holding vs. coverant control vs. combination of above vs. attention control vs. no-treatment control	5	5 wks.	amount of smoking	see Keutzer, 1968	return to pre-treatment level
emotional role playing (fear) vs. emotional role playing (shame) vs. cognitive role playing	1	–	amount of smoking	emotional role playing (fear) > shame = cognitive role playing	2 wks,; 50% of role play (fear) & 31% of cognitive role play maintain reduction

Table 13 cont.

Name	Diagnosis	No.	Sex	Age	Other	Description	No.
		Patient				Therapist	
Mann & Janis, 1968	smoking	57	57F	18–26	–	–	1
Marston & McFall, 1971	smoking	65	35F 30M	$\bar{x}=21$	$\bar{x}=26$ cigarettes/ day	psycholo- gists	2
McCallum, 1971	smoking	46	46M	18–22	–	–	–
McFall & Hammen, 1971	smoking	38	18F 20M	18–22	minimum = 20 cigar- ettes/day	psychology graduate students (3) & under- graduate students (3)	6
Miller & Gimpl, 1971	smoking	12	–	–	minimum = 20 cigar- ettes/day: under- graduate students	–	–
Ober, 1968	smoking	60	19F 41M	18–22	minimum = 20 cigar- ettes/day	psychology graduate students	2

Treatment			Outcomes		
Type	No. Sessions	Total Duration	Assessment Procedure	Results	Follow-up
role playing vs. exposure vs. no-treatment control	1	–	amount of smoking	role playing > exposure > no-treatment control	18 mos.; gains maintained
satiation vs. aversive conditioning vs. gradual reduction vs. "cold turkey"	6	3 wks.	amount of smoking	no significant between-condition differences; significant pre-post reductions within conditions	6 mos.; gains not maintained
satiation vs. covert sensitization vs. resolve-to-quit controls vs. attention vs. no-treatment control	6	1 wk.	amount of smoking	no significant between-condition differences; significant pre-post reduction within conditions (except no-treatment control)	2 mos.; gains maintained
fixed positive self-monitoring vs. positive self-monitoring vs. negative self-monitoring vs. minimal self-monitoring	6	3 wks.	amount of smoking	no significant between-condition differences; significant pre-post reductions within conditions	6 mos.; gains not maintained
self-instruction vs. self-monitoring vs. reinforcement	–	3 wks.	amount of smoking	no significant between-condition differences; significant pre-post reductions within conditions	–
self-control training vs. aversive conditioning vs. transactional analysis vs. no-treatment control	10	4 wks.	amount of smoking	all treatment groups > no-treatment control (based on N=50)	1 mo.; significant differences maintained

Table 13 cont.

Name	Diagnosis	No.	Sex	Age	Other	Description	No.
			Patient			Therapist	
O'Brien, 1972	smoking	100	–	–	–	graduate student	1
Pyke *et al.,* 1966	smoking	55	–	18–22	–	–	–
Resnick, 1968	smoking	60	30F 30M	17–28	$\bar{x}=23$ cigarettes/day	–	–
Sachs *et al.,* 1970	smoking	24	12F 12M	$\bar{x}=20$	–	–	2

Treatment			Outcomes		
Type	No. Sessions	Total Duration	Assessment Procedure	Results	Follow-up
negative practice groups vs. covert sensitization vs. attention monitoring	–	1 wk.	amount of smoking	no significant between-condition differences; significant pre-post reductions within conditions	6 mos.; gains not maintained
systematic desensitization + discussion & feedback + self-monitoring vs. self-monitoring (extensive) vs. self-monitoring (minimal)	20	10 wks.	amount of smoking	systematic desensitization + discussion & feedback + self-monitoring > self-monitoring groups	4 mos.; significant gains not maintained
satiation (triple normal) vs. satiation (double normal) vs. no-treatment control	–	1 wk.	amount of smoking	satiation (triple) > no treatment control	4 mos.; gains maintained & satiation (double) controls
covert sensitization vs. graduated self-control vs. placebo control	3	3 wks.	amount of smoking	covert sensitization > self-control; significant pre-post reductions within experimental conditions	1 mo.; gains maintained

Table 13 cont.

Name	Patient					Therapist	
	Diagnosis	No.	Sex	Age	Other	Description	No.
Sushinsky, 1972	smoking	–	–	–	–	–	–
Upper & Meredith, 1970	smoking	51	–	–	–	–	–
Wagner & Bragg, 1970	smoking	54	28F 26M	$\bar{x}=40$	$\bar{x}=30$ cigarettes/day	psychologists	2
Whitman, 1969	smoking	73	39F 34M	$\bar{x}=42$	$\bar{x}=29.7$ cigarettes/day	male paraprofessionals	3

Treatment			Outcomes		
Type	No. Sessions	Total Duration	Assessment Procedure	Results	Follow-up
satiation vs. individual effort vs. minimal treatment	–	–	amount of smoking	no significant between-condition differences; significant pre-post reductions within conditions	2 mos.; all groups returned to baseline
timer control vs. attention vs. no-treatment control	–	6 wks.	amount of smoking	timer control yielded 53% reduction, other groups 16% & 15%, respectively	–
systematic desensitization + covert sensitization vs. systematic desensitization vs. relaxation vs. counseling vs. no-treatment control	8	31 days	amount of smoking	no significant between-condition differences	7, 30, 90 days, significant reduction in all treatments maintained
aversive conditions vs. information dissemination vs. incompatible behavior vs. no-treatment control	5	5 wks.	amount of smoking	no significant between-treatment differences; significant pre-post reductions within conditions	3 mos.; gains not maintained

Table 13 cont.

Name	Diagnosis	No.	Sex	Age	Other	Description	No.
		Patient				Therapist	

Type 2B: Psychotherapist 1 vs. psychotherapist 2 for patients X

Name	Diagnosis	No.	Sex	Age	Other	Description	No.
Streltzer & Koch, 1968	smoking	30	30F	18–22	–	female under-graduate student; male physician	2

Level 3. Bidifferential prescriptions
Type 3A: Psychotherapy A vs. psychotherapy B for patients X vs. patients Y

Name	Diagnosis	No.	Sex	Age	Other	Description	No.
Berecz, 1972	smoking	110	70M 40F	17–30	moderate: 50–130 cigar-ettes/wk.; heavy: 130–236 cigar-ettes/wk.	–	–

Treatment			Outcomes		
Type	No. Sessions	Total Duration	Assessment Procedure	Results	Follow-up
emotional role playing (with hi status co-actor) vs. emotional role playing (with lo-status co-actor) vs. no-treat-ment control	1	–	amount of smoking; attitude scale	both role play conditions > no-treatment control; hi status group > lo status group in un-favorable smoking atti-tudes	3–4 wks.; results main-tained
shock for actual smoking vs. shock for imagined smoking vs. minimal con-tact control vs. placebo control vs. wait control	6	3 wks.	amount of smoking	for male, heavy smokers only: shock for imag-ined smoking > shock for actual smoking > placebo control; for moderate male smokers: imagined smoking = actual smoking; imagined smoking > placebo; for females: all treatments equal	5 wks.; results unspec-ified

Obesity

The research literature on the psychotherapeutic modification of obesity, in which weight loss is the explicit and primary goal of treatment, has been dominated by several behavior therapy approaches. In particular, these approaches may be organized into the following categories: (1) aversive conditioning procedures, especially covert sensitization, which attempt to instill a motivation to avoid situations and foods associated with overeating, (2) self-regulatory procedures, which are designed to manipulate the relationships between overt and covert behaviors and their positive consequences (e.g., contingency contracting, self-monitoring and self-reward, coverant control), and (3) the omnibus use of individually tailored operant conditioning techniques, which are designed to manipulate the antecedent, behavioral, and consequent variables that are functionally related to overweight. Unfortunately, there is currently no substantial body of evidence speaking to the relative merits of these approaches in either the treatment of obesity, in general, or specifying how they may differentially interact with characteristics of the patient. Although some operant conditioning approaches have seriously attempted to match specific treatments to the unique situational and behavioral aspects of each patient (e.g., Stuart, 1967; Stuart & Davis, 1972), as yet no empirically based prescriptions have emerged from this orientation.

On a nondifferential level, the majority of studies that have examined the association between covert sensitization and weight loss have reported statistically significant effects (e.g., Janda & Rimm, 1972; Manno & Marston, 1972; Meynen, 1970; Murray & Harrington, 1972; Sachs & Ingram, 1972). In contrast, however, Foreyt and Hagen (1973) found no difference in weight change between covert sensitization, an attention (placebo) group, and a no-treatment control group. Typically, in these studies covert sensitization involved instructions to imagine approaching a highly desired but forbidden food, followed immediately by suggestions that the individual feels nauseous and begins vomiting. Escape from these situations is accompanied by imagined feelings of comfort and satisfaction. Some investigators (e.g., Stuart, 1967) have largely reserved the use of covert sensitization to the alteration of specific associations between situations and overeating that have been refractory to other (positive reinforcement-based) procedures.

The explicit manipulation and rearrangement of the relationships between

274

consummatory behavior and its positive consequence have been attempted through coverant conditioning procedures and contingency contracting techniques. Coverant conditioning was first described by Homme (1965) as a means of affecting alterations in the "operants of the mind" (coverants) that exert a controlling influence on behavior. It is based on the "Premack principle" of reinforcement, which asserts that any low probability behavior may be reinforced if it is immediately followed by a higher probability behavior. For example, it may be possible to increase the likelihood of unpleasant thoughts about being overweight as well as pleasant ideas about being slender by a high probability activity contingent upon the prior occurrence of these thoughts. In this fashion, the probability of thoughts that are incompatible with eating behavior are increased and eating itself may become less probable. Unfortunately, as yet the small amount of research with this procedure for regulating weight-loss is unimpressive and unencouraging (e.g., Horan & Johnson, 1971; Tyler & Straughan, 1970).

More promising results have been reported with the use of "contingency contracting" procedures. As the term implies, this procedure basically involves an agreement between the patient and the therapist about the rules that define explicit behavioral prerequisites necessary for the patient to receive a particular reinforcer. For example, Mann (1972) devised a contingency contract with eight obese adults who, prior to treatment, surrendered to the therapist a large number of items each considered valuable. The patients signed a legal contract which stated the rate of weight-loss and ultimate loss necessary to earn back the valuables (reinforcements). Moreover, the contract specified that certain weight gains and weight-loss rates below the agreed-upon rate would result in a permanent forfeiture of a portion of the valuables. Results indicated an average loss of 1.65 pounds per week (range = −6.1 to −.2) for as long as the contract was in effect. Unfortunately, there was no follow-up data presented, particularly after an interval in which the contingency contract was inoperative. It is possible that once the contract expired the patient would return to his "pre-contract ways," particularly in light of Mann's finding that removal of the scheduled consequences was accompanied by weight gains that were similar in magnitude to the weight losses achieved in the presence of the contingency contract. Nevertheless, the results are quite encouraging and the procedure is amply flexible to permit the therapist to individualize the procedure with each patient yet retain the essential features and ingredients. For example, Mahoney, Moura, and Wade (1973) had obese patients deposit $21.00 into an account. The money was transformed into 21 shares, whose value increased when other participants forfeited their deposits or did not meet the behavioral requirements necessary to avoid monetary loss. The patients began the program with an empty account and could "self-reward" by requesting that a deposit (e.g., two shares) be made into their account for a particular weight-loss (e.g., one pound). This form of contingency contracting was significantly more effective than self-punishment, self-monitoring, or attention control procedures in producing weight-loss.

A third approach that has been impressively successful in the treatment of obesity involves the concurrent use of a variety of operant conditioning techniques. For example, Harris (1969, 1971) trained obese subjects in the use of self-monitoring techniques which focused on (1) the principles of positive and negative reinforcement and how these notions could be applied to restraints from eating, (2) the stimulus control of eating behavior and how manipulations of the environment can affect the probability of eating (e.g., not walking past the refrigerator), and (3) an analysis of the actual behaviors involved in eating and how changes in parameters of the eating response can affect the amount consumed (e.g., slowing the rate of eating by swallowing the last bite before putting more food into the mouth). Some subjects also received training in covert sensitization which, in this experiment, was shown to be inert in its effects. The operant conditioning program, on the other hand, resulted in a significantly greater weight loss when compared to subjects that were merely asked to try to lose weight on their own. In a similar fashion, Stuart (1967) documented the results of an operant-based treatment program designed to teach the participants "self-control" of overeating. To accomplish this goal, Stuart outlined six general learning points and corresponding behavioral exercises to promote the acquisition of control of overeating. These are summarized in Table 14. Throughout a one-year treatment period, there was an average regular weight loss of approximately one pound per week.

Penick, Filion, Fox, and Stunkard (1971) also reported on the successful use of operant conditioning procedures in the promotion of weight-loss. These investigators compared the effects of a behavior modification program against those obtained from a "supportive group psychotherapy." The three-month behavioral program (a) required the subjects to keep daily records of the amount, the time, and the circumstances of their eating, (b) encouraged the subjects to confine eating to one place to establish discriminative control over stimuli governing eating, (c) provided techniques to foster the self-control of eating (e.g., counting each mouthful), and (d) reinforced behaviors which served to delay or control eating (e.g., points transferable for money were contingently presented for implementing suggested control procedures during a meal or for devising an alternative to eating when a subject was tempted to eat). The results were analyzed by determining the percent of subjects in each group that lost more than 20 pounds, more than 30 pounds, or more than 40 pounds. Approximately twice as many subjects in the behavior modification program lost the amount of weight at each respective level compared to subjects in the supportive group psychotherapy program. However, despite a greater average weight-loss for the behavior modification subjects, large individual differences in responsiveness to the standardized program precluded

Table 14. Learning Principles and Treatment Techniques for the Self-Control of Eating

Learning Point	*Behavioral Exercise*
Eating is a response which can be analyzed into component parts which can be successively mastered.	Interrupt a meal for initially brief but progressively longer periods of time.
Become aware of the behaviors which facilitate eating a proper amount of food and which interfere with overeating.	Remove food from all places in the house, other than the kitchen, and keep only foods that require preparation.
Make eating independent from other behaviors which may be serving a discriminative function over eating.	Associate eating with no other activity (e.g., reading, watching TV).
Aspects of the eating response can be manipulated, controlled, and result in a lower quantity of food as well as a higher qualitative enjoyment of the food.	Put only a small amount of food in the mouth and put utensils down until finished swallowing.
Acquire a new response to well-established discriminative stimuli for eating.	Practice alternative, high probability (reinforcing), non-eating behaviors at times eating usually occurs.
Associate desired foods with unpleasant thoughts to reduce their attractiveness.	Covert sensitization.

statistically reliable differences between the treatments on this variable.

In an attempt to be directly responsive to the unique situational determinants that control overeating for each individual as well as taking into account the nutritional and energy expenditure factors that contribute to one's weight, Stuart and Davis (1972) have developed an elaborate and extensive treatment program for the modification of obesity. In general, the program represents an extension of the behavior modification principles developed previously by Stuart (1967) and his co-workers in conjunction with dietary management and physical exercise plans. The specific details of the program are presented fully in Stuart and Davis' excellent book, *Slim Chance in a Fat World* (1972). Briefly, the behavioral component of the program employs operant conditioning techniques designed to suppress antecedent and consequent conditions that interfere with controlled eating behaviors and concurrently strengthen the events which foster these behaviors. The following are examples of recommended procedures:*

1. Arrange to eat in only one room.
2. Arrange to eat at only one place in that room.
3. Do not engage in any other activity while eating.
4. Avoid the purchase of problematic foods.
5. Do not serve high-calorie condiments at meals.
6. Allow children and spouses to take their own sweets.
7. Clear plates directly into the garbage.
8. Make problematic eating as difficult as possible.
9. Reprogram the social environment to render the use of food as constructive as possible.
10. Have others monitor eating patterns.
11. Minimize contact with excessive food.
12. Make small portions of food appear to be as large as possible.
13. Control states of deprivation.
14. Provide a reasonable array of acceptable food choices.
15. Provide feedback about the amount which can be eaten.
16. Save allowable foods from meals for snacks.
17. Make acceptable foods as attractive as possible.
18. Slow the pace of eating.
19. Respond neutrally to all negative deviations from a weight-control plan.
20. Bring into focus the ultimate and immediate aversive consequences of overeating.
21. Update eating, exercise, and weight-change graphs daily.
22. Arrange for the provision of material reinforcement following completion of eating and exercise requirements and/or weight-loss.
23. Provide social reinforcement for all constructive efforts to modify weight-relevant behaviors.

According to Stuart and Davis (1972),

> The various steps suggested are illustrative of the techniques used successfully with an all-female experimental sample over 200 strong. In each instance it was found expedient to individualize specific procedures within the rubric of a general approach to situational management. When the overeater lives with others . . .it has proven essential to include significant others in the initial planning and execution of the program. . . Eighty-three percent of those subjects who could name and work with another person to aid in cueing and reinforcing appropriate eating lost 20 percent or more of body weight and maintained this loss for at least a 12-month post-treatment follow-up. Only 31 percent of those who did not have the cooperation of at least one other person met with this same degree of success. (p. 95–96)

In conclusion, the application of *operant conditioning procedures which are designed to alter a wide range of personally relevant antecedent, behavioral, and consequent variables* currently appears as the nondifferential pre-

---

*Adapted from R.B. Stuart and B. Davis. *Slim chance in a fat world.* Champaign, Ill.: Research Press, 1972.

scriptive treatment of choice for the modification of obesity. This includes both the omnibus use of behavioral principles, as described by Stuart and his colleagues, as well as the techniques of *contingency contracting* which can be conceptually and practically assimilated into a "broad-spectrum" program of treatment.

Table 15. OBESITY

Name	Patient					Therapist	
	Diagnosis	No.	Sex	Age	Other	Description	No.

Level 1. Nondifferential prescriptions
  Type 1A: Psychotherapy A for patients X

Name	Diagnosis	No.	Sex	Age	Other	Description	No.
Foreyt & Hagen, 1973	obesity	39	39F	18–24	at least 10% overweight	psychologists	2
Foreyt & Kennedy, 1971	obesity	12	12F	$\bar{x}$=40	TOPS members	–	–
Janda & Rimm, 1972	obesity	18	15F 3M	–	undergraduate volunteers, $\bar{x}$=41 lbs. overweight	psychology graduate student	1
R. A. Mann, 1972	obesity	8	7F 1M	18–33	agreed to lose 25 lbs. or more	–	–
Murray & Harrington, 1972	obesity	16	all F	–	TOPS members	2 male Ph.D. psychologists, 2 female trainees	4
Stuart, 1967	obesity	8	8F	$\bar{x}$=32	weight= 172–224 lbs.	–	–
Swanson & Dinello, 1970	obesity	25	1F 24M	23–55	long history of obesity; at least 50% overweight	unspecified	–

Treatment			Outcomes		
Type	No. Sessions	Total Duration	Assessment Procedure	Results	Follow-up
covert sensiti- zation vs. attention vs. no-treatment control	18	9 wks.	weight change	covert sensiti- zation = attention = no-treatment control	9 wks.
fear condi- tioning vs. no-treatment control	22	9 wks.	weight change	fear condition- ing > no-treat- ment control	48 wks.; change not main- tained
covert sensiti- zation + covert reinforcement vs. attention vs. no-treatment control	6	6 wks.	weight change	covert sensiti- zation + covert reinforcement > attention = no treat- ment control	6 wks,; signifi- cant change main- tained
contingency contracting	—	up to 200 days	weight change	substantial weight loss for all Ss ($\bar{x}$=2.1 lbs./ wk.)	
covert sensiti- zation	13–15	10 wks.	weight change	significant de- crease in weight loss	6 mos.; $\bar{x}$=.4 lbs. gained
"behavioral curriculum"	18	16 wks.	weight change	$\bar{x}$ weight loss= 37 lbs.	12 mos.
starvation (hospitalized)	—	$\bar{x}$=38 days	weight change	initial loss = 67 lbs.	12 mos.; −20/25 Ss re- gained weight back to original level

Table 15 cont.

Name	Diagnosis	Patient				Therapist	
		No.	Sex	Age	Other	Description	No.

Level 2. Unidifferential prescriptions
  Type 2A: Psychotherapy A vs. psychotherapy B for patients X

Harmatz & Lapuc, 1968	obesity	21	21M	29–48	psychiatric inpatients; $\bar{x}$ weight = 195.7 lbs.	–	–
Harris, 1969	obesity	24	15F 9M	–	at least 15 lbs. overweight	–	–
Harris & Bruner, 1971	obesity	32	26F 6M	18–48	desired to lose at least 20 lbs.	psychology graduate student	1
Horan & Johnson, 1971	obesity	96	96F	–	20–30% overweight; college students	counseling graduate students	7
Mahoney et al., 1973	obesity	53	48F 5M	$\bar{x}$=40	minimum of 10% overweight; $\bar{x}$= 166.3 lbs.	–	–

Treatment			Outcomes		
Type	No. Sessions	Total Duration	Assessment Procedure	Results	Follow-up
behavior modification (loss of money deposit for weight gain) + diet vs. group therapy + diet vs. diet only	6	6 wks.	weight change; semantic differential	behavior modification + diet = group therapy + diet only	4 wks.; behavior modification + diet group therapy + diet = diet only
self-monitoring (relaxation + lectures) + covert sensitization vs. self-monitoring vs. instructed control	20	10 wks. variable	weight change	self-monitoring + covert sensitization > self-monitoring > instructed control	—
contracting vs. self-control vs. attention control	—	12 wks.	weight change	contracting > self-control; significant pre-post reduction for contracting & self-control	10 mos.; no difference between groups
coverant conditioning vs. scheduled coverants vs. attention (diet) control vs. no-treatment control	3	8 wks.	weight change	coverant conditioning = attention control > no-treatment control	—
self-reward plus self-punishment vs. self-reward vs. self-punishment vs. self-monitoring vs. information control	8	4 wks.	weight change	self-reward > self-monitoring = information control	4 mos.; self-reward & self-reward + punishment > self-punishment or control

Table 15 cont.

Name	Patient					Therapist	
	Diagnosis	No.	Sex	Age	Other	Description	No.
Manno & Marston, 1972	obesity	41	36F 5M	–	desired to lose at least 15 lbs.	psychology graduate student	1
Meynen, 1970	obesity	36	36F	18–45	at least 20% over-weight	–	–
Penick *et al.,* 1971	obesity	32	24F 8M	$\bar{x}=42$	at least 20% over-weight; physical rehab. patients	internist (1) nurse (1); ex-perienced	4
Sachs & Ingram, 1972	obesity	10	–	–	adolescents	psychology graduate students	–
Stollack, 1967	obesity	99	–	18–55	20–30% overweight	psychology graduate & undergrad-uate students	6

Treatment			Outcomes		
Type	No. Sessions	Total Duration	Assessment Procedure	Results	Follow-up
covert sensiti- zation (positive) vs. covert sensi- tization (neg- ative) vs. mini- mal treatment control	6	4 wks.	weight change	covert sensiti- zation (pos- tive) = covert sensitization (negative) > minimal treat- ment control	3 mos.; signifi- cant change main- tained
covert sensiti- zation vs. sys- tematic desen- sitization vs. relaxation + application vs. no-treatment control	8	8 wks.	weight change	covert sensiti- zation = sys- tematic de- sensitization = relaxation + application > no-treatment control	–
behavior modi- fication (moni- toring + control of stimuli discrim. eating + rein- forcement, etc.) vs. group therapy	12	12 wks.	weight change	behavior modi- fication > group therapy	3,6 mos.; gains main- tained
covert sensitiza- tion (forward) vs. covert sen- sitization (back- ward)	2	3 wks.	weight change	no significant condition differences, significant pre- post weight loss within each condition	–
food assoc. shock + diary + contact vs. nonspecific shock + diary + control vs. con- tact + diary vs. no contact + diary vs. no contact – aware of experiment vs. no contact – unaware of experiment	16	8 wks.	weight change	contact plus diary > all other groups	10 wks.; signifi- cant change not main- tained

Table 15 cont.

Name	Diagnosis	No.	Sex	Age	Other	Description	No.
		Patient				Therapist	
Tyler & Straughan, 1970	obesity	57	57F	$\bar{x}$=39.4	$\bar{x}$ weight = 186.4 lbs.	–	–
Wollersheim, 1970	obesity	79	all F	18–36	$\bar{x}$% over-weight = 28.6 lbs.	–	–

Treatment			Outcomes		
Type	No. Sessions	Total Duration	Assessment Procedure	Results	Follow-up
coverant conditioning vs. breath holding vs. relaxation	7	9 wks.	weight change	coverant conditioning = breath holding = relaxation	–
social pressure group vs. insight-oriented group vs. operant conditioning group vs. no-treatment control	10	12 wks.	weight change	operant cond. group = social pressure group = insight group > no-treatment control	8 wks.; no difference between groups

Insomnia

As yet, the research literature on insomnia is quite limited, both in terms of the total number of studies reported as well as the breadth of the treatments investigated. As shown in the summary table, all studies have examined the effectiveness of various forms of muscular relaxation, either alone (e.g., Borkovec & Fowles, 1973; Kahn *et al.*, 1968) or in conjunction with other specific active therapeutic ingredients (e.g., Davison *et al.*, 1973). Results from these studies are consistent with the conclusion that *deep muscular relaxation training* is associated with a significant reduction in the amount of time required to fall asleep as well as with the number of awakenings during sleep. To possibly enhance its effectiveness, it is suggested that the *relaxation training be presented as a self control technique* (Goldfried, 1971) which emphasizes the active role of the individual in applying this new coping skill so as to increase the likelihood that the individual will cognitively attribute improvement to his own behavior change effects (e.g., Weil & Goldfried, 1972). This is consistent with the research evidence gathered by Davison *et al.* (1973), which suggests that attributing therapeutic improvement to one's own efforts serves to enhance the maintenance of the positive gains.

Table 16. INSOMNIA

	Patient					Therapist	
Name	Diagnosis	No.	Sex	Age	Other	Description	No.

Level 1. Nondifferential prescriptions
  Type 1A: Psychotherapy A for patients X

Kahn *et al.*, 1968	insom- nia	17	15M 2F	–	college under- graduates & graduate students	unspecified	–

Level 2. Unidifferential prescriptions
  Type 2A: Psychotherapy A vs. psychotherapy B for patients X

Borkovec & Fowles, 1973	insom- nia	37	all F	–	college student volunteers	males, graduate students	4
Davison *et al.*, 1973	insom- nia	15	10M 5F	19–25	college students	unspecified	–
Nicassio & Bootzin, 1974	insom- nia	30	9M 21F	$\bar{x}$=45.1	non- medicated	psychologist	1

Treatment			Outcomes		
Type	No. Sessions	Total Duration	Assessment Procedure	Results	Follow-up
relaxation (autogenic training)	2	2 wks.	self-report	84% improved	1 yr.; results maintained
relaxation vs. hypnotic relaxation vs. self-relaxation vs. no-treatment control	3	3 wks.	behavior; self-report; physiological measures	relaxation = hypnotic relaxation = self-relaxation > no-treatment control	none
stimulus control + relaxation + drug + instructions about expected effectiveness of drug (minimal vs. maximal)	—	1 wk.	behavior; self-report of restedness	stimulus control + relaxation + drug + instruction of minimal effectiveness > stimulus control + relaxation + drug + instruction of maximal effectiveness	none
relaxation vs. autogenic training vs. self-relaxation control vs. no-treatment control	4	4 wks.	self-report of sleep behavior; spouse or roommate reports; pupillography	relaxation= autogenic training > self-relaxation= no-treatment control	6 mos.; results maintained

Psychosis

SCHIZOPHRENIA

There exists considerable evidence to suggest that schizophrenia, more than any other disorder considered in this book, is most appropriately viewed as a *group of disorders* — the schizophrenias — or, as Rosenthal (1968) suggests, "the schizophrenic spectrum." Beyond possible etiological differences, the several schizophrenic disorders differ in the degree to which they consist of or reflect disturbances of mood, of social behaviors, of anxiety, of certain skill deficits, etc. Stated otherwise, an array of characteristics and syndromes differentially constitute and reflect the schizophrenic disorders. It follows, therefore, that an array of prescriptions is warranted.

For anxiety, mood disturbances, hyperactivity, and other "high arousal" states associated with certain of the schizophrenias, psychopharmacological interventions appear to be the prescriptions of choice. Psychotherapy, in several forms, may be an appropriate secondary prescription for these patient characteristics, but not a especially powerful one. That is, in a number of investigations, "drugs plus psychotherapy" yielded results no more favorable than "drugs" alone.

Apathy and withdrawal may be effectively decreased and social interaction and communication effectively increased by participation in a *token economy* or exposure to related contingency management or *reinforcement*-based procedures. It is of interest that certain other psychotherapies — such as milieu, therapeutic community, companionship and socioenvironmental — also yield incremental, if perhaps less consistent, effects upon interaction and communication. Interpersonal attention is a central feature of these therapies, and it appears to be prescriptively parsimonious to note that interpersonal attention is commonly viewed as a generalized social reinforcement, which can yield significant, behavior-change effects. Thus, reinforcement procedures remain sufficient as the prescriptive basis for apathy reduction and social interaction facilitation.

Given reduced apathy and increased interaction potential, certain types of schizophrenics (e.g., chronic, poor premorbid) may possess marked skill deficits. Such patients have been shown to benefit from *skill training*. The

293

skill training therapies demonstrated to yield significant gains in this regard are *activity, structured learning,* and *habit training.*

With regard to the therapies we have prescribed above, as well as those found ineffective on post-measurement, follow-up examination for later effectiveness is exceedingly rare. Thus the prescriptions offered for the schizophrenias are especially tentative; long-term examination of their continued efficacy is an especially desirable prescriptive research task yet undone.

A substantial and prescriptively relevant body of literature has emerged during the past two decades that speaks to the role of the therapist's personality in the treatment of schizophrenia (Chartier, 1971; Raxin, 1971). Whitehorn and Betz (1954) were the first to differentiate between psychotherapists who obtained relatively high success rates (approximately 75%) from those who obtained relatively low success rates (approximately 27%) with hospitalized schizophrenics. The more successful therapists were designated as type A and the less successful as type B. In addition to differentiating A-B therapists in terms of patient improvement rate, Betz and Whitehorn (1956) found that on the Strong Vocational Interest Blank, A-therapists tended to score high on the "lawyer" and "CPA" scales and low on the "printer" and "mathematics-physical science teacher" scales. B-therapists exhibited the opposite pattern on these scales. In addition, both A- and B-therapists had elevations in the "physician," "psychologist," and "public administrator" scales. More importantly, the two types of therapists were found to differ in the following clinical dimensions which were shown to be related to the differential improvement rates:

1. *The type of relationship:* A's were better able to gain the confidence of their patients;

2. *The type of personal formulation of the patient's problems:* A's tended to understand the motivation and meaning of patient's behavior, while B's tended to formulate their understanding solely in narrative, biographical terms;

3. *Types of strategic goals selected:* A's tended to formulate as goals (a) the patient's developing a better understanding of his capabilities and potentialities for constructive conflict resolution; (b) the development of a dependable, meaningful relationship between the patient and therapist that would serve to foster a new start toward greater confidence and growth in maturity and personality . . .;

4. *The type of tactical pattern used:* A's were actively, personally involved. They were characterized by initiative in sympathetic understanding, honest disagreement, challenging of self depreciation in patients, setting of realistic limits on patient's behavior; while B's adopted passive, interpretive and/or instructional, or practical case patterns. (Razin, 1971, p. 2)

In brief, A-therapists may be characterized as problem-solvers, noncoercive, and able to empathically understand and communicate this understanding in an accepting and persuasive manner (Razin, 1971). In contrast, B-therapists appear to be more opinionated, rigid, demand conformity to conventions, and do not communicate a sense of empathic understanding of the schizophrenic patient's phenomenological experiences.

The prescriptive utility of these findings, however, are limited by the gross designation of the treatment as "psychotherapy" in studies that have examined the influence of A-B therapist styles with schizophrenics. The need for a more prescriptive approach in the analysis of A-B therapist characteristics is highlighted by the finding that the type of treatment does, in fact, interact with the therapist style. For example, Whitehorn and Betz (1957) found no differences in the success rates of A and B therapists when insulin treatment accompanied "psychotherapy." In addition to treatment variables, characteristics of the schizophrenic patient are also crucial determinants which relate to differential success by A and B therapists. Thus, Betz (1963) found A and B therapists differentially successful with process schizophrenics but equally effective with nonprocess schizophrenics. According to Carson (1967) ". . .the difference in therapeutic effectiveness of A and B therapists may be limited to only the most inaccessible and severely disturbed patients . . ." (pp. 47–48), and that ". . .A's in relation to distrustful-extrapunitive others, and B's in relation to trusting-intrapunitive others, tend to respond with relatively greater perceived collaboration, activity and efficacy, and they appear to develop a greater sense that the other person is behaving flexibly and cooperatively" (p. 52).

Table 17. SCHIZOPHRENIA

Name	Diagnosis	No.	Sex	Age	Other	Description	No.
		Patient				Therapist	

Level 1. Nondifferential prescriptions
  Type 1A: Psychotherapy A for patients X

Name	Diagnosis	No.	Sex	Age	Other	Description	No.
Atthowe & Krasner, 1968	schizo-phrenia (chronic)	60	60M	mdn = 57	mdn years hospitalized = 22	Es; ward staff	–
Baker, 1971	schizo-phrenia (chronic)	18	4F 14M	x̄=53	x̄ years hospitalized = 29; mute	nurses	–
Bennet & Robertson, 1955	schizo-phrenia (chronic)	20	20M	x̄=37.5	x̄ length of illness = 15 yrs.	–	–
Bookhammer et al., 1966	schizo-phrenia (acute)	51	–	15–35	–	–	–
Eliseo, 1964	schizo-phrenia (chronic)	84	–	x̄=40.4	x̄ years hospitalized = 7.75 yrs.	nursing assistants	7
Foreyt & Felton, 1970	schizo-phrenia	67	35F 37M	17–86; x̄-35.6	18 Ss non-psychotic	–	6

Treatment			Outcomes		
Type	No. Sessions	Total Duration	Assessment Procedure	Results	Follow-up
token economy	—	14 mos.	behavioral ratings; discharge	improved social inter-action and communication, greater dis-charge rate	—
reinforcement for verbal responsive-ness vs. reinforce-ment for silence	26	13 wks.	behavioral ratings of communi-cations	reinforcement for verbal re-sponsiveness > reinforce-ment for si-lence	1 yr.; results main-tained
habit training vs. no-treatment control	—	2 yrs.	behavioral ratings, inter-views, percep-tual & cog-nitive tests	no significant between-con-dition differences. Significant pre-post improvement in behavioral ratings for habit training in per-sonal appearance	—
direct analysis vs. regular hos-pital treatment	—	—	staff ratings of change in self-con-cept, attitude toward others, work status, etc.	direct analysis = regular hos-pital treat-ment	5.0–5.5 yrs.
remotivation vs. no-treatment con-trol vs. remotiva-tion + occupational therapy	24	24 wks.	adjustment scale; social-ization ratings	remotivation = no-treatment control = remot-ivation + occu-pational therapy	—
milieu	—	variable	behavioral ratings	change propor-tional to length of treatment	—

Table 17 cont.

Name	Diagnosis	No.	Sex	Age	Other	Description	No.
		Patient				Therapist	
Gorham & Green, 1970	schizophrenia (chronic)	66	66M	$\bar{x}$=43	$\bar{x}$ years hospitalized = 18	nurses; aides	–
Grinspoon *et al.*, 1967	schizophrenia (chronic)	10	all M	18–35	minimum years hospitalized = 3	analytically oriented senior staff	18
Horwitz *et al,*, 1958	schizophrenia	12	–	–	–	John Rosen	1
Katkin *et al.*, 1971	schizophrenia	72	72F	$\bar{x}$=43	outpatients	female volunteers	–
Ludwig, 1968	schizophrenia (chronic)	30	14F 16M	21–50	$\bar{x}$ duration of hospitalization = 6.7 years	–	–
Maley *et al.*, 1973	schizophrenia (chronic)	40	40F	$\bar{x}$=36.7	$\bar{x}$ years hospitalized = 8 years	–	–
Meichenbaum & Cameron, 1973	schizophrenia	10	10M	$\bar{x}$=36	$\bar{x}$ years hospitalized = 1½ years	–	1
Mendel & Rapport, 1963	schizophrenia	166	166F	$\bar{x}$=32	$\bar{x}$ yrs. hospitalized = 2.6 yrs.	hospital staff (all categories)	–

Treatment			Outcomes		
Type	No. Sessions	Total Duration	Assessment Procedure	Results	Follow-up
token economy	–	9 mos.	behavioral ratings	decreased withdrawal, disorganized thinking, & suspiciousness	–
analytic + drugs vs. analytic + placebo	mini- mum of 92	2 yrs.	behavioral ratings, patient diaries	analytic + drugs > analytic + placebo	–
direct analysis	daily	$\bar{x}=2-3$ mos.	therapist rating of stability & absence of psychotic episodes	no Ss met outcome standard of emotional stability & no psychotic episodes	10 yrs.
supportive vs. no-treatment control	24 maxi- mum	12 mos.	rehospi- talization rate	supportive > no-treatment control	–
contingency management + milieu vs. milieu treatment	–	10 wks.	behavioral ratings, ad- justment scales	contingency management + milieu > milieu treatment on several behav- ioral & scale dimensions	–
token economy vs. no-treatment control	–	22–31 wks.	behavioral ratings, standardized interview	token economy > no-treatment control on mood, cooperation, communication	–
self-instruction vs. no-treatment control	8	3 wks.	interview, projective, behavioral ratings	self-instruction > no-treatment control on attentional criteria	–
existential	51	51 mos.	interview, rehospital- ization	70% of Ss remained out of the hospi- tal	–

Table 17 cont.

Name	Patient					Therapist	
	Diagnosis	No.	Sex	Age	Other	Description	No.
Roos et al., 1963	schizophrenia	52	–	$\bar{x}=52$	–	–	–
Schaefer & Martin, 1966	schizophrenia (chronic)	40	40F	–	apathetic	nurses; aides	–
Schnore, 1961	schizophrenia (chronic)	24	24M	$\bar{x}=47$	$\bar{x}$ years hospitalized = 18	physical, occupational & music therapists	–
Stevenson & Viney, 1973	schizophrenia (chronic & organic)	100	25F 75M	$\bar{x}=56$	$\bar{x}$ yrs. hospitalized =21	nonprofessional volunteers; 8 males, 42 females	50
Weingaertner, 1970	schizophrenia (paranoid)	45	45M	–	hallucinatory	–	–

Treatment			Outcomes		
Type	No. Sessions	Total Duration	Assessment Procedure	Results	Follow-up
remotivation vs. no-treatment control (regular care)	—	6 wks.	behavioral ratings	remotivation = no-treatment control (regular care)	6 wks.
contingent reinforcement of desirable behaviors vs. noncontingent reinforcement control	—	3 mos.	behavioral ratings of apathy	contingent reinforcement > noncontingent reinforcement control	—
activity vs. no-treatment control	—	2 yrs.	intelligence, projective, adjustment scales	activity > no-treatment control on symptom reduction	
companionship vs. no treatment control	—		behavioral ratings	companionship = no-treatment control on withdrawal, belligerence, depression & disorganization	—
self-administered shock vs. placebo vs. no-treatment control	—	2 wks.	staff ratings	self-administered shock = placebo = no-treatment control on hallucinatory behavior (pre-post significant decrease in all conditions)	—

Table 17 cont.

Name	Patient					Therapist	
	Diagnosis	No.	Sex	Age	Other	Description	No.

Level 2. Unidifferential prescriptions
  Type 2A: Psychotherapy A vs. psychotherapy B for patients X

Appelby, 1963	schizo-phrenia (chron-ic)	53	53F	$\bar{x}$=38	$\bar{x}$ yrs. hos-pitalized = 12	hospital staff (several categories)	—
Azima *et al.*, 1958	schizo-phrenia	18	18F	$\bar{x}$=35	$\bar{x}$ yrs. hos-pitalized = 10	psychiatrist & occupa-tional ther-apist	2
Baker & Thorpe, 1956	schizo-phrenia (chron-ic)	48	—	—	$\bar{x}$ yrs. hos-pitalized = 15	nurses	3
Cockshott, 1971	schizo-phrenia (process)	36	36F	—	—	—	—

Treatment			Outcomes		
Type	No. Sessions	Total Duration	Assessment Procedure	Results	Follow-up
continuous therapist vs. total push vs. hospital treatment vs. no-treatment control	—	1 yr.	behavioral ratings, adjustment scales	continuous therapist = total push = hospital treatment > no-treatment control on communication improvement; significant pre-post change on morbidity, self-care & social responsibility across the experimental groups	20 mos.
object relations (presentation of symbolic infantile situations) vs. occupational psychotherapy	120	6 mos.	therapist ratings	no statistical comparisons; apparent improvement in object relations group in communication & reality testing	2 yrs.; gains apparently maintained in moderately but not severely regressed Ss
habit training vs. electroconvulsive shock vs. regular hospital care	—	17 wks.	behavioral ratings	habit training > electroconvulsive shock on less daytime sleeping, more conversing & self-dressing	—
induced anxiety vs. attention vs. no-treatment control	8	8 wks.	adjustment scales, adjective check list, MMPI; ward behavior	induced anxiety > attention = no-treatment control	—

Table 17 cont.

Name	Patient					Therapist	
	Diagnosis	No.	Sex	Age	Other	Description	No.
Gelbart, 1971	schizo-phrenia	28	28M	–	unassertive & with-drawn	–	–
Gutride *et al.*, 1973	schizo-phrenia	78	33F 45M	$\bar{x}=37$	socially withdrawn	trained under-graduates	20
Gutride *et al.*, 1974	schizo-phrenia	92	43F 49M	$\bar{x}=40$	socially withdrawn	trained under-graduates	40
Hartlage, 1970	schizo-phrenia (chron-ic)	44	44F	$\bar{x}=42$	$\bar{x}$ yrs. hos-pitalized = 17	student nurses	22
Hogan, 1966	schizo-phrenia	50	–	–	–	psycholo-gists	–

Treatment			Outcomes		
Type	No. Sessions	Total Duration	Assessment Procedure	Results	Follow-up
systematic desensitization vs. relaxation	36	3 mos.	behavioral ratings, self-ratings	systematic desensitization = relaxation	−
structured learning (modeling, role playing & social reinforcement) vs. traditional vs. no-treatment control	12	4 wks.	behavioral ratings, mood scales	structured learning > traditional > no-treatment control on increased social interaction	−
structured learning + transfer training vs. structured learning vs. companionship vs. no-treatment control	15	5 wks.	behavioral ratings, mood scales	structured learning + transfer training = structured learning > companionship = no-treatment control on increased social interaction	−
reinforcement vs. "traditional" (i.e., interpretation, relationship)	35	7 wks.	adjustment scales, therapist ratings	reinforcement > traditional on adjustment & therapist criteria	−
implosive vs. insight-oriented therapy	−	$\bar{x}$=4.9–8.2 mos.	MMPI, discharge	implosive > insight-oriented therapy	1 yr.; gains maintained

Table 17 cont.

Name	Patient					Therapist	
	Diagnosis	No.	Sex	Age	Other	Description	No.
King *et al.,* 1960	schizo-phrenia (chron-ic)	48	48M	$\bar{x}=34$	$\bar{x}$ yrs. hos-pitalized = 9; with-drawn	experienced	3
Marks *et al.,* 1968	schizo-phrenia (chron-ic)	22	22M	$\bar{x}=36$	$\bar{x}$ yrs. hos-pitalized = 15	ward staff	9
May, 1968	schizo-phrenia	228	–	16–45	first ad-missions	psychiatrists	41
May & Tuma, 1965	schizo-phrenia	100	53F 47M	$\bar{x}=27$	–	psychiatric residents, psychiatrists	17
Meichenbaum, 1966	schizo-phrenia (acute)	64	64M	$\bar{x}=39$	$\bar{x}$ mos. hospital-ization = 13	–	–
Morris, 1968	schizo-phrenia (acute)	70	–	–	$\bar{x}$ yrs. hos-pitalized = 9	–	–

Treatment			Outcomes		
Type	No. Sessions	Total Duration	Assessment Procedure	Results	Follow-up
operant interpersonal vs. recreation vs. attention vs. no-treatment control	45 to > 90	15 wks.	ward observation; adjustment scales, verbal behavior	operant interpersonal > recreation = attention = no-treatment control on several criteria	–
token economy vs. relationship (crossover design)	–	20–26 wks.	adjustment scales, language & self-concept measure	token economy = relationship (pre-post significant increase in both)	–
supportive + drugs vs. each alone vs. milieu	$\bar{x}=49$	–	self- & therapist ratings, adjustment scales, MMPI	supportive + drugs = drugs > supportive = milieu	–
analytic + drugs vs. each alone vs. electroconvulsive shock vs. regular hospital care	–	1 yr. maximum	therapist ratings, rehospitalization, length of hospitalization, ward behavior	analytic + drugs = drugs > analytic = electroconvulsive shock = regular hospital care	–
contingent vs. noncontingent reinforcement for abstractness vs. punishment for nonabstractness vs. no-treatment control	2	2 days	proverbs test for level of abstraction	contingent reinforcement > all other conditions on posttest & generalized abstraction	–
systematic desensitization + assertiveness vs. systematic desensitization vs. concentration vs. visualization vs. no-treatment control	–	–	behavioral ratings, self-ratings	significant prepost anxiety reduction for systematic desensitization (both types)	–

Table 17 cont.

Name	Patient					Therapist	
	Diagnosis	No.	Sex	Age	Other	Description	No.
Pentony, 1971	schizo-phrenia	48	–	–	–	psycholo-gists	4
Rogers et al., 1967	schizo-phrenia	48	24F 24M	–	stratified on sex, age, & SES	psycholo-gists	8
Serber & Nelson, 1971	schizo-phrenia	24	9F 15M	21–68	$\bar{x}$ length of hos-pitaliza-tion = 4 mos.	–	2
Steinmetz, 1971	schizo-phrenia	38	–	$\bar{x}$=37	$\bar{x}$ yrs. hos-pitalized = 13	author	1
Tourney et al., 1960	schizo-phrenia (chronic)	40	20F 20M	$\bar{x}$=31.8	$\bar{x}$ yrs. hos-pitalized = 7	hospital staff (all categories)	–

Treatment			Outcomes		
Type	No. Sessions	Total Duration	Assessment Procedure	Results	Follow-up
systematic desensitization vs. implosive vs. attention vs. regular hospital care	10	–	therapist ratings, self-ratings, MMPI	systematic desensitization = implosive = attention = regular hospital care	–
client-centered vs. milieu vs. no-treatment control (non-patients)	–	2 mos. to 2½ yrs.	projective, relationship, behavioral ratings	client-centered = milieu = no-treatment control	1 yr.; no significant differences
systematic desensitization + assertiveness training vs. each alone	18 max.	6 wks.	behavioral ratings, self-rating	systematic desensitization + assertiveness training = systematic desensitization = assertiveness training	6 mos.; results maintained for systematic desensitization only
reinforcement vs. modeling vs. no-treatment control	12	4 wks.	observation of work persistence	reinforcement = modeling = no-treatment control; significant (pre-post) increase in work persistence within reinforcement condition	–
regular hospital care vs. resocialization	–	9 mos.	adjustment scale, behavioral ratings	significant pre-post improvement on adjustment scales for males only. No significant between-condition differences	20 mos.; gains not maintained

Table 17 cont.

| Name | Patient | | | | | Therapist | |
	Diagnosis	No.	Sex	Age	Other	Description	No.
Ullmann *et al.*, 1965	schizo-phrenia (chron-ic)	60	60M	$\bar{x}=41$	$\bar{x}$ yrs. hos-pitalized = 7	psychology graduate students	5
Wilson & Walters, 1966	schizo-phrenia	12	12M	$\bar{x}=46$	minimal speech	–	–
Zeisset, 1968	schizo-phrenia	48	48M	$\bar{x}=40$	$\bar{x}$ mos. hospital-ized = 8	psychology graduate student	1

Level 3. Bidifferential prescriptions
  Type 3A: Psychotherapy A vs. psychotherapy B for patients X vs. patients Y

| Ludwig & Marx, 1971 | schizo-phrenia | 28 | 14F 14M | $\bar{x}=31$ | $\bar{x}$ yrs. hos-pitalized = 10; soc-ially with-drawn vs. responsive | – | – |

Treatment			Outcomes		
Type	No. Sessions	Total Duration	Assessment Procedure	Results	Follow-up
reinforcement of healthy talk vs. sick talk vs. plural nouns	1	20 min.	amount sick talk	reinforcement of healthy talk > reinforcement of sick talk = reinforcement of plural nouns on decrease in sick talk	–
modeling + reinforcement vs. modeling vs. no-treatment control	16–30	–	behavioral ratings of speech output	modeling + reinforcement = modeling > no-treatment control on verbal productivity	–
systematic desensitization vs. relaxation + application vs. attention vs. no-treatment control	4	2 wks.	behavioral & self-ratings of anxiety	systematic desensitization = relaxation + application > attention = no-treatment control on anxiety reduction	–
attention + structure vs. each alone vs. no-treatment control (crossover design)	–	24 wks.	behavioral ratings, adjustment scales	socially withdrawn Ss: attention + structure > attention = structure > no-treatment control. Socially responsive Ss: attention + structure > no-treatment control > attention > structure	–

Table 17 cont.

Name	Patient					Therapist	
	Diagnosis	No.	Sex	Age	Other	Description	No.
Weinman *et al.*, 1972	schizo-phrenia	63	63M	$\bar{x}=45$	$\bar{x}$ yrs. hos-pitalized = 12; un-assertive & with-drawn; younger (31.9 yrs.) vs. old-er (54.2 yrs.)	psycholo-gists & parapro-fessional trainees	9

Type 3B: Psychotherapist 1 vs. psychotherapist 2 for patients X vs. patients Y

Name	Patient					Therapist	
Karon & Vandenbos, 1970	schizo-phrenia	36	–	–	–	psychiatrists & psycholo-gists; exper-ienced vs. inexper-ienced	12

Treatment			Outcomes		
Type	No. Sessions	Total Duration	Assessment Procedure	Results	Follow-up
socioenvironmental vs. systematic desensitization vs. relaxation	36	3 mos.	behavioral ratings, anxiety scale	socioenvironmental > systematic desensitization = relaxation for older Ss; socioenvironmental best with older Ss, no treatment difference with younger Ss	—
analytic + drug vs. analytic vs. supportive + drugs	60 (analytic groups only)	1 yr.	concept formation test, length of hospitalization	pooled analytic > supportive on shorter hospitalization & less thought disorder. Inexperienced therapists + unmedicated Ss led to longer hospitalization but lower thought disorder; inexperienced therapists + medicated Ss led to briefer hospitalization but little improvement in thinking	—

Summary and Conclusions

In this section of the book we have examined the psychotherapy research literature for the purpose of identifying combinations of patient, therapist, and treatment variables that are predictive of specific therapeutic outcomes. In addition, for each diagnostic category reviewed, the currently most optimal psychotherapeutic prescription was derived. Table 18 is a summary of these prepotent prescriptions. When presented in this capsule form, the importance, desirability, and clinical utility of differential treatment becomes evident. The "paradigm shift" away from unidimensional psychotherapy studies and toward factorially designed investigations, with its emphasis on the interaction between patient, therapist, and treatment variables, has provided an initial but substantial body of clinically relevant knowledge about which patients may benefit in specific ways from different forms of treatment. Much less is currently known, however, about the therapist's contribution to the change process. In all but a few studies the specific active therapist ingredients remained obscured and unanalyzed. Certainly, one future direction of prescriptive research should be directed toward identifying the manner in which known therapist dimensions within particular therapeutic approaches interact with patient characteristics operating across different treatment contexts. A second and equally crucial implication is the need to develop a conceptual system that serves to integrate and explain the empirically derived prescriptive relationships. While we have shown that diagnostic assessment is indeed relevant to the conduct of psychotherapy, it does not necessarily follow that differentiation between patients in terms of diagnostic labels is the most optimal approach for prescriptive purposes. Rather, what appears needed is a conceptual and technical system of assessment that differentiates between the heterogeneity that surely exists within existing diagnostic categories as well as one which meaningfully relates to the active therapist and technique variables operative during treatment. When this is accomplished, therapists would certainly be in a better position to derive specific treatments or combinations of treatments that are idiosyncratized to the unique characteristics of the individual patient. Currently, the behaviorally oriented therapies have generally adapted this framework, in which assessment and treatment are conceptually and pragmatically interrelated; this may, in part, account for the extensive contributions and prominence of this approach in the formulation of current prepotent psychotherapeutic prescriptions.

Table 18: SUMMARY OF CURRENT PREPOTENT CLINICAL PRESCRIPTIONS

Diagnosis	Patient Characteristics	Therapist	Treatment	Outcome
Psychoneuroses				
Phobic reactions				
acrophobia	female	—	contact desensitization	decreases in self-report of anxiety; behavioral improvement
agoraphobia	—	—	unknown	—
aquaphobia	college students	nonprofessionals	*in vivo* desensitization	decreases in self-report of anxiety; behavioral improvement
aviation fears	pilots	—	systematic desensitization	decreases in self-report of anxiety
fears of sickness or death	—	—	thought stopping	decreases in anxiety and precipitating thoughts
nonassertiveness	college students	nonprofessionals	behavioral rehearsal	decreases in self-report of anxiety; behavioral improvement
social anxiety	college students	nonprofessionals	behavioral rehearsal	decreases in self-report of anxiety; behavioral improvement
speech anxiety	college students	professionals & nonprofessionals	systematic desensitization; behavioral rehearsal; implosive therapy; fixed role therapy	decreases in self-report of anxiety; behavioral improvement
test anxiety	elementary, high school, college students	professionals & nonprofessionals	systematic desensitization (plus cognitive problem solving)	decreases in self-report of anxiety; improved grades
Obsessive compulsive	adult males & females	—	paradoxical intention; *in vivo* desensitization; flooding	decreases in self-report of anxiety; behavioral improvement

Diagnosis	Patient Characteristics	Therapist	Treatment	Outcome
Hysteria	—	—	unknown	—
Depression	adults	professionals	contingency management	decreases in frequency of depressed behaviors
	adult females	professionals	supportive therapy; interpersonal problem solving	improved social adjustment
Psychophysiological Disorders				
Bronchial asthma	adults & children	professionals	systematic desensitization	reduction in asthmatic attacks, improved respiration
Ulcerative colitus	persons with well-differentiated object relations	professionals	psychoanalysis	symptom improvement; improved adjustment
	persons with poorly differentiated object relations	professionals therapy	nondirective therapy	symptom improvement; improved adjustment
Hypertension & hypertensive headaches	adult males & females	—	biofeedback	reduction in blood pressure & frequency of headaches
Migraine	adult males & females	—	systematic desensitization; autogenic training	reduced frequency of migraine attacks
Sexual Deviations				
Sexual orientation disturbance (homosexuality)	adult males; history of pleasurable heterosexual interests	professionals	aversive conditioning; psychoanalysis	decreased homosexual arousal & increased heterosexual arousal

Table 18 cont.

Diagnosis	Patient Characteristics	Therapist	Treatment	Outcome
Orgasmic dysfunction (frigidity)	introverted females; well educated	professionals	systematic desensitization; "Masters & Johnson" program	increased frequency of orgasms
Orgasmic dysfunction (impotence)	erective failure (males)	professionals	systematic desensitization; "Masters & Johnson" program	increased satisfaction in sexual intercourse; decrease in erective failures
Fetishism & transvestism	adult males	—	aversive conditioning	decrease in covert & overt problem behaviors
Exhibitionism	adult males	professionals	covert sensitization	decrease in covert & overt exhibitionist behaviors
Anti-social behavior	adolescents & adults	professionals & nonprofessionals	reality therapy	reduction in parole violations
Smoking	adult males & females	—	emotional role playing	reduction in cigarettes smoked
Obesity	adult males & females	professionals & nonprofessionals	operant conditioning procedures; contingency contracting	weight-loss
Insomnia	adult males & females	professionals & nonprofessionals	relaxation training (self-control procedure)	decrease in time to fall asleep
Psychosis Schizophrenia	hospitalized adult males & females	professionals & nonprofessionals	contingency management	decrease in apathy & increase in social interaction
	hospitalized adult males & females	professionals & nonprofessionals	structured learning therapy	increase in social skills

REFERENCES

Agras, W. S. Transfer during systematic desensitization therapy. *Behaviour Research and Therapy,* 1967, **5,** 193–199.

Alexander, A. B. Systematic relaxation and flow rates in asthmatic children: Relationship to emotional precipitants and anxiety. *Journal of Psychosomatic Research,* 1972, **16,** 405–410.

Alexander, A. B., Miklich, D. R., & Hershkoff, H. The immediate effects of systematic relaxation training on peak expiratory flow rates in asthmatic children. *Psychosomatic Medicine,* 1972, **34,** 388–394.

Alexander, F., & Flagg, G. W. The psychosomatic approach. In B.B. Wolman (Ed.), *Handbook of clinical psychology.* New York: McGraw-Hill, 1965. 855–947.

Alexander, L. Contribution of physical treatment to the process and goals of psychotherapy. *American Journal of Psychiatry,* 1966, **123,** 87–91.

Allen, G. J. Effectiveness of study counseling and desensitization in alleviating test anxiety in college students. *Journal of Abnormal Psychology,* 1971, 77, 282–289.

Allen, G. J. The behavioral treatment of test anxiety: Recent research and future trends. *Behavior Therapy,* 1972, 3, 253–262.

Allen, G. J. Treatment of group-administered or self-administered relaxation and study counseling. *Behavior Therapy,* 1973, **4,** 349–360.

American Psychiatric Association. *Diagnostic and statistical manual of mental disorders.* Washington, D.C., 1968.

Appleby, L. Evaluation of treatment methods for chronic schizophrenics. *Archives of General Psychiatry,* 1963, 8, 8–21.

Arbuckle, D. S., & Boy, A. V. Client-centered therapy in counseling students with behavior problems. *Journal of Counseling Psychology,* 1961, 8, 136–139.

Astin, A. W. The functional autonomy of psychotherapy. *American Psychologist,* 1961, **16,** 75–78.

Atthowe, J. M., & Krasner, L. Preliminary report on the application of contingent reinforcement procedures (token economy) on a "chronic" psychiatric ward. *Journal of Abnormal Psychology,* 1968, 73, 37–43.

Auld, F., Jr., & Murray, E. J. Content-analysis studies of psychotherapy. *Psychological Bulletin,* 1955, **52,** 377–395.

Azima, H., Wittkower, E. D., & Latendresse, J. Object relations therapy in schizophrenic states. *American Journal of Psychiatry,* 1958, **115,** 60–62.

Azrin, N. H., & Powell, J. Behavioral engineering: The reduction of smoking behavior by a conditioning apparatus and procedure. *Journal of Applied Behavior Analysis,* 1968, **1,** 193–200.

Bach, G. R. *Intensive group psychotherapy.* New York: Ronald Press, 1954.

Baker, A. A., & Thorpe, J. G. Deteriorated psychotic patients – their treatment and its assessment. *Journal of Mental Science,* 1956, **102,** 780–789.

Baker, R. The use of operant conditioning to reinstate speech in mute schizophrenics. *Behaviour Research and Therapy,* 1971, 9, 329–336.

Barlow, D. H. Increasing heterosexual responsiveness in the treatment of sexual deviation: A review of the clinical and experimental evidence. *Behavior Therapy,* 1973, 4, 655–671.

Beck, A. T. *Depression: causes and treatment.* Philadelphia: University of Pennsylvania Press, 1967.

Beier, E. G. *The silent language of psychotherapy.* Chicago: Aldine, 1966.

Bennet, D. H., & Robertson, J. P. S. The effects of habit training on chronic schizophrenic patients. *Journal of Mental Science,* 1955, **101**, 664.

Bensen, H. Shapiro, D., Turskey, B., & Schwartz, G. Decreased systolic blood pressure through operant conditioning techniques in patients with essential hypertension. *Science,* 1971, **173**, 740–741.

Berecz, J. Modification of smoking behavior through self-administered punishment of imagined behavior: A new approach to aversion therapy. *Journal of Consulting and Clinical Psychology,* 1972, **38**, 244–250.

Bergin, A. E., & Strupp, H. H. *Changing frontiers in the science of psychotherapy.* Chicago: Aldine, 1972.

Bernstein, D. A. Modification of smoking behavior: An evaluative review. *Psychological Bulletin,* 1969, **71**, 418–440.

Betz, B. Validation of the differential treatment success of "A" and "B" therapists with schizophrenic patients. *American Journal of Psychiatry,* 1963, **119**, 1090–1091.

Betz, B. J., & Whitehorn, J. C. The relationship of the therpist to the outcome of therapy in schizophrenia. *Psychiatric Research Reports,* 1956, **5**, 89–105.

Beyme, J. Hyperesthesia of taste and touch treated by reciprocal inhibition. *Behaviour Research and Therapy,* 1964, **2**, 7–14.

Bhattacharyya, D. D., & Singh, R. Behavior therapy of hysterical fits. *American Journal of Psychiatry,* 1971, **128**, 602–606.

Bieber, B., Bieber, I., Dain, H. J., Dince, P. R., Drellich, M. G., Grand, H. G., Grundlach, R. H., Kremer, M. W., Wilber, C. B., & Bieber, T. D. *Homosexuality.* New York: Basic Books, 1963.

Birk, L., Huddleston, W., Miller, E., & Cohler, B. Avoidance conditioning for homosexuality. *Archives of General Psychiatry,* 1971, **25**, 313–323.

Blocher, D. What counseling can offer clients: Implications for research on selection. In J. M. Whiteley (Ed.), *Research in counseling.* Columbus, Ohio: Merrill, 1968, 5–21.

Blumberg, R. W. Therapist leadership and client dogmatism in a therapy analogue. *Psychotherapy: Theory, Research and Practice,* 1972, **9**, 132–138.

Bond, I. K., & Hutchinson, H. C. Application of reciprocal inhibition therapy to exhibitionism. *The Canadian Medical Association Journal,* 1960, **83**, 23–25.

Bookhammer, R. S., Meyers, R. W., Schober, C. C., & Piotrowski, Z. A. A five-year clinical follow-up study of schizophrenics treated by Rosen's "Direct analysis" compared with controls. *American Journal of Psychiatry,* 1966, **123**, 602–604.

Borkovec, T. D., Fowles, D. C. Controlled investigation of the effects of progressive and hypnotic relaxation on insomnia. *Journal of Abnormal Psychology,* 1973, **82**, 153–158.

Boulougouris, J. C., Marks, I. M., & Marset, P. Superiority of flooding (implosion) to desensitization for reducing pathological fear. *Behaviour Research and Therapy,* 1971, **9**, 7–16.

Brady, J. P. Brevital-relaxation treatment of frigidity. *Behaviour Research and Therapy,* 1966, **4**, 71–77.

Braginsky, B. M., Braginsky, D. D., & Ring, K. *Methods of madness.* New York: Holt, Rinehart & Winston, 1969.

Breger, L., & McGaugh, J. Critique and reformulation of learning theory approaches to psychotherapy and neurosis. *Psychological Bulletin,* 1965, **63**, 338–358.

British Tuberculosis Association. Hypnosis for asthma – controlled trial. A report to the research committee of the British Tuberculosis Association. *British Medical Journal,* 1968, **4**, 71–76.

Brody, B. Freud's case-load. *Psychotherapy: Theory, Research and Practice,* 1970, **7**, 8–12.

Brown, B. M. Cognitive aspects of Wolpe's behavior therapy. *American Journal of Psychiatry,* 1967, **124,** 854–859.

Brown, D. G., & Bettley, F. R. Psychiatric treatment of eczema: A controlled trial. *British Medical Journal,* 1971, **2,** 729–734.

Budzynski, T., Stoyva, J., & Adler, C. Feedback induced muscle relaxation: Application to tension headache. Paper presented at the Ninth Annual Meeting of the Society for Psychophysiological Research, Monterey, California, October 1969.

Burchard, J. Systematic socialization: A programmed environment for the habilitation of anti-social retardates. *Psychological Record,* 1967, **17,** 461–476.

Burchard, J. D., & Barrera, B. An analysis of time-out and response cost in a programmed environment. *Journal of Applied Behavior Analysis,* 1972, **5,** 271–282.

Burgess, E. P. The modification of depressive behaviors. In R. D. Rubin and C. M. Franks (Eds.), *Advances in behavior therapy, 1968.* New York: Academic Press, 1969, 193–199.

Buss, A. H. *Psychopathology.* New York: Wiley, 1966.

Carson, R. C. A and B therapist "types": a possible critical variable in psychotherapy. *Journal of Nervous and Mental Disease,* 1967, **144,** 47–54.

Cartwright, D. S. Annotated bibliography of research and theory construction in client-centered therapy. *Journal of Counseling Psychology,* 1957, **4,** 82–100.

Chapman, R. F., Smith, J. W., & Layden, T. Elimination of cigarette smoking by punishment and self-management training. *Behaviour Research and Therapy,* 1971, **9,** 255–264.

Chartier, G. M. A-B therapist variable: Real or imagined? *Psychological Bulletin,* 1971, **75,** 22–33.

Cockshott, J. B. The efficacy of induced anxiety with chronic hospitalized schizophrenics. *Dissertation Abstracts International,* 1971, **32,** 3631.

Cohen, R. The effects of group interaction and progressive hierarchy presentation on desensitization of test anxiety, *Behaviour Research and Therapy,* 1969, **7,** 15–26.

Cole, N. J., Branch, C. H. H., & Allison, R. B. Some relationships between social class and the practice of dynamic psychotherapy. *American Journal of Psychiatry,* 1962, **118,** 1004–1012.

Collison, D. R. Hypnotherapy in the management of asthma. *The American Journal of Clinical Hypnosis,* 1968, **11,** 6–11.

Cooper, A. J. Outpatient treatment of impotence. *The Journal of Nervous and Mental Disease,* 1969, **149,** 360–371.

Cooper, A. J. Frigidity, treatment and short-term prognosis. *Journal of Psychosomatic Research,* 1970, **14,** 133–147.

Crighton, J., & Jehn, D. Treatment of examination anxiety by systematic desensitization or psychotherapy in groups. *Behaviour Research and Therapy,* 1969, **7,** 245–248.

Croft, M., Stephenson, G., & Granger, C. A controlled trial of authoritarian and self-governing regimes with adolescent psychopaths. *American Journal of Orthopsychiatry,* 1964, **34,** 543–554.

Curran, D., & Parr, D. Homosexuality: An analysis of 100 male cases seen in private practice. *British Medical Journal,* 1957, **1,** 797–801.

Davison, G. C., Tsujimoto, R. N., & Glaros, A. G. Attribution and the maintenance of behavior change in falling asleep. *Journal of Abnormal Psychology,* 1973, **82,** 124–133.

Devine, D. A., & Fernald, P. S. Outcome effects of receiving a preferred, randomly assigned and non-preferred therapy. *Journal of Consulting and Clinical Psychology,* 1973, **41,** 104–107.

DiLoreto, A. O. A comparison of the relative effectiveness of systematic desensitization, rational-emotive and client-centered group psychotherapy in the reduction of interpersonal anxiety in introverts and extroverts. *Dissertation Abstracts International,* 1970, **30,** 5230–5231.

DiLoreto, A. O. *Comparative psychotherapy, an experimental analysis.* Chicago: Aldine-Atherton, 1971.

Donner, L. Automated group desensitization – a follow-up report. *Behaviour Research and Therapy,* 1970, **8,** 241–248.

Donner, L,, & Guerney, B. G. Automated group desensitization for test anxiety. *Behaviour Research and Therapy,* 1969, **7,** 1–13.

Druss, R. G., O'Connor, J. F., & Stern, L. O. Psychologic response to colectomy: *II.* Adjustment to a permanent colostomy. *Archives of General Psychiatry,* 1969, **20,** 419–427.

Dua, P. S. Comparison of the effects of behaviorally oriented action and psychotherapy reeduction of introversion-extroversion, emotionality, and internal-external control. *Journal of Counseling Psychology,* 1970, **17,** 567–572.

D'Zurilla, T. J., & Goldfried, M. R. Problem solving and behavior modification. *Journal of Abnormal Psychology,* 1971, **78,** 107–126.

Eliseo, T. Effectiveness of remotivation technique with chronic psychiatric patients. *Psychological Reports,* 1964, **14,** 171–178.

Elliot, R., & Tighe, T. Breaking the cigarette habit: Effects of a technique involving threatened loss of money. *Psychological Record,* 1968, **18,** 503–513.

Ellis, A. The effectiveness of psychotherapy with individuals who have severe homosexual problems. *Journal of Consulting Psychology,* 1956, **20,** 191–195.

Emery, J. R., & Krumboltz, J. D. Standard versus individualized hierarchies in desensitization to reduce test anxiety. *Journal of Counseling Psychology,* 1967, **14,** 204–209.

Engeln, R. G. A comparison of desensitization and aversive conditioning as treatment methods to reduce cigarette smoking. *Dissertation Abstracts International,* 1969, **30,** 1357.

Evans, D. R. Masturbatory fantasy and sexual deviation. *Behaviour Research and Therapy,* 1968, **6,** 17–19.

Evans, D. R. Subjective variables and treatment effects in aversion therapy. *Behaviour Research and Therapy,* 1970, **8,** 147–152.

Eysenck, H. J. The effects of psychotherapy. In H. J. Eysenck (Ed.), *Handbook of abnormal psychology: An experimental approach.* New York: Basic Books, 1961, 697–725.

Faulk, M. Factors in the treatment of frigidity. *British Journal of Psychiatry,* 1971, **119,** 53–56.

Feinsilver, D. B. & Gunderson, J. G. Psychotherapy for schizophrenics – is it indicated? A review of the relevant literature. *Schizophrenia Bulletin,* 1972, **6,** 11–23.

Feldman, M. P., & MacCulloch, M. J. The application of anticipatory avoidance learning to the treatment of homosexuality. *Behaviour Research and Therapy,* 1965, **2,** 165–183.

Feldman, M. P., & MacCulloch, M. J. The results of aversion therapy on a series of homosexual patients. In M. P. Feldman and M. J. MacCulloch, *Homosexual behavior: Therapy and assesment.* New York: Pergamon Press, 1971, 65–94.

Foreyt, J. P., & Felton, G. S. Change in behavior of hospitalized psychiatric patients in a milieu therapy setting. *Psychotherapy: Theory, Research, and Practice,* 1970, **1,** 139–142.

Foreyt, J. P., & Hagen, R. L. Covert sensitization: Conditioning or suggestion? *Journal of Abnormal Psychology,* 1973, **82,** 17–23.

Foreyt, J. P., & Kennedy, W. A. Treatment of overweight by aversion therapy. *Behaviour Research and Therapy,* 1971, **9,** 29–34.

Frank, J. D. *Persuasion and healing: A comparative study of psychotherapy.* Baltimore: Johns Hopkins Press, 1961.

Franks, C. M., Fried, R., & Ashem, B. An improved apparatus for the aversive conditioning of cigarette smokers. *Bahaviour Research and Therapy,* 1966, **4**, 301—308.

Freeling, N. W., & Shemberg, K. M. The alleviation of test anxiety by systematic desensitization. *Behaviour Research and Therapy,* 1970, **8**, 293—299.

Freund, K. Some problems in the treatment of homosexuality. In H. J. Eysenck (Ed.), *Behavior therapy and the neuroses.* London: Pergamon Press, 1960, 312—326.

Friedman, D. The treatment of impotence by brevital relaxation therapy. *Behaviour Research and Therapy,* 1968, **6**, 257—261.

Gardner, G. G. The psychotherapeutic relationship. *Psychological Bulletin,* 1964, **61**, 426—437.

Garlington, W. K., & Cotler, S. B. Systematic desensitization of test anxiety. *Behaviour Research and Therapy,* 1968, **6**, 247—256.

Gelbart, P. A study of the use of systematic desensitization with relaxation and relaxation alone with withdrawn hospitalized male schizophrenic patients. *Dissertation Abstracts International,* 1971, **32**, 1334.

Gelder, M. G., & Marks, I. M. Severe agoraphobia: A controlled prospective trial of behavior therapy. *British Journal of Psychiatry,* 1966, **112**, 309—319.

Gelder, M. G., & Marks, I. M. Desensitization and phobia: A cross-over study. *British Journal of Psychiatry,* 1968, **114**, 323—328.

Gerson, P., & Lanyon, R. I. Modification of smoking behavior with an aversion — desensitization procedure. *Journal of Consulting and Clinical Psychology,* 1972, **38**, 399—402.

Gerz, H. O. Experience with the logotherapeutic technique of paradoxical intention in the treatment of phobic and obsessive-compulsive patients. *American Journal of Psychiatry,* 1966, **123**, 548—553.

Glasser, W. *Reality therapy: A new approach to psychiatry.* New York: Harper and Row, 1965.

Glen, A. Psychotherapy and medical treatment for duodenal ulcer compared using the augmented histamine test. *Journal of Psychosomatic Research,* 1968, **12**, 163—169.

Glick, B. S. Conditioning therapy with phobic patients: Success and failure. *American Journal of Psychotherapy,* 1970, **24**, 92—101.

Goldfried, M. R. Systematic desensitization as training in self control. *Journal of Consulting and Clinical Psychology,* 1971, **37**, 228—234.

Goldfried, M. R., & Pomeranz, D. M. Role of assessment in behavior and modification. *Psychological Reports,* 1968, **23**, 75—87.

Goldstein, A. P. *Therapist-patient expectancies in psychotherapy.* New York: Pergamon Press, 1962.

Goldstein, A. P. Domains and dilemmas. *International Journal of Psychiatry,* 1969, **7**, 128—134.

Goldstein, A. P. *Psychotherapeutic attraction.* New York: Pergamon Press, 1971.

Goldstein, A. P. *Structured learning therapy: Toward a psychotherapy for the poor.* New York: Academic Press, 1973.

Goorney, A. B. Treatment of aviation phobias by behavior therapy. *British Journal of Psychiatry,* 1970, **117**, 535—544.

Gorham, D. R., & Green, L. W. Effect of operant conditioning techniques on chronic schizophrenics. *Psychological Reports,* 1970, **27**, 223—234.

Grace, W. J., Pinsky, R. H., & Wolff, H. G. The treatment of ulcerative colitis. *Gastroenterology,* 1954, **26**, 462—468.

Graff, R. W., MacLean, G. D., & Loving, A. Group reactive inhibition and reciprocal inhibitions therapies with anxious college students. *Journal of Counseling Psychology,* 1971, **18**, 431—436.

Grimaldi, K. E., & Lichtenstein, E. Hot, smoky air as an aversive stimulus in the treatment of smoking. *Behaviour Research and Therapy,* 1969, **7,** 275–282.

Grimshaw, L. The outcome of obsessional disorder: A follow-up study of 100 cases. *British Journal of Psychiatry,* 1965, **111,** 1051–1056.

Grinker, R. R. Emerging concepts of mental health and models of treatment: The medical point of view. *American Journal of Psychiatry,* 1969, **125,** 865–869.

Grinspoon, L., Ewalt, J. R., & Shader, R. Long term treatment of chronic schizophrenia: A preliminary report. *International Journal of Psychiatry,* 1967, **4,** 116–128.

Grossberg, J. M. Behavior therapy: A review. *Psychological Bulletin,* 1964, **62,** 73–88.

Gutride, M. E., Goldstein, A. P., & Hunter, G. F. The use of modeling and role playing to increase social interaction among asocial psychiatric patients. *Journal of Consulting and Clinical Psychology,* 1973, **40,** 408–415.

Gutride, M., Goldstein, A. P., & Hunter, G. F. Structured learning therapy for increasing social interaction skills. *Journal of Clinical Psychology,* 1974, July, 277–280.

Guttmacher, J. A., & Birk, L. Group therapy: What specific therapeutic advantages. *Comprehensive Psychiatry,* 1971, **12,** 546–556.

Haley, J. *Strategies of psychotherapy.* New York: Grune and Stratton, 1963.

Hark, R. D. An examination of the effectiveness of coverant conditioning in the reduction of cigarette smoking. *Dissertation Abstracts International,* 1970, **31,** 2958.

Harmatz, M. G., & Lapuc, P. Behavior modification of overeating in a psychiatric population. *Journal of Consulting and Clinical Psychology,* 1968, **32,** 583–587.

Harper, R. A. *Psychoanalysis and psychotherapy,* Englewood Cliffs, N. J.: Prentice Hall, 1959.

Harris M. B. Self-directed program for weight control: A pilot study. *Journal of Abnormal Psychology,* 1969, **74,** 263–270.

Harris, M. B., & Bruner, C. G. A comparison of a self-control and a contract procedure for weight control. *Behaviour Research and Therapy,* 1971, **9,** 347–354.

Harris, M. B., & Rothberg, C. A. Self-control approach to reducing smoking. *Psychological Reports,* 1972, **31,** 165–166.

Hartlage, L. C. Subprofessional therapists' use of reinforcement versus traditional psychotherapeutic techniques with schizophrenics. *Journal of Consulting and Clinical Psychology,* 1970, **34,** 181–183.

Heller, K. A broader perspective for interview therapy. Presented at Midwestern Psychological Association, Chicago, 1965.

Hersen, M., Eisler, R. M., Alford, G. S., & Agras, W. S. Effects of token economy on neurotic depression: An experimental analysis. *Behavior Therapy,* 1973, **4,** 392–397.

Herzog, Elizabeth. *Some guidelines for evaluative research.* (United States Department of Health, Education and Welfare, Social Security Administration Children's Bureau, pamphlet) Washington, D. C.: Government Printing Office, 1959.

Hobbs, N. Sources of gain in psychotherapy. *American Psychologist,* 1962, **17,** 741–747.

Hodgson, R., Rachman, S., & Marks, M. The treatment of chronic obsessive-compulsive neurosis: Follow-up and further findings. *Behaviour Research and Therapy,* 1972, **10,** 181–189.

Hoehn-Saric, R., Frank, J. D., Imber, S. D., Nash, E. H., Stone, A. R., & Battle, C. C. Systematic preparation of patients for psychotherapy. I. Effects on therapy behavior and outcome. *Journal of Psychiatric Research,* 1964, **2,** 267–281.

Hogan, R. A. Implosive therapy in the short term treatment of psychotics. *Psychotherapy: Theory, Research, and Practice,* 1966, **3,** 25–32.

Homme, L. Perspectives in psychology: XXIV. Control of coverants, the operants of the mind. *Psychological Record,* 1965, **15,** 501–511.

Homme, L., Csany, A. P., Gonzales, M. A., & Rechs, J. R. *How to use contingency contracting in the classroom.* Champaign, Ill.: Research Press, 1970.

Horan, J. J., & Johnson, R. G. Coverant conditioning through a self-management application of the Premack principle: Its effect on weight reduction. *Journal of Behaviour Therapy and Experimental Psychiatry,* 1971, **2**, 243–249.

Horwitz, W., Polatin, P., Kolb, L., & Hoch, P. A study of cases of schizophrenia treated by "direct analysis." *American Journal of Psychiatry,* 1958, **114**, 780–783.

Hussain, M. Z. Desensitization and flooding (implosion) in treatment of phobias. *American Journal of Psychiatry,* 1971, **127**, 1509–1514.

Ingram, I. M. Obsessional illness in mental hospital patients. *Journal of Mental Science,* 1961, **107**, 382–402.

James, L. E., & Foreman, M. E. A-B status of behavior therapy technicians as related to success of Mower's conditioning treatment for enuresis. *Journal of Consulting and Clinical Psychology,* 1973, **47**, 224–229.

Janda, L. H., & Rimm, D. C. Covert sensitization in the treatment of obesity. *Journal of Abnormal Psychology,* 1972, **80**, 37–42.

Janis, I. L., & Mann, L. Effectiveness of emotional role-playing in modifying smoking habits and attitudes. *Journal of Experimental Research in Personality,* 1965, **1**, 84–90.

Johnson, S. M., & Sechrest, L. Comparison of desensitization and progressive relaxation in treating test anxiety. *Journal of Consulting and Clinical Psychology,* 1968, **32**, 280–286.

Johnson, T., Tyler, V., Thompson, R., & Jones, E. Systematic desensitization and assertive training in the treatment of speech anxiety in middle-school students. *Psychology in the Schools,* 1971, **8**, 263–267.

Kahn, M., & Baker, B. Desensitization with minimal therapist contact. *Journal of Abnormal Psychology,* 1968, **73**, 198–200.

Kahn, M., Baker, B. L., & Weiss, J. M. Treatment of insomnia by relaxation training. *Journal of Abnormal Psychology,* 1968, **73**, 556–558.

Kanfer, F., & Phillips, J. *Learning foundations of behavior therapy.* New York: Wiley, 1970.

Kanfer, F. H. & Saslow, G. Behavioral diagnosis. In C. M. Franks (Ed.), *Behavior therapy: Appraisal and status.* New York: McGraw-Hill, 1969, 417–444.

Karon, B. P., & Vandenbos, G. R. Experience, medication, and the effectiveness of psychotherapy with schizophrenics. *British Journal of Psychiatry,* 1970, **116**, 427–428.

Karst, T. O., & Trexler, L. D. Initial study using fixed-role and rational-emotive therapy in treating public-speaking anxiety. *Journal of Consulting and Clinical Psychology,* 1970, **34**, 360–366.

Karush, A., Daniels, G. E., O'Connor, J. F., & Stern, L. O. The response to psychotherapy in chronic ulcerative colitus. *Psychomatic Medicine,* 1969, **31**, 201–226.

Katahn, M., Strenger, S., & Cherry, N. Group counseling and behavior therapy with test anxious college Ss. *Journal of Consulting Psychology,* 1966, **30**, 544–549.

Katkin, S., Ginsburg, M., Rifkin, M. J., & Scott, J. T. Effectiveness of female volunteers in the treatment of outpatients. *Journal of Counseling Psychology,* 1971, **18**, 97–100.

Kellam, S. G., Goldberg, S. C., Schooler, N. R., Berman, A., & Schelzev, J. L. Ward atmosphere and outcome of treatment of acute schizophrenia. *Journal of Psychiatric Research,* 1967, **5**, 145–163.

Kelly, F. S., Farina, A., & Mosher, D. L. Ability of schizophrenic women to create a favorable or unfavorable impression on an interviewer. *Journal of Consulting and Clinical Psychology,* 1971, **36**, 404–409.

Keutzer, C. S. Behavior modification of smoking: The experimental investigation of diverse techniques. *Behaviour Research and Therapy,* 1968, **6**, 137–157.

Keutzer, C. S., Lichtenstein, E., & Himes, K. H. "Emotional" role playing and changes in smoking attitudes and behavior. *Proceedings of the 77th Annual Convention of the*

American Psychological Association, 1969, **4,** 373–374.

Keutzer, C. S., Lichtenstein, E., & Mees, H. L. Modification of smoking behavior: A review. *Psychological Bulletin,* 1968, **70,** 520–533.

Kiesler, D. J. Some myths of psychotherapy research and the search for a paradigm. *Psychological Bulletin,* 1966, **65,** 110–136.

King, G. F., Armitage, S. G., & Tilton, J. R. A therapeutic approach to schizophrenics of extreme pathology: An operant-interpersonal method. *Journal of Abnormal and Social Psychology,* 1960, **61,** 276–286.

Klett, C. J., & Moseley, E. C. The right drug for the right patient. Cooperative Studies in Psychiatry, Veterans Administration, Report No. 54, November 1963.

Koenig, K. P., & Masters, J. Experimental treatment of habitual smoking. *Behaviour Research and Therapy,* 1965, **3,** 235–243.

Kondas, O. Reduction of examination anxiety and "stage fright" by group desensitization and relaxation. *Behaviour Research and Therapy,* 1967, **5,** 275–281.

Kringlen, E. Obsessional neurotics. *British Journal of Psychiatry,* 1965, **111** 709–722.

Kumar, K., & Wilkinson, J. C. M. Thought stopping: A useful treatment in phobias of "internal stimuli." *British Journal of Psychiatry,* 1971, **119,** 305–307.

Kushner, M., & Sandler, J. Aversion therapy and the concept of punishment. *Behaviour Research and Therapy,* 1966, **4,** 179–186.

Lawson, D. M., & May, R. B. Three procedures for the extinction of smoking behavior. *Psychological Record,* 1970, **20,** 151–157.

Laxer, R. M., Quarter, J., Kooman, A., & Walker, K. Systematic desensitization and relaxation of high test-anxious secondary school students. *Journal of Counseling Psychology,* 1969, **16,** 446–451.

Laxer, R. M., & Walker, K. Counterconditioning versus relaxation in the desensitization of test anxiety. *Journal of Counseling Psychology,* 1970, **17,** 431–436.

Lazarus, A. A. The treatment of chronic frigidity by systematic desensitization. *Journal of Nervous and Mental Disease,* 1963, **136,** 272–278.

Lazarus, A. A. Behavior rehearsal vs. non-directive therapy vs. advice in effecting behavior change. *Behaviour Research and Therapy,* 1966, **4,** 209–212.

Lazarus, A. A. In support of technical eclecticism. *Psychological Reports,* 1967, **21,** 415–416.

Lazarus, A. A. Learning theory and the treatment of depression. *Behaviour Research and Therapy,* 1968, **6,** 83–89.

Lennard, H. L., & Bernstein, A. *The anatomy of psychotherapy.* New York: Columbia University Press, 1960.

Lewinsohn, P. M., & Atwood, G. E. Depression: A clinical-research approach. *Psychotherapy: Theory, Research, and Practice,* 1969, **6,** 166–171.

Lewinsohn, P. M., & Shaffer, M. Use of home observations as an integral part of the treatment of depression: Preliminary report and case studies. *Journal of Consulting and Clinical Psychology,* 1971, **37,** 87–94.

Lichtenstein, E., & Keutzer, C. S. Experimental investigation of diverse techniques to modify smoking: A follow-up report. *Behaviour Research and Therapy,* 1968, 7, 139–140.

Lichtenstein, E., & Keutzer, C. S. Modification of smoking behavior: A later look. In R. D. Rubin, H. Fensterheim, A. A. Lazarus, C. M. Franks (Eds.), *Advances in behavior therapy, 1969.* New York: Academic Press, 1971.

Lichtenstein, E., Keutzer, C. S., & Himes, K. H. "Emotional" role playing and changes in smoking attitudes and behavior. *Psychological Reports,* 1969, **25,** 379–387.

Liebert, R. M., & Morris, L. W. Cognitive and emotional components of test anxiety: A distinction and some initial data. *Psychological Reports,* 1967, **20,** 975–978.

London, P. *The modes and morals of psychotherapy.* New York: Holt, Rinehart, and Winston, 1964.

Love, L. R., Kaswan, J., & Bugental, D. E. Differential effectiveness of three clinical interventions for different socialeconomic groupings. *Journal of Consulting and Clinical Psychology,* 1972, **39,** 347–360.

Ludwig, A. M. The influence of nonspecific healing techniques with chronic schizophrenics. *American Journal of Psychotherapy,* 1968, **22,** 382–404.

Ludwig, A. M., & Marx, A. J. The response of chronic schizophrenics to attention and structure. *British Journal of Psychiatry,* 1971, **118,** 447–450.

Lyons, J. *Experience. An introduction to a personal psychology.* New York: Harper and Row, 1973.

MacCulloch, M. J., Birtles, C. J., & Feldman, M. P. Anticipatory avoidance learning for the treatment of homosexuality: Recent developments and an automatic aversion therapy system. *Behavior Therapy,* 1971, **2,** 151–169.

MacCulloch, M. J. & Feldman, M. P. Personality and the treatment of homosexuality. *Acta Psychiatrica Scandinavica,* 1967, **43,** 300–317.

Magaro, P. A. A prescriptive treatment model based upon social class and premorbid adjustment. *Psychotherapy: Theory, Research and Practice,* 1969, **6,** 57–70.

Mahoney, M. J., Moura, N. G., & Wade, T. C. Relative efficacy of self-reward, self-punishment, and self-monitoring techniques for weight loss. *Journal of Consulting and Clinical Psychology,* 1973, **40,** 404–407.

Maletzky, B. M. "Assisted" covert sensitization in the treatment of exhibitionism. *Journal of Consulting and Clinical Psychology,* 1974, **42,** 34–40.

Maley, R. F., Feldman, G. L., & Ruskin, R. S. Evaluation of patient improvement in a token economy treatment program. *Journal of Abnormal Psychology,* 1973, **82,** 141–144.

Malmo, R. B. Emotions and muscle tension: The story of Anne. *Psychology Today,* 1970, **3,** 64–67, 83.

Mann, J. Vicarious desensitization of test anxiety through observation of videotaped treatment. *Journal of Counseling Psychology,* 1972, **19,** 1–7.

Mann, L. The effects of emotional role playing on desire to modify smoking habits. *Journal of Experimental Social Psychology,* 1967, **3,** 334–348.

Mann, L. and Janis, I. L. A follow-up study on the long-term effects of emotional role-playing. *Journal of Personality and Social Psychology,* 1968, **8,** 339–342.

Mann, R. A. The behavior-therapeutic use of contingency contracting to control an adult behavior problem: Weight control. *Journal of Applied Behavior Analysis,* 1972, **5,** 99–109.

Manno, B., & Marston, A. R. Weight reduction as a function of negative covert reinforcement (sensitization) versus positive covert reinforcement. *Behaviour Research and Therapy,* 1972, **10,** 201–207.

Marcia, J. E., Rubin, B. M., & Efran, J. S. Systematic desensitization: Expectancy change or counterconditioning. *Journal of Abnormal Psychology,* 1969, **74,** 382–387.

Marks, I. M. Agoraphobic syndrome: Phobic anxiety state. *Archives of General Psychiatry,* 1970, **23,** 538–553.

Marks, I. M., & Gelder, M. G. Transvestism and fetishism: Clinical and psychological changes during faradic aversion. *British Journal of Psychiatry,* 1967, **113,** 711–729.

Marks, I., Gelder, M., & Bancroft, J. Sexual deviants two years after electric aversion. *British Journal of Psychiatry,* 1970, **117,** 173–185.

Marks, I. M., Gelder, M. G., & Edwards, G. Hypnosis and desensitization for phobias: A controlled prospective trial. *British Journal of Psychiatry,* 1968, **114,** 1263–1274.

Marks, I., Marset, P., Boulougouris, J., & Huson, J. Physiological accompaniments of neutral and phobic imagery. *Psychological Medicine,* 1971, **1,** 299–307.

Marks, I., Sonoda, B., & Schalock, R. Reinforcement vs. relationship therapy for schizophrenics. *Journal of Abnormal Psychology,* 1968, 73, 397–402.

Marsden, G. Content-analysis studies of therapeutic interviews: 1954–1964. *Psychological Bulletin,* 1965, 63, 298–321.

Marston, A. R., & McFall, R. M. Comparison of behavior modification approaches to smoking reduction.*Journal of Consulting and Clinical Psychology,* 1971, 36, 153–162.

Martinson, W. D., & Zerface, J. P. Comparison of individual counseling and a social program with nondaters. *Journal of Counseling Psychology,* 1970, 17, 36–40.

Massimo, J. L., & Shore, M. F. Comprehensive vocationally oriented psychotherapy: A new treatment technique for lower-class adolescent delinquent boys. *Psychiatry,* 1967, 30, 229–236.

Masters, W. H., & Johnson, V. E. *Human sexual inadequacy.* Boston: Little, Brown and Company, 1970.

May, P. R. A. *Treatment of schizophrenia.* New York: Science House, 1968.

May, P. R. A., & Tuma, A. H. Treatment of schizophrenia: An experimental study of five treatment methods. *British Journal of Psychiatry,* 1965, 111, 503–510.

McCallum, R. N. The modification of cigarette smoking behavior: A comparison of treatment techniques. *Dissertation Abstracts International,* 1971, 31, 6264.

McConaghy, N., & Barr, R. F. Classical, avoidance and backward conditioning treatments of homosexuality. *British Journal of Psychiatry,* 1973, 122, 151–162.

McConaghy, N. Aversive therapy of homosexuality: Measures of efficacy. *American Journal of Psychiatry,* 1971, 127, 1221–1224.

McFall, R. M., & Hammen, C. L. Motivation, structure, and self-monitoring: Role of nonspecific factors in smoking reduction. *Journal of Consulting and Clinical Psychology,* 1971, 37, 80–86.

McFall, R. M., & Lillesand, D. B. Behavior rehearsal with modeling and coaching in assertion training. *Journal of Abnormal Psychology,* 1971, 77, 313–323.

McFall, R. M., & Marston, A. R. An experimental investigation of behavior rehearsal in assertive training. *Journal of Abnormal Psychology,* 1970, 76, 295–303.

McGuire, R. J., & Vallance, M. Aversion therapy vs. electric shock: A simple technique. *British Medical Journal,* 1964, 1, 151–153.

McLachlan, J. F. C. Benefit from group therapy as a function of patient-therapist match on conceptual level. *Psychotherapy: Theory, Research and Practice,* 1972, 9, 317–323.

McMahon, A. W., & Shore, M. F. Some psychological reactions to working with the poor. *Archives of General Psychiatry,* 1968, 18, 562–568.

McMillan, J. R., & Osterhouse, R. A. Specific and generalized anxiety as determinants of outcome with desensitization of test anxiety. *Journal of Counseling Psychology,* 1972, 19, 518–521.

McNair, D. M., Callahan, D., & Lorr, Therapist "type" and patient response to psychotherapy. *Journal of Consulting and Clinical Psychology,* 1962, 26, 425–429.

McReynolds, W. T., & Tori, C. A further assessment of attention-placebo effects and demand characteristics in studies of systematic desensitization. *Journal of Consulting and Clinical Psychology,* 1972, 38, 261–264.

Meichenbaum, D. H. Effects of social reinforcement on the level of abstraction in schizophrenics. *Journal of Abnormal Psychology,* 1966, 71, 354–362.

Meichenbaum, D. H. Cognitive modification of test anxious college students. *Journal of Consulting and Clinical Psychology,* 1972, 39, 370–380.

Meichenbaum, D. H., Bowers, K. S., & Ross, R. R. Modification of classroom behavior of institutionalized female adolescent offenders. *Behaviour Research and Therapy,* 1968, 6, 343–353.

Meichenbaum, D., & Cameron R. Training schizophrenics to talk to themselves: A means of developing attentional controls. *Behavior Therapy,* 1973, **4**, 515–534.

Mendel, W., & Rapport, S. Outpatient treatment for chronic schizophrenic patients. *Archives of General Psychiatry,* 1963, **8**, 190–196.

Meyer, A. E. Psychoanalytic versus behavior therapy of male homosexuals: A statistical evaluation of clinical outcome. *Comprehensive Psychiatry,* 1966, **7**, 110–117.

Meynen, G. E. A comparative study of three treatment approaches with the obese: Relaxation, covert sensitization, and modified systematic desensitization. *Dissertation Abstracts International,* 1970, **31**, 2998.

Miller, A., & Gimpl, M. Operant conditioning and self-control of smoking and studying. *Journal of Genetic Psychology,* 1971, **119**, 181–186.

Miller, L. C., Barrett, C. L., Hampe, E., & Noble, H. Comparison of reciprocal inhibition, psychotherapy, and waiting list control for phobic children. *Journal of Abnormal Psychology,* 1972, **79**, 269–279.

Mitchell, K. R. A psychological approach to the treatment of migraine. *British Journal of Psychiatry,* 1971a, **119**, 533–534.

Mitchell, K. R. Note on treatment of migraine using behavior therapy techniques. *Psychological Reports,* 1971b, **28**, 171–172.

Mitchell, K. R., & Ng, K. T. Effects of group counseling and behavior therapy on the academic achievement of test anxious students. *Journal of Counseling Psychology,* 1972, **19**, 491–497.

Moore, N. Behavior therapy in bronchial asthma: A controlled study. *Journal of Psychosomatic Research,* 1965, **9**, 257–276.

Moore, R. F., Albert, R. S., Manning, M. J., & Glasser, B. A. Explorations in alternatives to hospitalization. *American Journal of Psychiatry,* 1962, **119**, 560–569.

Moorefield, C. W. The use of hypnosis and behavior therapy in asthma. *The American Journal of Clinical Hypnosis,* 1971, **13**, 162–168.

Morgenstern, F. S., Pearce J. F., & Rees, W. L. Predicting the outcome of behavior therapy by psychological tests. *Behaviour Research and Therapy,* 1965, **2**, 191–200.

Morris, F. G. Anxiety reduction in schizophrenics through the use of systematic desensitization. *Dissertation Abstracts International,* 1968, **28**, 4297–4298.

Murray, D. C., & Harrington L. G. Covert aversive sensitization in the treatment of obesity. *Psychological Reports,* 1972, **30**, 560.

Mylar, J. L., & Clement, P. W. Prediction and comparison of outcome in systematic desensitization and implosion. *Behaviour Research and Therapy,* 1972, **10**, 235–246.

Nicassio, P., & Bootzin, R. A comparison of progressive relaxation and autogenic training as treatments for insomnia. *Journal of Abnormal Psychology,* 1974, **83**, 253–260.

Ober, D. C. Modification of smoking behavior. *Journal of Consulting and Clinical Psychology,* 1968, **32**, 543–549.

O'Brien, R. M. Contingency factors in negative practice of smoking. *Dissertation Abstracts International,* 1972, **33**, 2352–2353.

O'Connor, J. F., Daniels, G., Karush, A., Moses, L., Flood, C., & Stein, L. The effects of psychotherapy on the course of ulcerative colitis – a preliminary report. *American Journal of Psychiatry,* 1964, **120**, 738–742.

Orne, M. I., & Wender, P. H. Anticipatory socialization for psychotherapy: Method and rationale. *American Journal of Psychiatry,* 1968, **124**, 1207–1212.

Orwin, A. Respiratory relief: A new and rapid method for the treatment of phobic states. *British Journal of Psychiatry,* 1971, **119**, 635–637.

Orwin, A. The running treatment: A preliminary communication on a new use for an old therapy (physical activity) in the agoraphobic syndrome. *British Journal of Psychiatry,* 1973, **122**, 175–179.

Osterhouse, R. A. Desensitization and study – skills training as treatment for two types of test anxious students. *Journal of Counseling Psychology,* 1972, **19**, 301–307.

Ovesey, L., Gaylin, W., & Hendin, H. Psychotherapy of male homosexuality. *Archives of General Psychiatry,* 1963, **9**, 19–31.

Parloff, M. B. Goals in psychotherapy: Mediating and ultimate. In A. R. Mahrer (Ed.), *The goals of psychotherapy.* New York: Appleton-Centary-Crofts, 1967. 5–19.

Paul, G. L. Insight vs. desensitization is psychotherapy: Two years after termination. *Journal of Consulting Psychology,* 1967, **31**, 333–348.

Paul, G. L. Behavior modification research: Design and tactics. In C. M. Franks (Ed.), *Behavior therapy: Appraisal and status.* New York: McGraw-Hill, 1969. 29–62.

Penick, S. B., Filion, R., Fox, S., & Stunkard, A. J. Behavior modification in the treatment of obesity. *Psychosomatic Medicine,* 1971, **33**, 49–55.

Pentony, J. F. A comparison of two techniques of behavior therapy. *Dissertation Abstracts International,* 1971, **31**, 6909.

Persons, R. W. Psychotherapy with sociopathic offenders: An empirical evaluation. *Journal of Clinical Psychology,* 1965, **21**, 205–207.

Persons, R. Psychological and behavioral change in delinquents following psychotherapy. *Journal of Clinical Psychology,* 1966, **22**, 337–340.

Phillip, R. L., Wilde, G. J. S., & Day, J. H. Suggestion and relaxation in asthmatics. *Journal of Psychosomatic Research,* 1972, **16**, 193–204.

Platt, E. S., Krassen, E., & Mausner, B. Individual variation in behavioral change following role playing. *Psychological Reports,* 1969, **24**, 155–170.

Powell, J., & Azrin, N. The effects of shock as a punisher for cigarette smoking. *Journal of Applied Behavior Analysis,* 1968, **1**, 63–71.

Powers, H. P. Psychotherapy for hysterical individuals. *Social Casework,* 1972, **33**, 435–440.

Prochaska, J. O. Symptom and dynamic cues in the implosive treatment of test anxiety. *Journal of Abnormal Psychology,* 1971, 77, 133–142.

Pyke, S., Agnew, N. Mck., & Kopperud, J. Modification of an overlearned maladaptive response through a relearning program: A pilot study on smoking. *Behaviour Research and Therapy,* 1966, **4**, 197–203.

Rachman, S., Hodgson, R., & Marks, M. The treatment of chronic obsessive-compulsive neurosis. *Behaviour, Reserach and Therapy,* 1971, **9**, 232–247.

Rapaport, D. The structure of psychoanalytic theory: A systematizing attempt. In S. Koch (Ed.), *Psychology: A study of a science Vol. 3.* New York: McGraw-Hill, 1959. 55–183.

Razin, A. M. A-B variable in psychotherapy: A critical review. *Psychological Bulletin,* 1971, **75**, 1–21.

Rehm, L. P., & Marston, A. R. Reduction of social anxiety through modification of self-reinforcement: An instigation therapy technique. *Journal of Consulting and Clinical Psychology,* 1968, **32**, 565–574.

Reisman, J. *Toward the integration of psychotherapy.* New York: Wiley, 1971.

Resnick, J. H. The control of smoking behavior by stimulus satiation. *Behaviour Research and Therapy,* 1968a, **6**, 113–114.

Resnick, J. H. Effects of stimulus satiation on the overlearned maladaptive response of cigarette smoking. *Journal of Consulting and Clinical Psychology,* 1968b, **32**, 501–505.

Richardson, F. C., & Suinn, R. M. A comparison of traditional systematic desensitization, accelerated massed desensitization and anxiety management training in the treatment of mathematics anxiety. *Behavior Therapy,* 1973, **4**, 212–218.

Ritter, B. The use of contact desensitization, demonstration plus participation, and demonstration alone in the treatment of acrophobia. *Behaviour Research and Therapy,* 1969a, **7**, 157–164.

Ritter, B. Treatment of acrophobia with contact desensitization. *Behaviour Research and Therapy,* 1969b, **7**, 41–45.

Rogers, C. R. The necessary and sufficient conditions of therapeutic personality change. *Journal of Consulting Psychology,* 1957, **21**, 95–103.

Rogers, C. R., Gendlin, E. T., Keiser, D. J., & Truax, C. B. *The therapeutic relationship and its impact: A study of psychotherapy with schizophrenics.* Milwaukee, Wisconsin: University of Wisconsin Press, 1967.

Roos, P., Hayes, R., Marion, R., & England, B. Evaluation of remotivation with institutionalized psychotics. *Journal of Clinical Psychology,* 1963, **19**, 341–343.

Rosenthal, D. The heredity-environment issue in schizophrenia: A summary of the conference and present status of our knowledge. In D. Rosenthal & S. Kety (Eds.) *The transmission of schizophrenia.* New York: Pergamon Press, 1968.

Rubinstein, E. A., & Parloff, M. B. (Eds.), *Research in psychotherapy.* Washington, D. C.: American Psychological Association, 1959.

Sachs, L. B., Bean, H., & Morrow, J. E., Comparison of smoking treatments. *Behavior Therapy,* 1970, **1**, 465–472.

Sachs, L. B., & Ingram, G. I. Covert sensitization as a treatment for weight control. *Psychological Reports,* 1972, **30**, 971–974.

Sanua, V. D. Sociocultural aspects of psychotherapy and treatment. *Progress in Clinical Psychology,* 1966, **7**, 151–190.

Sarason, I. G. Verbal Learning, modeling, and juvenile delinquency. *American Psychologist,* 1968, **23**, 254–266.

Sargent, J. D., Green, E. E., & Walters, E. D. Preliminary report on the use of autogenic feedback training in the treatment of migraine and tension headaches. *Psychosomatic Medicine,* 1973, **35**, 129–135.

Schaefer, H. H., & Martin, P. L. Behavioral therapy for "apathy" of hospitalized schizophrenics. *Psychological Reports,* 1966, **19**, 1147–1158.

Schill, T., Rollo, C., Emanual, G., Chapin, J., Heisler, G., Green, V., Plopper, J., & Oscos, A. A comparison of the effectiveness of four psychotherapeutic approaches in treating public speaking anxiety. Unpublished manuscript, Southern Illinois University, 1974.

Schmahl, D. P., Lichtenstein, E., & Harris, D. E. Successful treatment of habitual smokers with warm, smoky air and rapid smoking. *Journal of Consulting and Clinical Psychology,* 1972, **38**, 105–111.

Schnore, M. Re-evaluation of an activity treatment programme with regressed schizophrenic patients. *Canadian Psychiatric Association Journal,* 1961, **6**, 158–161.

Schofield, W. *Psychotherapy: The purchase of friendship,* Englewood Cliffs, New Jersey: Prentice-Hall, 1964.

Schultz, J. H., & Luthe, W. *Autogenic training: A psychophysiological approach in psychotherapy.* New York: Grune and Stratton, 1959.

Schwitzgebel, R. L. Short term operant conditioning of adolescent offenders on socially relevant variables. *Journal of Abnormal Psychology,* 1967, **72**, 134–142.

Semans, J. H. Premature ejaculation: A new approach. *Southern Medical Journal,* 1956, **49**, 353–357.

Serber, M., & Nelson, P. The ineffectiveness of systematic desensitization and assertive training in hospitalized schizophrenics. *Journal of Behavior Therapy and Experimental Psychiatry,* 1971, **2**, 107–109.

Shapiro, D. *Neurotic styles.* New York: Basic Books, 1965.

Shapiro, D., Tursky, B., & Schwartz, G. E. Differentiation of heart rate and systolic blood pressure in man by operant conditioning. *Psychosomatic Medicine,* 1970, **32**, 417–423.

Sherman, A. R. Real-life exposure as a primary therapeutic factor in the desensitization treatment of fear. *Journal of Abnormal Psychology,* 1972, **79**, 19–28.

Shipley, C. R., & Fazio, A. F. Pilot study of a treatment for psychological depression. *Journal of Abnormal Psychology*, 1973, **82**, 372–376.

Sifneos, P. E. Psychoanalytically oriented short-term dynamic or anxiety-provoking psychotherapy for mild obsessional neuroses. *Psychiatric Quarterly*, 1966, **40**, 271–282.

Sloane, R. B., Cristal, A. H., Pepenik, M. C., & Staples, F. R. Role preparation and expectation of improvement in psychotherapy. *Journal of Nervous and Mental Disease*, 1970, **150**, 18–26.

Smith, R. E., & Nye, S. L. A comparison of implosive therapy and systematic desensitization in the treatment of test anxiety. *Journal of Consulting and Clinical Psychology*, 1973, **41**, 37–42.

Snider, J. G., & Oetting, E. R. Autogenic training and the treatment of examination anxiety in students. *Journal of Clinical Psychology*, 1966, **22**, 111–114.

Solyom, L., & Miller, S. B. Reciprocal inhibition by aversion relief in the treatment of phobias. *Behaviour Research and Therapy*, 1967, **5**, 313–324.

Solyom, L., Heseltine, G. F. D., McClure, D. J., Ledwidge, B., & Kenny, F. A. Comparative study of aversion relief and systematic desensitization in the treatment of phobias. *British Journal of Psychiatry*, 1971, **119**, 299–303.

Solyom, L., McClure, O. J., Heseltine, G. F. D., Ledwidge, B., & Solyom, C. Variables in the aversion relief therapy of phobias. *Behavior Therapy*, 1972, **3**, 21–28.

Solyom, L., & Miller, S. A. Differential conditioning procedure as the initial phase of the behavior therapy of homosexuality. *Behaviour Research and Therapy*, 1965, **3**, 147–160.

Steinmetz, D. K. The use of modeling and reinforcement to increase task orientation with State Hospital patients. *Dissertation Abstracts International*, 1971, **31**, 3356–3357.

Stephens, J. H., & Astrup, C. Treatment outcome in "process" and "nonprocess" schizophrenics treated by "A" and "B" types of therapists. *Journal of Nervous and Mental Disease*, 1965, **140**, 449–456.

Stern, R. Treatment of a case of obsessional neurosis using thought-stopping technique. *British Journal of Psychiatry*, 1970, **117**, 441–442.

Stevenson, E. W., & Viney, L. L. The effectiveness of nonprofessional therapists with chronic, psychotic patients – an experimental study. *Journal of Nervous and Mental Disease*, 1973, **156**, 38–46.

Stieper, D. R., & Wiener, D. N. *Dimensions of psychotherapy: An experimental and clinical approach.* Chicago: Aldine, 1965.

Stollak, G. E. Weight loss obtained under different experimental procedures. *Psychotherapy: Theory, Research and Practice*, 1967, **4**, 61–64.

Streltzer, N. E., & Koch, G. V. Influence of emotional role-playing on smoking habits and attitudes. *Psychological Reports*, 1968, **22**, 817–820.

Strupp, H. H., & Bergin, A. E. Some empirical and conceptual bases for coordinated research in psychotherapy: A critical review of issues, trends, and evidence. *International Journal of Psychiatry*, 1969, **7**, 18–90.

Strupp, H. H., & Bloxom, A. L. Preparing the lower-class patient for psychotherapy. Development and evaluation of a role induction procedure. Unpublished manuscript, Vanderbilt University, 1971.

Strupp, H. H. & Luborsky, L (Eds.) *Research in psychotherapy.* Vol. 2. Washington, D. C.: American Psychological Association, 1962.

Stuart, R. B. Behavioral control of overeating. *Behaviour Research and Therapy*, 1967, **5**, 357–365.

Stuart, R. B. A three-dimensional program for the treatment of obesity. *Behaviour Research and Therapy*, 1971, **9**, 177–186.

Stuart, R. B., & Davis, B. *Slim chance in a fat world,* Champaign, Illinois: Research Press, 1972.

Suinn, R. M. The desensitization of test-anxiety by group and individual treatment. *Behaviour Research and Therapy,* 1968, **6,** 385–387.

Suinn, R. M., & Richardson, F. Anxiety management training: A nonspecific bahavior therapy program for anxiety control. *Behavior Therapy,* 1971, **2,** 498–510.

Sulzer, E. S. Reinforcement and the therapeutic contract. *Journal of Counseling Psychology,* 1962, **9,** 271–276.

Sushinsky, L. W. Expectation of future treatment, stimulus satiation, and smoking. *Dissertation Abstracts International,* 1972, **33,** 2825.

Swanson, D. W., & Dinello, F. A. Severe obesity as a habituation syndrome: Evidence during a starvation study. *Archives of General Psychiatry,* 1970, **22,** 120–127.

Szymanski, L., & Fleming, A. Juvenile delinquent and an adult prisoner: A therapeutic encounter? *Journal of the American Academy of Child Psychiatry,* 1971, **10,** 308–320.

Tanner, B. A. A comparison of automated aversive conditioning and a waiting list control in the modification of homosexual behavior in males. *Behavior Therapy,* 1974, **5,** 29–32.

Thorpe, J. G., Schmidt, E., Brown, P. T., & Castell, D. Aversion-relief therapy: A new method for general application. *Behaviour Research and Therapy,* 1964, **2,** 71–82.

Tourney, G., Senf, R., Dunham, H. W., Glen, R., & Gottlieb, J. The effect of resocialization techniques in chronic schizophrenic patients. *American Journal of Psychiatry,* 1960, **116,** 993–1000.

Trexler, L. D., & Karst, T. O. Rational-emotive therapy, placebo, and no-treatment effects on public speaking anxiety. *Journal of Abnormal Psychology,* 1972, **79,** 60–67.

Truax, C. B. Effective ingredients in psychotherapy: An approach to unraveling the patient-therapist interaction. *Journal of Counseling Psychology,* 1963, **10,** 256–263.

Tyler, V. O., & Brown, G. D. The use of swift, brief isolation as a group control device for institutionalized delinquents. *Behaviour Research and Therapy,* 1967, **5,** 1–9.

Tyler, V. O., & Straughan, J. H. Coverant control and breathholding as techniques for the treatment of obesity. *Psychological Record,* 1970, **20,** 473–478.

Uhlenhuth, E. H., Lipman, R. S., & Covi, L. Combined pharmachotherapy and psychotherapy. *Journal of Nervous and Mental Disease,* 1969, **148,** 52–64.

Ullmann, L. P., Forsman, R. G., Kenny, J. W., McInnis, T. L., Unikel, I. P., & Zeisset, R. M. Selective reinforcement of schizophrenics' interview responses. *Behaviour Research and Therapy,* 1965, **2,** 205–212.

Upper, D., & Meredith, L. A stimulus control approach to the modification of smoking behavior. *Proceedings of the Annual Convention of A. P. A.,* 1970, **5,** 739–740.

Victor, R. G., & Krug, C. M. "Paradoxical intention" in the treatment of compulsive gambling. *American Journal of Psychotherapy,* 1967, **21,** 804–814.

Wagner, M. K., & Bragg, R. A. Comparing behavior modification approaches to habit decrement – smoking. *Journal of Consulting and Clinical Psychology,* 1970, **34,** 258–263.

Watson, J. P., & Marks, I. M. Relevant and irrelevant fear in flooding – A crossover study of phobic patients. *Behavior Therapy,* 1971, **2,** 275–293.

Weil, G., & Goldfried, M. R. Treatment of insomnia in an eleven year old child through self-relaxation. Unpublished manuscript, SUNY at Stony Brook, 1972.

Weingaertner, A. H. The effects of self shock procedure on hallucinatory activity in hospitalized schizophrenics. *Dissertation Abstracts International,* 1970, **30,** 5704–5705.

Weinman, B., Gelbart, P., Wallace, M., & Post, M. Inducing assertive behavior in chronic schizophrenics: A comparison of socioenvironmental desensitization and relaxation therapies. *Journal of Consulting and Clinical Psychology,* 1972, **39,** 246–252.

Weinstock, H. J. Successful treatment of ulcerative colitis by psychoanalysis: A survey of 28 cases with follow-up. *Journal of Psychosomatic Research*, 1962, **6**, 243–249.

Weiss, J. H., Martin, C., & Riley, J. Effects of suggestion on respiration in asthmatic children. *Psychosomatic Medicine*, 1970, **32**, 409–415.

Weissman, M. M., Klerman, G. L., Paykel, E. S., Prusoff, B., & Hanson, B. Treatment effects on the social adjustment of depressed patients. *Archives of General Psychiatry*, 1974, **30**, 771–778.

Weitzman, B. Behavior therapy and psychotherapy. *Psychological Review*, 1967, **74**, 300–317.

Whitehorn, J. C., & Betz, B. J. A study of psychotherapeutic relationships between physicians and schizophrenic patients. *American Journal of Psychiatry*, 1954, **111**, 321–331.

Whitehorn, J. C., & Betz, B. A comparison of psychotherapeutic relationships between physicians and schizophrenic patients when insulin is used alone. *American Journal of Psychiatry*, 1957, **113**, 901–910.

Whitehorn, J. C., & Betz, B. J. Further studies of the doctor as a crucial variable in the outcome of treatment with schizophrenic patients. *American Journal of Psychiatry*, 1960, **117**, 215–223.

Whitman, T. L. Modification of chronic smoking behavior: A comparison of three approaches. *Behaviour Research and Therapy*, 1969, **7**, 257–263.

Wilkins, W. Desensitization: Social and cognitive factors underlying the effectiveness of Wolpe's procedure. *Psychological Bulletin*, 1971, **76**, 311–317.

Wilson, F. S., & Walters, R. H. Modification of speech output of near-mute schizophrenics through social-learning procedures. *Behaviour Research and Therapy*, 1966, **4**, 59–67.

Wilson, G. T., & Davison, G. C. Aversion techniques in behavior therapy: Some theoretical and metatheoretical considerations. *Journal of Consulting and Clinical Psychology*, 1969, **33**, 327–329.

Wine, J. Test anxiety and direction of attention. *Psychological Bulletin*, 1971, **76**, 92–104.

Wolff, H. G. *Headache and other head pain.* Cambridge: Oxford University Press, 1948.

Wollersheim, J. P. Effectiveness of group therapy based upon learning principles in the treatment of overweight women. *Journal of Abnormal Psychology*, 1970, **76**, 462–474.

Wolman, B. B. Interactional psychotherapy with schizophrenics. *Psychotherapy: Theory, Research and Practice*, 1966, **3**, 61–70.

Wolpe, J. *Psychotherapy by reciprocal inhibition.* Stanford: Stanford University Press 1958.

Woodward, M. The diagnosis and treatment of homosexual offenders. *British Journal of Delinquency*, 1958, **9**, 44–59.

Woody, R. H. *Psychobehavioral counseling and therapy.* New York: Appleton-Century-Crofts, 1971.

Woolson, A. M., & Swanson, M. G. The second time around: Psychotherapy with the "hysterical woman." *Psychotherapy: Theory, Research and Practice*, 1972, **9**, 168–175.

Yamamoto, J., James, Q. C., Bloombaum, M., & Hattem, J. Racial factors in patient selection. *American Journal of Psychiatry*, 1967, **124**, 630–636.

Yates, A. J. *Behavior therapy.* New York: Wiley, 1970.

Zax, M. & Klein, A. Measurement of personality and behavior changes following psychotherapy. *Psychological Bulletin*, 1960, **57**, 435–448.

Zechnich, R. Exhibitionism: Genesis, dynamics and treatment. *Psychiatric Quarterly*, 1971, **45**, 70–75.

Zeisset, R. M. Desensitization and relaxation in the modification of psychiatric patients' interview behavior. *Journal of Abnormal Psychology*, 1968, **73**, 18–24.

Author Index

Subject Index

TITLES IN THE PERGAMON GENERAL PSYCHOLOGY SERIES (Continued)